Simon Sterne

Constitutional History and Political Development of the United

States

Fourth Edition

Simon Sterne

Constitutional History and Political Development of the United States
Fourth Edition

ISBN/EAN: 9783337071233

Printed in Europe, USA, Canada, Australia, Japan

Cover: Foto ©Suzi / piuelia.de

CONSTITUTIONAL HISTORY

AND

POLITICAL DEVELOPMENT

OF THE

UNITED STATES.

BY

SIMON STERNE,
OF THE NEW YORK BAR.

———

FOURTH REVISED EDITION.

———

NEW YORK & LONDON
G. P. PUTNAM'S SONS
The Knickerbocker Press
1888

PREFACE.

THE request addressed to me by the publishers to write for non-professional readers a book on the Constitution of the United States led me to inquire whether, in the multiplicity of works on this, as on almost every other conceivable subject touching large popular interests, there is any room to say something novel, or put into a new form the old matter which has been said and written over and over again by abler tongues and pens than mine. It occurred to me that a sketch of the Constitution of the United States as it stands in text, and as it is interpreted by the Supreme Court, accompanied by a history of the political controversies which resulted in the formation of and changes in that instrument, together with the presentation of the actual situation of political parties and questions, which, in their turn, may produce constitutional changes, would, if given within a limited space, present such a view of the institutional condition of the United States as to justify this book to the student of political history.

At no time in the history of the United States have its institutions awakened such widespread and friendly interest as at present. It is true that dur-

ing the great civil war, from 1861 to 1865, the
news from the contending armies was read with
greater avidity than that which is awakened by the
items of a commercial, agricultural, and industrial
character, which now in the main fill the columns
of the press; but a far greater proportion of the
human family are more largely concerned in these
very items than then were in our military contests,
inasmuch as since that period the United States
has become the largest contributor to the food
supply of the world.

That period of the history of this country beginning with the close of the war is a most interesting
one to the student of political institutions. European statesmen doubted, and many thoughtful
Americans at times had misgivings, whether its
institutions could bear the strain of the conditions
in which at the close of the war the national government was placed. Every war issue has been
met and successfully disposed of. The ills of an
improperly laid and collected revenue, a bad civil
service, mischievous methods of taxation and corrupt municipal administration still exist, but not
one of these evils, properly speaking, can be said to
date from the war period, but the roots of them
were planted many years before the slavery agitation was at its height. Nigh a million of men, who
in the North and South were under arms at the

close of the war, were disbanded and absorbed again by the agricultural and industrial enterprises of the country, and no appreciable increase of crime or lawlessness was visible in the community. The government returned to a sound currency from a depreciated paper war currency, notwithstanding the fact that great masses believed the return to specie payment would be the ruin of individual enterprise. A large proportion of the debt created by the war has already been paid off; and the remainder, by the establishment of a financial credit second to none in the world, is refunded at so low a rate of interest that the burden of the debt, taking into consideration the increase of population, is but a third of what it was at the close of the war. The revenue of the country is so far in excess of its financial needs that but for the ingenuity of politicians to devise jobs to absorb public funds, a bad civil service and governmental extravagance, a still greater reduction would have been made. As it is, the debt of the United States, although the most recent of the great governmental debts of the world, may still be the first to be paid off.

All these evidences of elasticity of institutions, enabling them successfully to meet unlooked-for emergencies in the country's needs, have from time to time elicited the admiring expressions of publicists the world over, and caused them more closely viPREFACE.

to study institutions which, while they on the one
hand secure individual freedom of action, seem not
to be devoid of the power to produce such far-
reaching results as are supposed to be the special
advantages of the more paternal forms of government.

To attribute the whole of the prosperity of the
people of the United States to its institutions would
be puerile in the extreme. Any constitutional form
of government securing freedom of action in dealing with its practically exhaustless resources, among
which may be enumerated vast treasures of mineral
wealth, fruitful soil, and beneficent climate, coupled
with a geographical situation which almost wholly
prevents foreign complications, would have made
for the inhabitants of the vast domain known as
the United States a home filled with comfort, lux-
ury, and wealth, and have attracted seekers of fortune from every quarter of the globe.

That the institutions of the United States did,
however, largely favor the growth of material wealth
cannot be denied. Not to speak of other advantages
afforded to individual enterprise, the entire absence
of any inter-state custom-house from Maine to Florida, and from the Atlantic to the Pacific, has given
the inestimable and incalculable advantages of free
trade in its most absolute form over a larger surface and among more varied conditions of an indus-

trial and agricultural character than unimpeded exchanges exist elsewhere on the face of the globe. While it is true that in more recent years (since 1846) European nations have let down the barriers of protection toward each other, both by treaty and more liberal legislation, yet in the United States the practical advantages of the system of free trade commenced almost synchronously with the teaching of the doctrine by Adam Smith, in 1776. The errors of protection, which still govern the legislation of the United States in its relations with foreign countries, and to some degree counterbalance in evil the benefits thus conferred, bring loss, but in the limited ratio that foreign commerce bears to a nation's internal exchanges; and as the ratio of foreign commerce is at best not one to twenty of domestic interchange, the benefits conferred by the freedom of exchange within the United States must have been out of all proportion greater than the injury inflicted by the protective system inaugurated in 1861—a system which is, if the signs of the times do not mislead, fast crumbling away.

That there is ample scope for the political reformer, and much material to work upon in the United States as elsewhere, and in some respects more than elsewhere, will in the following pages be frankly admitted. The methods of legislation are wofully primitive and defective, and the practice ofttimes corrupt. The existing system of representation is inharmonious and unphilosophical; the tariff legislation a mass of injustice and incongruities, resulting in a collection of revenue at a most burdensome expense to the consumer. Municipal government is too easy a prey to jobbery and venality of every description. The civil service, notwithstanding recent improvements, still goes by favor rather than by merit. Political parties, although they divide upon numberless unimportant issues, seldom upon fundamental principles of government, almost constantly unite in favoring monopolies in disregard of individual rights and interests, and in almost every attack upon the public purse, frequently vieing with each other in bidding for popular favor at the sacrifice of the more permanent interests of the community. Yet these evils, mischievous as they are, are not without remedy. The one crowning merit of American institutions lies in the fact that an earnest and persistent appeal to the good sense of the people has, since the formation of the Constitution, always evoked a spirit able to cope with even more formidable national vices. We have, therefore, strong reason to expect that these lesser defects will be remedied by deliberately formulated constitutional changes adequate to extirpate them.

SIMON STERNE.

New York, *December*, 1881.

PREFACE

TO THE FOURTH AMERICAN EDITION.

THE demand for another edition of this essay on
the Constitution of the United States may surely
be taken as an indication that the book has met a
degree of acceptance at the hands of the public
justifying its issue from the press in 1882.

In bringing the subject matter down to date, the
author, in the preparation of this edition, has re-
written a considerable part of the work, and has
incorporated the suggestions of kindly critics who
have, both in the public press and in letters addressed to him personally, suggested amendments.

The march of national political events, since the
publication of the first edition of this book, has
been along a very narrow and smooth road. The
administrative machinery in the United States
has been improved in Federal, State, and municipal departments. As to the nation, an administration has been inaugurated free from scandal
in its executive functions. A serious attempt has

ix

fairly been made to meet the strong popular demand for civil service reform. While from the
point of view of the statesman there is still in this
particular much to be done, and the battle against
corruption is by no means ended by the disap-
pearance of the spoilsman from the field of active
politics, yet the more flagrant and repulsive elements of the spoils system have been eliminated,
and the removals and appointments which are made
in obedience to party dictation are made apologeti-
cally and with the consciousness that an awakened
public opinion upon this subject keeps the administration under constant surveillance, and requires
at its hands an explanation, if a justification is impossible, for the distribution of offices.

In matters of State administration, considerable
of a curb has been placed upon the growth of old
forms of monopolistic elements, and in some of the
Western States the demand for municipal home
rule has been met by legislation which promises to
bear good fruit in the near future. In several of
the States, constitutional limitations have been set
to the growth of public debts and to the appropriation of public moneys, thereby arresting the advancing strides of municipal and State indebtedness.
Indeed the statistics in that regard, particularly in
relation to the ratio of increase of public debts

since 1882, both State and municipal, are a gratifying exhibit as compared with the ratio of increase in the decade preceding 1882. In matters of municipal administration, the success with which citizens' movements have disturbed and dumfounded party organizations, compelling the latter to recognize the strength and possible success of such revolts against their dominion at the polls, has increased the value of character as an element of availability for municipal public offices, and considerably lessened the power, in municipal bodies, of the urban dependent proletariat elements. Notably is this the case in influencing the selections for judicial offices, which have in municipal districts considerably improved—an improvement in part due to increased salaries and longer terms of service. The same awakened public opinion which holds the United States Government to a strict accountability in the distribution of offices, is equally potent in relation to municipal administration in its effects upon local political leaders ; and finally the success which has attended some of the criminal prosecutions of corrupt public officials, is a most hopeful sign of improvement. On the other hand, the artificially fomented discontent of handicraftsmen and laborers under the goad of demagogues and labor agitators, aided by a portion of the public press which finds its profit in feeding any excitement prevailing in the community—circulation depending upon excitement—is a menace of very considerable magnitude to the safety of property and even to the permanence of the institutions of the country. When we take into consideration that in no other nation in the world is labor so well remunerated as it is in the United States, and that at no time in the history of the United States has labor received such an advancing ratio of its proportion of the common resulting product of the combined efforts of capital and labor as it receives at the present time, we should naturally look for contentment and happiness among the non-capitalist class instead of strife and threats to overturn the existing social order. The wages of labor have advanced from twenty to thirty per cent. within a decade, and the products consumed by labor in the way of necessaries of life, more especially cereals and all articles of clothing, have decreased in price from twenty to fifty per cent. during the same period of time. The dissatisfaction, therefore, on the part of the laboring elements does not arise from any present grievance as compared with any prior condition, but seeks its justification in the theory now hotly advocated that all remuneration to capital is an usurpation, and that private ownership in land, particularly in larger cities, unfairly intercepts a considerable proportion of the wages of labor, and is therefore a violation of the fiat of the Almighty and the natural rights of man. [As by the original constitution of every State of the Union, and by the amendments to the National Constitution, protection to private ownership, both of lands and of personal property, is prominent among the main purposes of those instruments, this attack from a numerous and organized body of fellow citizens, is nothing less than an assault upon the principles which lie at the very foundation of our government.] An examination of the reasons supposed to justify this attack, and the answers to them, will be found in the addenda.

The persistence in the policy of a tariff laid mainly for purposes of stimulating and rewarding manufacturing industry is to be accounted for only by the power of concentrated organized interests in few hands as against the larger interests of the many not organized, and also by a very considerable disparity of business habits between the contending forces. The protectionists are men of business in every sense of the word,—that is, they are the extensive manufacturers of the country who have achieved success in their respective industries, and they therefore carry into the campaign for a continuance of legislation favorable to their interests a considerable amount of accumulated capital and thoroughly well trained commercial habits. On the other hand, the revenue reformers and free traders are largely under the guidance of college professors and theoretical political economists who have no such training for the actual warfare of life, and no taste nor personal interest as spurs to action, and they are overborne by their adversaries in organization and power to influence Congress.

However, the demonstrated and demoralizing effect of a surplus in the United States Treasury and the numerous devices suggested for the distribution of that surplus, particularly those which come from the insatiable claimants for pensions for services rendered during the war of the Rebellion, together with the economic disturbances which the accumulation of funds laid up in the federal treasury produce in the money market and upon values, have persuaded a large number of our fellow citizens that such an accumulation of a surplus must hereafter be prevented, and many politicians of both political parties are, by the logic of events and force of experience, compelled to acquiesce in this view. This situation necessitates a reduction of the revenue. This reduction may be brought about by the adoption of either one of two courses—a diminution of the tariff rate upon raw products and upon such manufactured articles as are consumed by the poorer people of the United States, or by an abolition of the internal revenue raised mainly from whiskey and tobacco. The protectionists, who are in favor of a reduction of the revenue so as to avoid an annual surplus, naturally favor a reduction or a complete abolition of the excise on whiskey and tobacco, which would, as they think, require leaving the tariff untouched.

The revenue reformer, on the other hand, who believes in larger and freer trade with other nations, recognizes the fact that the tax upon these luxuries, results in the largest possible returns to the treasury with the least possible injury to the consumer, and favors an abolition of duties upon raw materials and a reduction of those upon the necessaries of life which are more advantageously imported from abroad than produced at home. In all probability the current session of Congress, stimulated by the President's message, which presents the issue boldly and clearly from the revenue reformer's point of view upon this question, will begin a political controversy dividing parties upon vital political questions, and for a few years to come, at least, make political contests turn upon questions of economic principles instead of upon merely personal considerations for the holding of office, which have characterized the national contests of the past decade.   •

Lastly, by the Interstate Commerce Act, a great progress and reform was inaugurated, as well as an entirely new departure taken in the line of governmental supervision of business affected by a public interest. It can scarcely be doubted that this step will be followed by further guardianship of general interests by Congress, in opposition to special and sinister interests which in the United States, no less than elsewhere, have so great a tendency to create imperial powers stronger than the government itself.

In the passage of this bill by the Congress of 1886–1887, an assertion of a long-neglected federal governmental authority was made. It is proper to concede that this failure to insist upon subordinating the great railway interest of the country to federal law came from a desire to avoid over-legislation, and to let private interests take care of themselves, a position based in general upon an undeniably sound political principle in dealing with strictly private affairs. The transportation and road constructing institutions are, however, largely and preponderatingly matters of public concern ; therefore the abstention from federal interference in an interest which had outgrown the power of regulation by the individual States, had resulted in many oppressive abuses by the railway companies, which the enforcement of the Interstate Commerce Act is in process of removing. Hereafter, the fear of over-legislation will be less potent in deterring the imposition of restraints by Congress in all such cases as tend to grow to such magnitude and overshadowing proportions, that it may seriously be apprehended that a refusal to exercise control is likely to result in private wrongs and tyrannizing of citizens far greater than any evils to be looked for from the exercise of governmental authority. The passage of the law regulating interstate commerce, and the organization of a commission thereunder commanding public confidence, have been perhaps, in this day and generation, the most important administrative advance taken by the Government of the United States to obliterate State authority where State authority has proved impotent and ineffectual, and to protect the public from the dangers of encroachments on the rights of the individual by agencies which in power had outgrown State control.

To avoid too much interference with stereotyped

plates, addenda to the book following page 274 carry the history of the Constitution and the political development of the United States from 1882 down to the close of 1887, instead of interweaving them in the separate chapters.

NEW YORK, *February* 16, 1888.

CONTENTS.

xix

XX CONTENTS.

CONSTITUTIONAL HISTORY

OF THE

UNITED STATES.

CHAPTER I.

CONSTITUTION OF THE UNITED STATES.

It would far transcend the limits of a book intended for popular purposes, to enter into an elaborate investigation of all the causes which contributed to the creation of the United States Constitution, or to trace in detail the reasons why the constitutions of the American States all came to be written documents, instead of being unwritten and elastic principles of government, like the Constitution of Great Britain. Without much sacrifice of space, however, a few salient elements may properly here have attention drawn to them.

The powers of the governments of the English colonies in America, before the Revolutionary war, beginning in 1775, were all written instruc-

1

tions, accompanied by charters and grants of title
and formulated frameworks of government. The
English colonists were thus accustomed to written
documents as the source of governmental power,
and the meaning of their provisions was the test
of governmental limitations.

At an early date in the history of the origin and
settlement of Virginia no taxes were to be levied
by the Governor without the consent of the General Assembly, and when raised they were subject
to an appropriation by the Legislature of the
colony. The Plymouth colonists, who were the
settlers in New England, acted originally under a
form of voluntary compact; but found it difficult
to obtain proper respect for governmental authority under this voluntary form of association, and as early as January, 1629, by a patent
from the Council under the charter of King James
of 1020, obtained sanction and authority for the
laws which they subsequently enacted. The fact
that this Patent lacked royal assent was the excuse for its withdrawal by Charles II., and it was
not until 1691, under the charter granted by
William and Mary, that unquestioned royal
authority was granted for the laws enacted by the
New England colonists.

At an early period in the history of the English

colonies in America the rights of the inhabitants
to personal liberty were based upon Magna Charta
and on the Petition and Bill of Rights; and the
common law, except in so far as it may have been
modified by special charters, was the prevailing
law of the land.

The principle upon which the common law was
thus recognized as the prevailing law, was that it
was the birthright and inheritance of every emi-
grant in so far as it was applicable to his condition.

There were three classes of government, instituted
in America by the English crown. One was the
provincial establishments, in which the Governor
was made supreme; under this form of government New Hampshire, New York, New Jersey,
Virginia, the Carolinas, and Georgia were administered. The second was called proprietary governments, which embraced grants to individuals with
governmental powers; under this form, in their
earliest history under the English crown, Maryland, Pennsylvania, and Delaware were constituted.
The third was charter governments, of which
Massachusetts was the leading example, and Connecticut and Rhode Island as derivative forms from
the Massachusetts grant. Under all these forms,
in process of time, local Legislatures were established, which drew to themselves a considerable

proportion of the governmental power which had originally been parceled out to the governors of the colonies. In both the proprietary and charter governments, the colonists, during all their early struggles with the crown, insisted that they had an inherent right of representation ; the crown, on the other hand, insisted that it was a mere privilege, held at its will. In some of the colonies the laws were required to be sent to the King for his approval ; in others, they were not so required. The general feeling on the part of the colonists that it was their right to make their own laws is best expressed in the declaration drawn up by the Congress of the nine colonies assembled at New York in October, 1765, wherein they are made to say, " that they owe the same allegiance to the crown of Great Britain that is owing from his subjects born within the realm, and all due subordination to that august body, the Parliament of Great Britain ; that the colonists are entitled to all the inherent rights and liberties of his natural-born subjects within the kingdom of Great Britain ; that it is inseparably essential to the freedom of a people and the undoubted right of Englishmen that no taxes be imposed upon them but with their own consent, in person or by their representatives ; that the people of the colonies are not, and from their local circumstances cannot, be represented in the House of Commons; that the only representatives of the colonies are persons chosen by themselves; that no taxes could be constitutionally imposed upon them but by their respective Legislatures; that the. supplies of the crown being free gifts of the people, it is unreasonable and inconsistent with the principle and spirit of the British Constitution for the people of Great Britain to grant to His Majesty the property of the colonies; and that trial by jury is an inherent and invaluable right of every British subject in the colonies."

The united colonies admitted the right of Parliament to pass general acts for the amendment of the common law to which the colonies were subject, or general acts for the regulation of trade and commerce throughout the whole empire, but denied the right of Parliament to pass special acts applicable only to a part of His Majesty's subjects, to wit, the inhabitants of the colonies, and more particularly special acts imposing taxation. The Stamp Act being such a special act, the colonies, at the invitation of Massachusetts, assembled by their representatives in September, 1774, at Philadelphia, in a Congress, and thus established, for the first time in the history of the English-American colonies, a general deliberative body, deriving its authority from the people of the colonies alone. This Congress continued to exercise power until March, 1781, and was then superseded by the Congress of the Confederation, which came into existence during the latter part of the War of Independence; it then being manifest that a new nation would be born. The Continental Congress avoided creating jealousy between the several colonies, by placing them all, independent of size or numerical strength, on the same footing; inasmuch as the combined delegation from each separate colony had but a single vote.

The second session of this Congress of delegates met in May, 1775, immediately after the opening of the war of Independence by the battles of Lexington and Concord. This Congress then assumed supreme direction of the war of Independence, and was, to all intents and purposes, the government of the united colonies after the 4th of July, 1776, when, by the promulgation of the Declaration of Independence, they declared their severance from the British crown, their right to make treaties with foreign governments, and their establishment as a nation. It appointed the officers of the army; it pledged the credit of the united colonies for the payment of the expenses of military organization; it apportioned the amounts which each State was to pay toward the general expenses; it adopted rules for the government of the army and navy; it granted commissions by letters of marque to capture the vessels of Great Britain; and exercised, in short, substantially all the powers which subsequently, first by the Articles of Confederation and then more fully by the Constitution of the United States, were ceded by the several States to the general or national government.

The severance of the colonies from Great Britain, both by the result of the war and by the formal Declaration of Independence, made each particular colony a sovereign and independent State, except in so far as it might voluntarily consent to subject its sovereignty, by cession, to the general government of all the States. Although this is true of the original thirteen States, it is not equally true of the remaining twenty-five, as their very existence as States depended upon the fiat of the Federal Congress.

Several of the States, between the breaking out of the War of Independence and the formation of the Articles of Confederation, framed constitutions of their own, in which they formally declared their independence of the mother country, and reënacted such parts of Magna Charta and the Bill of Rights as were applicable to their condition, together

with statements of the rights of man expressive of
the wider views and the more revolutionary principles which had found acceptance with the colonists from the freedom of movement and independence of character incident to and formed by
American colonial conditions. These views, as to
forms of expression, were very considerably influenced by the theoretical teachings of the French
Encyclopædists, whose works, to no small degree,
quickened the thoughts and influenced the methods of expression of Jefferson, Adams, Madison,
and Hamilton, who were the leading minds of the
Continental Congress.

Virginia, New Hampshire, New York, and South
Carolina had, before 1778, passed constitutions for
the people of their States as sovereignties, and
subsequently every State of the Union, after the
Articles of Confederation were formed, by a properly delegated convention of its people, put in
shape, and, by subsequent submission to the people,
caused the passage of organic laws, called constitutions, by which the general framework of the
institutions under which they were living was
mapped out, the division of Executive, Judicial,
and Legislative functions clearly defined, and the
rights inherent in the people beyond governmental
control, expressed and insisted upon.

The revolutionary Congress, recognizing the fact that its existence would end with the struggle, and acting on the assumption that the struggle would result favorably to the colonies, appointed in June, 1776, a committee composed of one member from each colony, to consider the form of Articles of Confederation to be entered into between the colonies, as the basis of a permanent form of government. These Articles of Confederation formed the subject of debate in Congress until the 15th of November, 1777, when they were adopted. A circular letter was prepared to the several States requesting authority from the States to authorize their delegates to Congress to subscribe the Articles of Confederation. The States proposed many amendments, which were all rejected by Congress, because Congress deemed it inexpedient to accept any amendments for fear of the delay. A draft was thereupon prepared and sent to all the States on the 26th of June, 1778, and was ratified by them all, except Delaware and Maryland, which respectively withheld their ratifications, the one until 1779 and the other until 1781.

From the moment of the organization of government under the Articles of Confederation, the question of the ownership of the lands which theretofore had belonged to the crown, in the several States, was an irritating subject between

1*

the States, as was also the not-clearly defined
boundaries between the States. The only way to
overcome the difficulty first named, was to conform
to the suggestion of Congress, that the several
States should cede the crown lands within their
borders to the general government, as lands belonging to the people at large. The name of the confederacy was the United States of America. Under
it the following powers of government were secured
to the nation and ceded by the States:

Congress was empowered to determine on peace
or war with foreign nations, to send and receive
ambassadors, and to make treaties of commerce ;
but each State was free to levy whatever import or
export duties it saw fit, to determine upon the rules
of capture by land or sea, and to appoint courts
for the trial of cases of captures on high seas and
piracy. In all cases of dispute between the States,
if the agents of the States could not by joint consent agree upon judges to try their causes as they
might arise, Congress was empowered to constitute
a court by a most cumbersome method. Three
persons were appointed from each State, and then
the disputing States struck out one each, until
thirteen remained, from which number Congress
drew out seven or nine by lot, a majority of which
determined the cause finally.

Congress was also empowered to regulate the coinage, to afford postal facilities, and to appoint the officers for the land and naval forces.

During the recess of Congress, its powers were conferred upon a committee of the States—one delegate from each State—with the limitation, however, that upon almost every important question it required the assent of nine States before the measure could become operative as a law.

Under these Articles of Confederation the treaty of peace with England was concluded and the American nation was governed until the final adoption of the Constitution of the United States. The main defect of the Articles of Confederation was, that although powers sufficient to create a government were ceded, there was no power to raise revenue, to levy taxes, or to enforce the law, except with the consent of nine States; and although the government had power to contract debts, there were no means provided to discharge them. The government had power to raise armies and navies, but no money wherewith to pay them, unless the funds were voted by the States themselves; it could make treaties with foreign powers, but had no means to coerce a State to obey such treaty. In short, it was a government which had the power to make laws, but no power to pun-

ish infractions thereof. Washington himself said.
" The Confederation appears to me to be little
more than the shadow without the substance, and
Congress a nugatory body."

Chief Justice Story, in summing up the leading
defects of the Articles of Confederation, says :
"There was an utter want of all coercive authority
to carry into effect its own constitutional measures ;
this of itself was sufficient to destroy its whole
efficiency as a superintendent government, if that
may be called a government which possessed no
one solid attribute of power. In truth, Congress
possessed only the power of recommendation.
Congress had no power to exact obedience or punish disobedience of its ordinances ; they could
neither impose fines nor direct imprisonments, nor
divest privileges, nor declare forfeitures, nor suspend refractory officers. There was no power to
exercise force."

This absence of all coercive power was most
directly and injuriously felt in the financial administration of the nation. The requisitions of Congress
for money were disregarded at will. The consequence was, that the treasury of the United States
was empty ; the credit of the confederacy was gone ;
and while public burdens were increasing, public
faith was prostrate. Even the interest of the pub-

lic debt remained unpaid, and the bills of credit that had been issued during the Revolution and immediately subsequent thereto sank to so low a value that the public debt was substantially repudiated. As an illustration of this fact, it may be remarked that of the requisitions for the payment of the interest upon the domestic debt from 1782 to 1786, which amounted to more than six million dollars, only a million was paid. Each State saw fit to exercise its sovereign power to regulate commerce with the other States, and this created dissensions among the States; so that in 1784 the national Congress formally declared its inability to maintain the public credit or to enforce obedience to its own dictates, and from time to time, up to 1787, declared in various public ordinances its inability even to enforce its own treaty power.

This state of things became intolerable, and was, by the leading men who had guided the colonies through the struggles of the War of Independence and aided in the formation of the Articles of Confederation, recognized as a mischief which would result in the disintegration of the union of the States. Hence an active propaganda was instituted in all the States for the preparation of more perfect articles of union and the creation of a government representing the States as a nation. In February,

1787, a resolution was adopted by Congress recommending a convention in Philadelphia of delegates from the several States for the purpose of revising the Articles of Confederation, and reporting to Congress and the several Legislatures such alterations and provisions therein as should, when agreed to in Congress and confirmed by the several States acting as sovereigns, be adequate to the exigencies of government and the preservation of the Union.

The convention met, and, after very full consideration, determined that amendments to the Articles of Confederation would be inadequate for the purposes of the government, and prepared a new Constitution, the ratification of the conventions of nine States to be deemed sufficient for the establishment of the constitution among the States so ratifying the same. This Constitution was submitted to the several States, and was ratified by eleven of them, North Carolina and Rhode Island standing out, the former until November, 1789, and the latter until May, 1790.

Although the government was organized by the ratification by eleven States, the ratification by all the States made that instrument the supreme law of the land, and that Constitution, with its amendments, from that time forth, remained the charter under which the government of the United States has been administered in all its foreign and inter-state relations.

In the interpretation of this chart of government it must be remembered that the government of the United States is one of delegated powers; that in theory the States possess all the sovereign powers not delegated, either expressly or by necessary implication, to the general government : and that the vast body of law, known as constitutional law, in the United States, deals first with the interpretation of these powers delegated to the general government, and secondly with the reserved rights of the States under their respective State constitutions, and the reserved rights of the people never delegated either to the State or to the general government.

The history of the Constitution shows, first, that the compact between the States was intended to be indissoluble. The Articles of Confederation in terms said so, and when they were found inadequate for the purpose, the Constitution was framed, "to form a more perfect union." Likewise the States are indestructible. The Constitution is a compact of States, and the States are, therefore, an integral part of the nation ; without them there is no compact which can bind non-assenting States.

16 CONSTITUTIONAL HISTORY.

This has been decided in a recent case (Texas vs. White) by the Supreme Court of the United States.

The Constitution makes the national government, in all matters delegated to it, the supreme law of the land, and not only is it the supreme power in all such matters wherein the Congress of the United States has, in pursuance of constitutional authority, acted, but it is the supreme authority whenever it chooses to take up a subject which is delegated to the government of the United States, although the States, in the absence of such action on the part of the general government, have seen fit to pass laws of their own to meet the emergencies. A notable instance of this is bankruptcy. From time to time bankruptcy laws have existed in the United States, enacted by the general Congress, and have been repealed. During the period of repeal the various States have enacted insolvency and bankrupt laws which, on the instant when the general government again took up the subject by passing a new bankruptcy law, became dormant and inert, and remained in abeyance until the national law was in its turn repealed.

The Territories of the United States have no reserved rights. They can be dealt with by the general government in such way as it may see fit, and not until a Territory becomes sufficiently populous

to be admitted as and becomes a State is it entitled
to all the reserved rights of States, and when so
invested it is as sovereign and independent a community as though it had been one of the original
thirteen States which had entered into the compact.

Amendments to the Constitution are provided
for in two ways. In the one in which Congress
has the initiative, it may recommend amendments
by a vote of two-thirds of both Houses, and such
amendments shall become valid when ratified either
by the Legislatures of three-fourths of the several
States or by conventions of three-fourths thereof,
as one or the other of these modes of ratification
may be proposed by Congress. Another mode
provided by the Constitution is for Congress, on
the application of the Legislatures of the several
States, to call a convention for proposing amendments; the work of which convention must be
equally ratified by the Legislatures of three-
fourths of the States or by conventions in three-
fourths thereof. The only limitation upon the
power of amendment of the Constitution is, that no
State, without its consent, shall be deprived of its
equal suffrage in the Senate. This provision was
deemed necessary in order to prevent an amendment by the more populous and larger States which

should deprive the few smaller States, such as Rhode Island and Delaware, of their equal representation in the Senate. This power of amendment takes away all excuse for revolution, because the instrument which is the supreme law of the land provides a method by which the popular will can act upon it so as to remedy or remove any existing or supposed abuses.

The general provisions of the Constitution which do not fall under the divisions of Legislative, Judicial and Executive functions, are enumerated in the fourth and sixth articles of the Constitution of 1789, the amendments of 1789, and 1790, 1794, 1798, 1804, and what are known as the thirteenth, fourteenth and fifteenth amendments, which were the result of the Civil War. The earlier provisions in terms provide that full faith and credit shall be given in each State to the public acts, records, and judicial proceedings of every other State; that the citizens of each State shall be entitled to the privileges and immunities of the citizens of the several States; that persons who are fugitives from justice shall be delivered up to the State having jurisdiction of the crime; persons who were held to labor in one State were required to be extradited and delivered up if they fled into another for the purpose of escaping from such servitude. There is a section allowing States to be admitted into the Union, but prohibiting Congress from creating new States from existing States without the consent of the latter; and providing that the United States shall guarantee to every State in the Union a republican form of government, shall protect each against invasion, and on the application of the Legislature, or of the Executive of a State when the Legislature cannot be convened, shall protect it from domestic violence.

The first amendments which were deemed necessary to the Constitution after its formation were proposed almost immediately after its adoption, and were rather in the nature of after-thoughts better to protect the rights of individual liberty. The first article of the amendments provides that Congress shall make no law respecting the establishing of religion, or prohibiting the free exercise thereof, or abridging the freedom of speech, or of the press, or the right of the people peaceably to assemble, or to petition the government for a redress of grievances. The second article provides that a well-regulated militia being necessary to the security of a free State, the right of the people to keep and bear arms shall not be infringed. The third, that no soldier shall in time of peace be quartered at any house without the consent of the owner, nor

in time of war, but in a manner to be prescribed by
law. The fourth, that the right of the people to be
secure in their persons, houses, papers and effects
against unreasonable searches and seizures, shall
not be violated, and that no warrants shall issue but
upon probable cause supported by oath or affirmation, and particularly describing the place to be
searched and the person or things to be seized.
The fifth, that no person shall be held to answer for
a capital or otherwise infamous crime unless upon
a presentment or indictment of a grand jury, except
in cases arising in the land or naval forces, of the
militia when in actual service in time of war, or
public danger; and that no person shall, for the
same offense, be put twice in jeopardy of life or
limb, nor be compelled in any criminal case to
be a witness against himself, nor be deprived of
life, liberty, or property, without due process of
law, and that private property shall not be taken
for public use without just compensation. The
sixth is to the effect that in all criminal prosecutions the accused shall enjoy the right to a speedy
and public trial by an impartial jury of the State
and district wherein the crime shall have been
committed, which district shall have been previously ascertained by law, and to be informed of
the nature and cause of the accusation, to be con-

fronted with the witnesses against him, to have compulsory process for obtaining witnesses in his favor, and to have the assistance of counsel for his defense. The seventh, that in all suits at common law, where the value in controversy shall exceed twenty dollars, the right of trial by jury shall be preserved. The eighth is to the effect that excessive bail shall not be required, nor excessive fines imposed, nor cruel or unusual punishments inflicted. The ninth, to prevent any misconstruction by the courts, that rights not specially reserved by the people are not withheld from arbitrary power, specifically says that the enumeration in the Constitution of certain rights shall not be construed to deny or disparage others retained by the people. The tenth, that powers not delegated to the United States by the Constitution, nor prohibited by it to the States are reserved to the States respectively or to the people. The eleventh was proposed in September, 1794, by Congress, and was ratified in January, 1798, and is to the effect that the judicial power of the United States shall not be construed to extend to any suit in law or equity commenced or prosecuted against one of the United States by citizens of another State, or by citizens or subjects of any foreign State. The force and effect of the twelfth amendment, which was adopted in 1804, in relation to the election of the President of the United States, will be considered in connection with the creation and powers of the Executive department of the government. The thirteenth, fourteenth and fifteenth amendments were the result of the Civil War, 1861–1865. Their declared object, purpose and meaning were forever to abolish the system of slavery or domestic servitude, and to prevent thereafter all class distinctions or inequalities before the law arising from color, race, or previous condition of servitude. A stringent provision was made to prevent persons from holding office who had been in office and had taken an oath to support the Constitution of the United States prior to the rebellion, but who, notwithstanding such oath, were engaged subsequent thereto in insurrection or rebellion. It was provided, however, that Congress, by a vote of two-thirds of each House, might remove such disability. A provision was made to prevent the validity of the public debt of the United States from being questioned, and to prevent the United States, or any State, from assuming any debt or obligation incurred in aid of insurrection or rebellion against the United States, or recognizing any claim for the loss or emancipation of any slave, and that all such debts and obligations and claims shall be held illegal and void. The representative

system, by representation of majorities only in geo-
graphically defined districts, was adopted as the
cardinal and underlying principle upon which was
to be created the law-making power under the Constitution of the United States, and of the several
States. Wherever Congress is required to act, or
the people of the several States are required to
act, through their Legislatures, the intent is that
such congressional action or legislative action
shall be performed by a mere majority, unless otherwise declared.

In considering also the provisions of the Constitution, it must be borne in mind that they are
largely the result of compromise. The jealousy
of the States of each other was the cause of the
threatened dissolution of the Confederacy under
the system of government which prevailed in the
United States of America from the close of the war
in 1783 until 1789, the year of the adoption of the
Constitution of the United States.

When, in consequence of the pressure that arose
from the evident inadequacy of the Articles of
Confederation to create a permanent form of government, the people of the United States called
a convention to consider provisions for the formation of a more perfect union, the members of the
convention were, more or less, under the influence of this local jealousy, and the organization of

the Senate, giving to each State two members, independent of the numbers, wealth, or position of the State, was intended to placate the smaller States and to make them feel that, although under a system of representation dependent upon numerical strength they would lose power in the lower House, they would still, by the veto power that the upper House had over the legislation of the lower, preserve their dignity as States and prevent the possibility of the passage of laws detrimental to their interests. Thus, it happens, for instance, that the new State of Colorado, although having two Senators, has but one Representative, its numerical strength being just sufficient for a single Representative in the House of Representatives; yet its admission as a State entitles it to equal position in the Senate with the State of New York with its five millions of inhabitants.

From an early period in the history of the United States, down to the commencement of the Civil War, there was a wide divergence of opinion whether the Constitution of the United States was a dissoluble partnership, or was a framework of government which did not admit of the idea of separation. On the one hand it was contended that, as there is no political common umpire or tribunal authorized to decide as a last resort upon the powers and interpretation of the Constitution, each State had a right to construe the compact for itself. Such were the resolutions of Virginia as early as 1798 ; such was the resolution of South Carolina when it attempted to nullify the tariff legislation of the United States in 1832. But this theory is refuted by the very wording of the Constitution itself, which says that it is ordained and established by the people of the United States to create a more perfect union ; and, as all the States were parties to it, no one State could construe it against the rights of the other States. Such an interpretation is against the theory of government itself, which prohibits any State which has once delegated its powers to a sovereign, from reasserting such power, without the consent of such sovereign ; and leads to the absurdity of claiming the possibility of carrying on a government which would give to each member thereof the right to deny the very existence of the government itself whenever it feels the pressure of the governmental hand.

On all constitutional questions the Constitution appointed a tribunal which was to expound its provisions, and, therefore, no province was left to the Legislatures or courts of the several States to determine the limit of the United States Government. The Supreme Court of the United States was the

final interpreter of all the powers conferred upon
the general government. The Civil War of 1861–
1865 originating from the desire of the Southern
States to preserve slavery, uninterfered with by the
sentiments of the Northern States, and to maintain
the doctrine of State rights, resulting disastrously
to the South, took that branch of constitutional controversy out of American politics. By the amendments since 1865 the political fact has been established that the United States Government is indissoluble, and that the Constitution created not a
partnership between the States, but a form of government for the States, from which such States
could not withdraw; and that, instead of remitting
questions between the States to the arbitrament of
the sword, they had to find peaceful solution after
argument before the Supreme Court of the United
States, or by amendment of the Constitution itself.
The fourteenth amendment will have a tendency
to prevent unequal taxation within the States.
Heretofore there was no limitation upon States
(except in so far as some few State Constitutions
may have prevented) as to acts of confiscation
under the guise of tax laws ; but this amendment,
by securing equal protection of the laws, sets a
limit to spoliation under the forms of taxation.

CHAPTER II.

WE have thus far, in our examination of the provisions of the Constitution of the United States, shown that the reason why the Articles of Confederation failed to accomplish their purpose to create a nation, was because the national authority, as created by such Articles, was stripped of the element of sanction. There was, in the first place, no supreme executive power ; in the second place, the Federal Congress had simply power, until the adoption of the Constitution of 1789, to pass laws without enforcing them, and they were therefore in the nature of mere recommendations. The clear and unequivocal surrender of power on the part of the States of certain well-defined governmental functions to the national government, and the general transfer of power involved in that grant of the Constitution which says "that all legislative power by the Constitution granted shall be vested in a Congress of the United States which shall con-

27

sist of a Senate and House of Representatives," as interpreted by the Supreme Court of the United States, gives to the national Legislature power to pass laws on all subjects of which the United States has jurisdiction either by direct grant or by implication. The House of Representatives is composed of members chosen every second year by the people of the several States, and the qualifications requisite for electors are the same as those which the State constitutions require for electors of members in the same branch of the respective State Legislatures. The qualifications of representatives are that each representative shall have attained the age of twenty-five years, that he shall have been seven years a citizen of the United States ; and that he be an inhabitant of the State in which he shall be chosen. Under the Constitution of 1789 the representatives as well as direct taxes were apportioned among the several States according to the number of their inhabitants, which included all free persons and those bound to service for a term of years ; three-fifths of all other persons, which of course meant slaves, and excluded Indians not taxed. The first enumeration after the adoption of the Constitution was to be made within three years after the first meeting of the Congress, and thereafter every ten years. The number of representatives then fixed was

to be one for every thirty thousand, but each State
was to have at least one representative. This provision was subsequently changed by the fourteenth
amendment, to the requirement that the representatives should be apportioned among the several
States according to their respective numbers, counting the whole number of persons in each State, excluding Indians not taxed ; and that when the right
to vote at any election for the choice of electors for
President and Vice-President of the United States,
of Representatives in Congress, of the Executive
and Judicial officers of a State, or members of the
Legislature thereof, is denied to any one of the male
inhabitants of such State, being twenty-one years of
age and a citizen of the United States, or in any
way abridged, except for participation in rebellion
or other crime, the basis of representation therein
shall be reduced in the proportion which the number of male citizens shall bear to the whole number
of such male citizens twenty-one years of age in such
State.   The object of this amendment, which was
adopted in 1866, was to prevent the slave States,
which theretofore had been in rebellion, from
abridging or limiting the right of suffrage on the
part of the negroes for State offices, without incur-
ring the penalty of diminishing thereby their representation in the House of Representatives of the

United States.   Under the Constitution as it originally stood the States were at liberty to determine
as they saw fit the manner in which these representatives were to be elected within the States, or
Congress was at liberty to legislate upon the subject in furtherance of the constitutional provision
as to representation.

Congress did from time to time apportion the number of representatives to each State in conformity
with the census of each decade, so that in 1872,
under the census of 1870, an apportionment was
made by which the number of the members of
the House of Representatives was fixed at 292.*
As the population of the United States from
time to time increased, Congress likewise by law
advanced the limitation of the number of persons
who were entitled to single representatives, in
order that the popular body should not become too
numerous for purposes of deliberation ; so that
under the census of 1870, by act of 1872, each 130,000
of the population is entitled to one representative.
By the act of 1872 making such apportionment,
following the preceding acts of apportionment,
it is required that Representatives to Congress
shall be elected by districts composed of contiguous territory, containing as nearly as practicable
an equal number of inhabitants, and equal in

---

* Chap. 20, Laws of 1882, fixes the number at 325 and 8 delegates from Territories.

number to the number of representatives to which
the State in which they lie may be entitled in Congress, no one district electing more than one representative. This is followed by a provision that
as to the then immediately succeeding Congress
the additional representatives to which each State
should be entitled under the apportionment might,
until otherwise provided for by the Legislature, be
voted for upon a ticket at large. The only national
requirement, therefore, as to election of representatives is, that they shall be elected by contiguous
territories, one from each district. The manner in
which the apportionment is to be made, the way in
which districts are to be apportioned, the lines
forming such districts, are all left to the legislative
bodies of the several States. The apportionment
act of 1872, which is the last apportionment act in
force, provides the Tuesday after the first Monday
in November of every second year as the day of
election in all the States and Territories for representatives and delegates to the Congress of the
fourth day of March next thereafter. The time for
holding elections in any such district or territory
for representative or delegate to fill the vacancy is
prescribed by the laws of the several States and
Territories. The vote for representatives is required under the provisions of Congress to be by

ballot. The compensation of members of Congress is $5.000 a year, and an allowance for actual traveling expenses.

At the first session of Congress after every general election of representatives, the oath of office may be administered by any member of the House of Representatives to the Speaker, and by the Speaker to all the members and delegates present, and to the Clerk, previous to entering on any business, and to members and delegates as they afterward appear, previous to their taking their seats. Before the first meeting of each Congress the Clerk of the next preceding House of Representatives makes the roll of the representatives elected, placing thereon the names of those persons only whose credentials show that they were regularly elected, in accordance with the laws of the United States. The Sergeant-at-arms is charged with the duties of the Clerk in the event of any vacancy in that office, and in the event of the disability or absence of the Clerk; and in the event of the disability or absence of both Clerk and Sergeant-at-arms, the Door-keeper of the next preceding House of Representatives is charged with this duty. In the event of Congress being prevented, by a contagious disease or the existence of other circumstances, making it, in the opinion of the President, hazardous to the lives of members to convene at the seat of government, he is authorized to convene them at such other place as he may judge proper.

The Senate is constituted of the senators elected by the Legislature of each State. The election takes place on the second Tuesday after the meeting and organization of the Legislature ; and if an election fails to be made on the first day, at least one vote is required to be taken every day thereafter, during the session of the Legislature, until a Senator is chosen. A vacancy existing at the beginning of the session is filled in the same manner, and if a vacancy occurs during the session it is also filled by election, the proceedings for which are to be commenced on the second Tuesday after the Legislature has organized and has notice of such vacancy. The number of senators is fixed at two from each State, independent and irrespective of the size of the State or the number of its inhabitants; so that there are several instances of States, notably Oregon and Delaware and Nevada, which have two senators and but one representative.

No person can be a senator who has not attained the age of thirty years, been nine years a citizen of the United States, and who shall not have

2*

been, when elected, an inhabitant of the State from which he shall be chosen.

Senators are chosen for six years. They are divided into three classes, one class being chosen every second year. If vacancies happen, the Executive of a State may make a temporary appointment until the Legislature of the State can act.

The Vice-President of the United States is the President of the Senate, but without a vote, except in cases of equal division. The Senate chooses its other officers and also a President *pro tempore* in the absence of the Vice-President, or when he shall exercise the office of President.

The organization of the Senate is provided for by the act of June 1, 1789. The oath of office is administered by the President of the Senate to each senator elected previous to his taking his seat. When a President of the Senate has not taken the oath of office, it is administered to him by any member of the Senate.

Congress is the law-making power. One House contains the direct, immediate representatives of the people, the other the indirect representatives of the people; *i.e.*, the direct representatives of the States. Besides being part of the law-making power, the Senate shares with the President the power of appointment to office, of making treaties of peace and declarations of war. Although Congress cannot be said to be superior to the co-ordinate Judicial and Executive departments of the Government, it nevertheless has, from the nature of its functions, the superior power. The history of the United States since 1865 gives several instances of the manner in which both the Judicial and Executive departments of the United States Government may, in cases of conflict, be coerced to a considerable degree by the law-making power. Notable instances of this coercion are the acts of Congress interfering with the Executive discretion of President Johnson when he was in direct conflict with the majority of both Houses of Congress, and his subsequent impeachment and all but conviction and removal; and the increase in the number of the judges of the Supreme Court of the United States, when a decision had been rendered upon a quasi-political subject—the constitutionality of the Legal Tender act, which did not conform to the opinions of the Executive and Legislative departments, and which was, therefore, to be re-argued and reversed, an increase of personnel of the court of last resort being the coercive method found effective to secure such a result.

Among the formalities of the organization of Congress, not heretofore referred to, are constitutional provisions to the effect that Congress shall assemble at least once in every year, and that the meeting shall commence on the first Monday in December, unless by law a different day be appointed. Each House is made the judge of the elections, return, and qualifications of its own members. A majority is constituted a quorum for the transaction of business, but power is given to a smaller number to adjourn from day to day and to compel the attendance of absent members. Congress is empowered to make rules for its own government, and each House makes its own rules. The expulsion of a member is given to two-thirds of either House. Neither House has the power during the session to adjourn, without the consent of the other House, for more than three days, nor to any other place than the one appointed by law. No senator or representative is permitted, during the term for which he is elected, to be appointed to any civil office under the authority of the United States, which shall have been created or the emoluments whereof shall have been increased during such term of service, and no person holding any office under the United States shall be a member of either House during his continuance in office.

All revenue laws must originate in the House of Representatives. This includes all appropriation

bills, but the Senate is permitted to propose or
concur with amendments in the same manner as on
other bills. Power is given to Congress to levy
and collect taxes, duties, imposts, and excises; to
pay the debts, and provide for the common defense
and general welfare of the United States; but such
duties, imposts, and excises must be uniform
throughout the United States. We have already
referred to the fact that the absence of such a
power given in express terms, or even by necessary
implication, and the absence of any power to
enforce a system of taxation, was the main cause of
the failure of the United States to form a stable
government under the Articles of Confederation.

In many forms has the question of the constitutional exercise of this power been before the
Supreme Court of the United States. The result
of these decisions may be summed up as follows:
Congress has power to levy such taxes and imposts
as it may see fit for public purposes. It was
claimed that customs duties levied with the ulterior
purpose of protecting home industry, were an unconstitutional exercise of power under this grant,
for the reason that such duties are not levied with
the view to the raising of revenue, but, on the contrary, for the purpose of enabling manufacturers
within the United States to increase profits on

products for the benefit of their private operations. It was held by the Supreme Court of the United States, that if any revenue whatever was raised from this source, the motive could not be inquired into, and that the indirect benefit to classes in the community of this mode of raising revenue was one of the consequences which did not come within judicial cognizance It was held, however, by the Supreme Court of the United States in the case of Loan Association against Topeka, 20 Wallace, 655, that where, however, the tax is avowedly laid for a private purpose, it is illegal and void. In this case the tax, having been avowedly laid to aid a private corporation in creating a manufacturing establishment, was held to be an illegal exercise of the taxing power. This case has been followed in several of the States, and creates a line of cases which in time, as public opinion in the United States may be ripened and educated by politico-economical studies, may lead to a reversal by the Supreme Court of the United States of its opinion that taxation for incidental protection under the guise of revenue laws is a constitutional exercise of power. ˙Thus may possibly be given to the United States the full benefit of free-trade doctrines through an interpretation by the Supreme Court of the United States, namely, that all customs duties must be levied for purposes of revenue only, and that if it appears to the court that the object is not one of revenue, but the incidental benefit of persons or classes in the community, it is unequal taxation; is a burden laid not for purposes of government, but for private purposes, and is, therefore, unconstitutional and void.

Where Congress has the power to tax, the States are prohibited from exercising the same power, under the general exposition that what is granted to the government of the United States is taken away from the several States; and when Congress exempts from taxation in express terms, the States are *ipso facto* inhibited from imposing taxation upon the same, commodity or asset. For instance, the bonds of the United States are, by the contract of the bondholder with the federal government, incorporated into the law creating the bonds, exempted from taxation. Under those circumstances it would be an illegal exercise of power on the part of the States or municipalities to tax such bonds.

In a leading case decided by the Supreme Court of the United States it was fully recognized that the power to tax involved the power to destroy. As the Union and the State governments are coördinate branches of the polity of the United States, and as to tax the State governments or the municipalities created thereunder, would involve the power to destroy the States or such muncipalities, Congress is by the very nature of such institutions inhibited from levying any such tax. Congress, therefore, cannot tax the salaries of State officers, franchises created by a State, municipal corporation, of a State, processes of State courts, etc.

Congress is empowered to borrow money on the credit of the United States. The meaning of this clause is too clear to require judicial interpretation, and gives constitutional sanction to the funded debt of the United States. Congress is authorized to regulate commerce with foreign nations, and among the several States, and with the Indian tribes. This power to regulate commerce with foreign nations involves, of course, the treaty-making power; to make such arrangements in relation to the commerce, resting on mutual comity, as exigencies may from time to time demand. The power to regulate commerce between the several States involves, of course, the power to regulate commerce on the navigable rivers and streams which run between the several States. And more recently, in consequence of the growth of inter state traffic and the establishment of railways which run through many States, and of telegraphic lines which spread their net-work over the whole of the domain of the

United States, this power has been invoked by the people of the United States as a means of asserting uniform jurisdiction over corporate franchises coëxtensive in their exercise with the United States of America, although chartered under the several State laws.

The question of railway and telegraph monopoly has in recent years become much agitated in the United States, in consequence of the rapid growth of those several interests. The power of the National Congress to regulate such enterprises organized under State corporate franchises, but really carrying on inter-state commerce, has been recognized by the Supreme Court of the United States. Although ordinarily the safer course of legislation is toward decentralization of power, it is nevertheless true that in the case of industrial enterprises having a tendency to centralization within the area of the vast territory of the United States, the governmental power to regulate these enterprises, if they partake in the least of a monopoly character, must be equally coëxtensive with the territory they occupy. As the several States have shown themselves powerless to deal with the subject either in an efficient way or upon a uniform plan, the power of the United States, now placed beyond question by the decisions of the

Supreme Court of the United States, to regulate these gigantic industrial enterprises is well lodged in Congress.

Power is given to the Congress of the United States to establish a uniform rule of naturalization and uniform laws on the subject of bankruptcy throughout the United States. The grant of this power of naturalization has been followed by national legislation from time to time, by which persons who are residents of the United States for five years can become citizens thereof by following certain prescribed forms of identification, declaration of intentions, etc. Exceptions of an unimportant character are made in cases of minors.

The bankruptcy legislation of the United States has been extremely spasmodic. When a bankruptcy law exists the States are prohibited, by necessary implication, from enforcing insolvency laws in conflict with the bankruptcy laws. When the bankruptcy laws are repealed, as they frequently have been and as is the case at present, the State insolvent laws once more come into force. While the federal bankruptcy laws are on the statute book and in force, all State insolvent laws, if inconsistent, are for the time being superseded.

Congress is empowered to coin money and to regulate the value thereof and of foreign coin, and fix a standard of weights and measures. Under this grant of power, the right of the issue of the United States Treasury notes, made legal tender at the beginning of the Civil War, was seriously contested. At first a decision was had, under the presiding justiceship of Mr. Chase, who was Secretary of the Treasury when such notes were issued, declaring such issue to be in contravention of the Constitution of the United States. This decision was subsequently reversed by a court which had in the interim become enlarged, and it was held that this issue of legal tender notes, made during the war, though not justified strictly under the power granted, was the exercise of a war power, and was naturally limited to a condition either of domestic insurrection or foreign invasion. While this decision stands, there is no cause to apprehend that under the power to coin money and to regulate its value, any addition will be made to the legal tender issue of the United States.*

Congress is empowered to provide for the punishment of counterfeiting securities and current coin of the United States; to establish post-offices and post roads; promote the progress of science and useful arts by securing for limited times to authors and inventors the exclusive right to their respective writings and discoveries. Under this power the

---

* The decision in Juillard vs. Greenman, 110 U. S., 421 (1884), disappoints the hope expressed in the text. See Addenda.

Patent Office was organized, and patent, trade mark, and copy-right laws passed, securing for limited periods of time the rights of inventors and authors in their respective inventions and books.

Congress is empowered also to constitute tribunals inferior to the Supreme Court. In the third article creating the judicial power of the United States, such power is vested in the Supreme Court and in such inferior courts as Congress may from time to time ordain and establish. This article further provides that the judges, both of the Supreme and inferior courts, shall hold their office during good behavior, and shall at stated times receive for their services a compensation which shall not be diminished during their continuance in office. Under these two several sections of the Constitution of the United States, Congress, from 1789 to 1876, from time to time, passed judiciary laws under which district courts were organized, which give to each State, substantially, one district judge (to Pennsylvania, however, two, to New York two, to Ohio two, to Illinois two), and circuit courts of nine circuits with one judge for each circuit.* The judges of the Supreme Court of the United States when not sitting in banc likewise hold circuit courts. The Judicial department of the United States being created under a separate article

---

* Act of 1887 adds an additional circuit judge to New York.

of the Constitution, we will reserve our further examination into the organization of these courts and their jurisdiction until we reach that head. Congress has exclusive jurisdiction in defining and punishing felonies committed on the high seas, and offenses against the law of nations; to declare war, and grant letters of marque and reprisal, and to make rules concerning captures on land and water; to raise and support armies, but no appropriation of money to that end shall be for a longer term than two years; to provide and maintain a navy; to make rules for the government and regulation of the land and naval forces; to provide for calling forth the militia for executing the laws of the Union; to suppress insurrections and repel invasions; to provide for organizing the army and disciplining the militia, and for governing such part of them as may be employed in the service of the United States, reserving to the States respectively the appointment of the officers and the authority of training the militia according to the discipline prescribed by Congress. Under the power to make rules for the government of the land and naval forces, Congress has not the power to make any rules inconsistent with the position of the President of the United States as Commander-in-chief. The Constitution appoints him the first officer of the army, and the laws of war give to the first officer powers, of which, under the guise of rules and regulations, he cannot be stripped. The manner in which the President makes his requisition for militia is by a call upon the Executive of a State, but he is not required to recognize the chief Executive of a State; he can make his call directly upon the militia officers. Although the States have the power to appoint officers for the militia, they are all outranked by the Commander-in-chief, when called by him to the service of the United States, and outranked by any general or other officer who may be appointed over them.

The object in providing that no appropriation of money for army purposes shall be for a longer period than two years, is obviously that no Congress subservient to the Executive power shall create a standing army to be placed under the control of the chief Executive of the Union and make permanent provision therefor. The necessity to ask from time to time the popular consent for army appropriations through the instrumentality of Congress, will, it is supposed, forever prevent an army being created which shall be used in a manner opposed to the popular will.

Congress has power to exercise exclusive legislation in all cases whatsoever over such district, not exceeding ten miles square, as may, by a cession of particular States and the acceptance of Congress, become the seat of government of the United States, and to exercise like authority over all places purchased by the consent of the Legislature of the State in which the same shall be, for the erection of forts, magazines, arsenals, dockyards, and other needful buildings. Under this section of the Constitution the District of Columbia was ceded by the State of Maryland to the United States for the establishment of the seat of government at Washington on the Potomac, and Congress has exclusive jurisdiction over the government in that district. It provided the district with a municipal administration, which, however, in consequence of the abuses incident thereto, was abolished, and it is now governed directly by a committee of Congress.

Crimes committed within a fort, magazine, arsenal, or dock-yard, or other building of the United States, are cognizable only in the United States courts within their respective districts.

Congress is empowered to declare the punishment of treason, but no attainder of treason shall work corruption of blood, or forfeiture, except during the life of the person attainted.

Congress is further empowered to make all laws which shall be necessary and proper for carrying into execution the foregoing powers, and all other powers vested by the Constitution in the government of the United States, or in any department or officer thereof.

Although under this general grant of all power necessary to carry into execution the powers specifically enumerated, no new power has been granted, such a clause was, nevertheless, necessary for the purpose of preventing captious objections to the exercise of power by necessary implication arising from powers already granted, simply because such powers were not expressed in set terms. Under this grant of implied powers, it was held that Congress could charter a national bank, and that it could make appropriations for internal improvements. Under this grant of implied power, it was held by the Supreme Court of the United States that Congress might organize a form of State government for the States which were in insurrection, and which immediately after the Civil War for the time being had thereby lost their framework of government.

Shortly after the adoption of the Constitution, by reason of the serious controversy which was then threatening war with France, the so-called

Alien and Sedition laws were passed, by the first of which the President of the United States was empowered to order any aliens out of the country whose presence was supposed to be dangerous to the community, and this in time of peace. The Sedition laws made it a crime for persons unlawfully to combine or conspire together with the intent to oppose any measure or measures of the United States, etc., or to write, print, utter, or publish, or cause or procure to be written, etc., any false, scandalous and malicious articles against the government of the United States, or either House of Congress, so as to stir up sedition, etc. These laws, although upheld by the judiciary, were so obnoxious to many of the States of the Union that their presence upon the statute book resulted in the passage of resolutions by the Legislatures of several States—Virginia and Kentucky—by which they nullified such laws within their own States. Rather than force a conflict upon this point, the laws were repealed.

Under the ninth section of the first article of the Constitution, restricting the powers of Congress and of the States, it is provided that the migration or importation of such persons as any of the States now existing shall think proper to admit, shall not be prohibited by Congress prior to the

3

year 1808, but a tax or duty may be imposed on such importation, not exceeding ten dollars for each person. This was an awkward and obscure provision, adopted to prohibit Congress from preventing the importation of slaves until 1808. In that respect it resembles the provision requiring the States to surrender fugitives who were held to service in other States. The framers of the Constitution were evidently extremely unwilling to use the term slave in the instrument, and so in several instances resorted to a paraphrase.

Congress was forbidden to suspend the writ of habeas corpus, except when, in case of rebellion or invasion, the public safety may require it. It has, however, been expressly held by the Supreme Court of the United States that the power to suspend the writ of habeas corpus exists only in the case of war or insurrection as to the district which is the theatre of war or insurrection, and not where the civil tribunals exercise full and undisputed authority.

Congress is forbidden to pass any bill of attainder or *ex post facto* law. Although there is secured to each man accused of a crime the right to be confronted by his accusers, and to a trial by a jury, which would seem necessarily to forbid the passage of any bill of attainder, yet, to place the rights of the people beyond doubt, it was deemed expedient to put in express terms that no man shall be convicted by bill, and that no man shall be convicted of a criminal offense under a law passed subsequent to the committing of the act. Under this prohibition as to the passage of *ex post facto* laws, it has, however, been held that this does not forbid Congress from passing retroactive laws in civil matters.

No capitation or other direct tax is permitted to be laid unless in proportion to the decennial census or enumeration. No tax or duty shall be laid on articles exported from any State. Under this clause of the Constitution, it was held by the Supreme Court of the United States that the export duty on cotton, levied after the close of the Civil War, was unconstitutionally levied.

No preference is permitted to be given by any regulation of commerce or revenue to the ports of one State over those of another; nor are vessels bound to or from one State obliged to enter, clear, or pay duties in another. No money is permitted to be drawn from the Treasury except in consequence of appropriations made by law, and a regular statement of account of the receipts and expenditures of all public money is required to be published from time to time.

No title of nobility is permitted to be granted by the United States, and no person holding any office of profit or trust under its laws is allowed, without the consent of Congress, to accept any present, emolument, office, or title of any kind whatever from any king, prince, or foreign state. No State is permitted to enter into any treaty, alliance, or confederation; to grant letters of marque or reprisal, coin money or emit bills of credit, or make anything but gold and silver coin a tender in payment of debts; nor to pass any bill of attainder, *ex post facto* law, or law impairing the obligation of contracts, or grant any title of nobility.

Under these restrictions upon the powers of the States, the question which has been most frequently before the Supreme Court of the United States for interpretation has been, "What is a law impairing the obligation of contracts, and what contracts are under the protection of the Constitution of the United States?" While it is true that no one Legislature can tie the hands of a subsequent Legislature in matters strictly governmental, nevertheless the Legislature of a State may pass a law which constitutes a contract with individuals or corporations binding upon the State. Such a law cannot be subsequently impaired, changed or modified to the detriment of the other contracting party without the consent of such contracting party or its assigns. Under this head it has been held by the Supreme Court of the United States, that the State, as to a particular property, may forever surrender its taxing power. In a leading case, decided as early as 1819, known as the Dartmouth College case, it was held that the charter granted by a State to a college was a contract which the Constitution of the United States would not permit to be impaired.

As the result of this decision restricting the powers of States to alter and modify franchises granted by them, the States hastened to alter their respective Constitutions, so that it was thenceforth provided that all grants to corporations and all charters of corporations were subject to modification, alteration, and repeal at the will of the Legislature. This made the right of the Legislature to alter, modify, or repeal franchises granted to corporations, a part of the contract originally entered into with the corporation, and therefore the exercise of that right, however detrimental to the interests of the corporation, could not be said to be an impairment of the obligation of the contract embodied in its charter enacted subsequently to such constitutional amendment. When some of the Western States of the United States recently enacted laws by virtue of which commissioners were appointed to regulate the tariff of charges for freight and passengers to be levied by the railway corporations which had been chartered within the State, it was argued before the Supreme Court of the United States, by the bondholders and stockholders of the corporation, that such legislation was an impairment of the original contract made with the corporation, and that under such contract the bondholders and stockholders acquired rights which could not be subsequently destroyed by a reassertion of sovereign power on the part of the State, which had been impliedly bargained away. In those States, however, the constitutions provided that grants by the Legislature of corporate franchises were subject to modification and repeal, and the Supreme Court held that the bond and stock holders were without remedy. It has also been held that the remedial provisions of law by which the creditor could collect from his debtor within the respective States by judgment and execution a claim due him, could not be so altered as substantially to impair his rights; that the remedial legislation of the State under which contracts are made form part of the contract, and that to alter them to the detriment of the creditor was an impairment of his rights. On the other hand, it has been held by the

Supreme Court of the United States, in construing this provision of the Constitution, that a municipal corporation, being a subordinate branch of the sovereignty of the State, having delegated powers only, is subject to have its charter modified, altered or repealed at the will of the Legislature, and that such legislation never partakes of the nature of a contract. This is likewise true of all officers of the States whose salaries are fixed by the State, and whose functions are prescribed by State laws.

It has also been held that a State cannot by contract bargain away the essential powers of sovereignty. The State, therefore, cannot deprive itself of the right to appropriate private property to public use under the power of eminent domain.

Even exclusive privileges in the nature of legislative contracts are upheld. If the State, for instance, grants a privilege to a corporation to build a bridge, and couples such grant with an agreement not to charter a bridge within a certain given point, the State is held to such a contract after the bridge is built. On the other hand, whatever may appropriately be deemed to fall within police powers cannot be contracted away. A man who buys a large stock of liquors under existing laws by which no license is required, cannot claim as against the State that his contract is impaired because the State subsequently either restricts the sale or imposes conditions upon the business in which he is engaged.

No State is permitted, without the consent of Congress, to lay any imposts or duties on imports or exports except such as may be absolutely necessary for executing its inspection laws, and the net produce of all duties and imposts laid by any State on imports or exports shall be for the use of the Treasury of the United States, and all such laws shall be subject to the revision and control of Congress.

No State is permitted, without the consent of Congress, to lay any duty of tonnage, keep troops or ships of war in time of peace, enter into any agreement or contract with another State or with a foreign power, or to engage in war unless actually invaded or in such imminent danger as will not admit of delay.

Under these provisions it has been held that an immigrant tax imposed by State law upon vessels entering the port of New York, of one dollar per head, collected from ships which brought the emigrants, and the purpose and object of the expenditure of such head-money was undoubtedly of an extremely useful character to both emigrants and ship owners, was an unconstitutional impost. The Emigration Commission, which for many years in the City of New York performed a very praiseworthy function in protecting the immigrants, from the moment of their landing until their departure from the City of New York, against frauds and swindles of every description which had theretofore been practiced upon them, providing hospitable accommodations for them, and for a year after their landing exercising some degree of guardianship in relation to their affairs, had its usefulness, after thirty years' duration, suddenly endangered by a decision of the Supreme Court of the United States adverse to the levy of the fund which supported it.

Full faith and credit is required to be given in each State to the public acts, records, and judicial proceedings of every other State, and Congress is required by general laws to prescribe the manner in which such acts, records, and proceedings shall be proved, and the effect thereof. Under this section exemplification acts exist under which the acts and records of the several States are made evidence in the courts of law of other States.

The citizens of each State are, under the Constitution, entitled to all the privileges and immunities of citizens in the several States. Under this clause special license laws, by which citizens of one State

were prohibited from seeking trade in other States
except on taking out licenses which were not required to be taken out by the citizens of the State,
were held to be unconstitutional. In some of the
courts of the United States, however, it has been
held that by the term citizens of each State who
are entitled to such protection is meant natural
citizens, and not artificial creations like corporations, and that, therefore, a State is at liberty to
impose terms upon corporations of other States
as a condition of their doing business therein
which they do not impose upon their own corporations.

A person charged in any State with treason,
felony, or other crime, who shall flee from justice
and be found in another State, shall, on demand
of the Executive authority of the State from
which he fled, be delivered up to be removed to
the State having jurisdiction of the crime. This
creates without treaty between the States a provision for extradition by which all criminals are
delivered by one State to another, so that such
criminals can be tried within the State where the
crime has been committed.

The constitutional provision that no person
held to service or labor in one State under the
laws thereof, escaping into another, shall, in con-

sequence of any law or regulation therein, be discharged from such service or labor, but shall be
delivered up on claim of the party to whom such
service or labor may be due, was mainly applicable
to a condition of slavery, now happily passed away,
when negro bondmen escaped from the Southern
to the Northern States, and is now applicable only
to cases of apprenticeship, for which it is not likely
to be invoked.

The United States is required to guarantee to
every State in the Union a republican form of
government, and to protect each of them against
invasion, and on application of the Legislature, or
of the Executive when the Legislature cannot be
convened, against domestic violence.

The provision requiring that full faith and credit
shall be given in each State to the acts, etc., of
every other State is intended to prevent any such
weakening of the bonds of the Federal Union as
might follow from the States disregarding what
was due to courtesy and comity when their respective proceedings should come under consideration,
and thus opening anew the controversies and questions which, in the jurisdiction having properly and
primarily the control of them, had once been
determined.   This clause relates only to judgments
in civil actions, and not to judgments on criminal

60

CON$TITUTIONAL HISTORY.

prosecutions. In the latter respect the relation of the States to each other is wholly unaffected by the Constitution.

The clause giving to the citizens of each State all the privileges and immunities of citizens in the several States, was not intended to give the laws in one State the slightest force in another State. It simply secures to the citizens of each State in every other State, not the laws or peculiar privileges which they may be entitled to in their own State, but such protection and benefit of the laws of every and any other State as are common to the citizens thereof in virtue of their being citizens.

Under the section making it imperative upon the United States to guarantee to every State in the Union a republican form of government, a question was raised by the friends of woman's suffrage, before the Supreme Court of the United States, whether a government that excluded women from the suffrage was a republic, and the court held that it was.

When the senators and representatives of a State are admitted to the council of the Union, the authority of the government under which they are appointed, as well as its republican character, is recognized by the proper constitutional authority.

Congress has power to dispose of and make all

needful rules and regulations respecting the territory or other property belonging to the United States. Under this grant of power it has been held that Congress has the absolute right to prescribe the times, the conditions, and the mode of transferring the public domain, or any part of it, and to designate the persons to whom the transfer shall be made; that no State legislation can interfere with this right, or embarrass this exercise, and that no State law, whether by limitation or otherwise, can defeat the title of the United States to public lands within the limits of the State.

By the sixth article of the Constitution, it is provided that all debts contracted and engagements entered into before the adoption of the Constitution shall be as valid against the United States under the Constitution as under the Confederation.

The second section provides that the Constitution and the laws of the United States which shall be made in pursuance thereof, and all treaties made, or which shall be made, under the authority of the United States, shall be the supreme law of the land, and the judges in every State shall be bound thereby, anything in the constitution or laws of any State to the contrary notwithstanding. This supremacy gives to the United States Government, as contradistinguished from a State Government, its true sovereignty. Without it the Union could not maintain itself. There would have been a constant clashing of interests and of laws, and endless interpretations by the several State courts conflicting with each other as to the meaning of clauses of the Constitution of the United States. The declaration of supremacy of the Constitution of the United States and the laws thereunder, and the organization of the Supreme Court of the United States to determine all questions arising under the Constitution of the United States, or under a United States law, or when the Constitution of the United States, or the United States statutes are invoked or called into question, has created a homogeneity of decisions and interpretation which gives stability to and respect for its laws.

A treaty is regarded as equivalent to an act of Congress, and has precisely the same validity. Congress has, therefore, the power by a subsequent law to repeal clauses in a treaty if the subsequent enactments are in necessary conflict with the treaty. It is only the foreign governments, the compact with which has been violated, which have a ground of complaint for an infraction of the treaty, not the citizens of the United States.

Although the Constitution thus places the United States government and its legislation above that of States, it nevertheless takes from the States their power to legislate in but three cases. First, where they are expressly prohibited from legislating; second, where exclusive power is expressly vested in the United States; and third, where power vested in the United States is in its nature exclusive.

It has now been expressly held by the Supreme Court of the United States, that when a State becomes one of the United States, it enters into an indissoluble relation. The act which consummates its admission into the Union is something more than a compact; it is the incorporation of a new member into the political body; it is final. The union is as complete, as perpetual, and as indissoluble as the union between the original States.

The senators and representatives, and the members of the several State Legislatures, and all Executive and Judicial officers both of the United States and of the several States, are required by the Constitution to be bound by an oath or affirmation to support the Constitution; but no religious test is ever required as a qualification for any office or public trust under the United States. Shortly after the war of the rebellion a new oath was prescribed by Congress to all office-holders, known as the "iron-clad" oath, by which the officer swore that he had not aided or abetted the rebellion in any form or manner, and abjured the heresy of secession. This oath was, after solemn argument, declared to be an unconstitutional imposition as a test for office, as the Constitution required nothing further than an oath to support the Constitution.

Shortly after the adoption of the Constitution, amendments were proposed, and by the States in due form ratified, which limited the powers of Congress; the first eleven were in their nature a sort of Declaration of Rights of the people against arbitrary interference by the federal authority, and have already been commented upon.

CHAPTER III.

THE Executive power of the Federal Government under the Constitution of the United States is vested in a President, who is to hold his office for the period of four years, and who, together with the Vice-President chosen for the same term, is elected by an Electoral College composed of electors of each State equal to the whole number of senators and representatives to which the State is at the time of such election entitled in Congress. The manner of the election of the members of the Electoral College is determinable by the Legislatures of the several States, with the limitation only that no senator or representative, or person holding an office of trust or profit under the United States, shall be appointed an elector. Under the Constitution, Congress was vested with power to determine the time of choosing the electors and the day on which they shall give their votes; such day, however, to be the same throughout the United

65

States. By an amendment to the Constitution, adopted in September, 1804, these electors were constituted into electoral colleges, to meet not as one body, but in their respective States, and to vote by ballot for President and Vice-President, one of whom at least shall not be an inhabitant of the same State with themselves. The ballots for President shall be separate from those for Vice-President, and after having made distinct lists of all persons voted for as President and of all persons voted for as Vice-President, and of the numbers of votes for each, the lists are required to be signed and certified and transmitted sealed to the seat of government of the United States, directed to the President of the Senate. The President of the Senate then shall, in the presence of the Senate and House of Representatives, open all the certificates, and the votes shall then be counted. The person having the greatest number of votes for President shall be President, if such number be a majority of the whole number of electors appointed. If no person have such majority, then from the persons having the highest number of votes, not exceeding three, on the list thus voted for as President, the House of Representatives shall immediately choose by ballot the President. When that contingency arises the members of the House of

Representatives cease to vote in their individual capacity, but vote by States, each delegation or a majority of each delegation, casting the vote of the State. For this purpose the quorum to constitute the House of Representatives must consist of a member or members from two-thirds of the States, and a majority of all the States is necessary to a choice.*

In the event of the House of Representatives failing to choose a President, when the right of choice thus devolves upon them, before the fourth day of March next following the election, then the Vice-President, elected as hereinafter stated, shall act as President, as in case of the death or other constitutional disability of the President.†

The person having the greatest number of votes as Vice-President shall be the Vice-President, if such number be a majority of the whole number of electors. If no person has a majority, then from the two highest numbers on the list the Senate shall choose the Vice-President. A quorum for this purpose shall consist of two-thirds of the whole number of senators, and a majority of the whole number shall be necessary to a choice. No person is eligible for the position of President unless he be a natural-born citizen or a citizen of the United States at the time of the adoption of

---

* *See* Addenda, Law of 1886 on Presidential count.
† *See* Addenda, Law of 1887 on Presidential succession.

CONSTITUTIONAL HISTORY.

years of age, and have been fourteen years a resident within the United States.

The difference between the amendment and the
Constitution as it originally stood, lies mainly in
the fact that under the original Constitution the
electors voted by ballot for two persons, and that
they made a list of all the persons voted for and the
number of votes for each, and the person having
the highest number of votes, if such number was a
majority of the whole number, became the President, and the next person having the highest
number of votes became the Vice-President. The
idea which the framers of the Constitution enter-
tained as to the manner in which these electoral
colleges should exercise their function was that
the people of each State would, in such manner as
the Legislature directed, select the wisest and best
men in the State to determine upon the fittest and
best citizens for the offices of President and Vice-
President respectively. Alexander Hamilton says
in the *Federalist*, "It was desirable that the sense
of the people should operate in the choice of the
persons to whom so important a trust was to be
confided. This end will be answered by committing the right of making it not to any preëstab-
lished body, but to men chosen by the people for

the special purpose at a particular juncture. It was equally desirable that the immediate election should be made by men most capable of analyzing qualities adapted to the station. . . . A small number of persons selected by their fellow-citizens from the general mass would be most likely to possess the information and discernment necessary for so complicated an investigation."

The end which was intended to be achieved by preventing the merger of the State electors in any general body, was mainly to preserve State action to such a degree as to prevent State jealousy in the selection of the President, so that each State should feel that in the performance of so important a task as the selection of a President of the United States it preserved its separate action; secondarily, by this system of double election to secure the best possible result as to persons to fill the important offices of President and Vice-President.

At a very early period after the adoption of the Constitution the practical result of this method of selection was the very opposite from that which was intended by the framers of that instrument. National conventions of parties predetermined who the nominees of the party should be for such offices, and the election of electors under the forms of the Constitution at a subsequent period was

merely a method whereby to test the party strength
in the several States; the electors to be voted for
were likewise to be determined by a party convention within the State; and the majority in any
State would elect either Federal or Republican
electors, subsequently Whig or Democratic, and
at a still later period Republican or Democratic
electors, by a majority vote which determined
which party should prevail in each particular
State. The electors so elected became and are
mere registering machines to cast the vote of the
party in conformity with the nomination of the
party; and so strong are party ties in the United
States, that there is no instance of any elector so
elected disregarding his obligation to his party
and exercising an independent choice for President
of the United States. Therefore, after the November election preceding the March when the President of the United States is to be inaugurated, and
considerably preceding the period of the meeting
of the electoral colleges, the selection of electors
is deemed the conclusion of the contest, and when
such electors are elected, who is to become the
President and Vice-President of the United States
is immediately thereupon declared and known.
The subsequent meeting of the electoral colleges
on the first Wednesday in December following the

Tuesday after the first Monday of November, when the election takes place, has degenerated into a mere matter of form, to which nobody pays anything more than a mere passing attention. The Revised Statutes of the United States, sections 132–151, provide a uniform time for the choice of the electors, their number, the manner for filling vacancies, the certificates for the electors, the manner of making their returns, their compensation; there is a provision for the contingency of a new election in the event of the Presidency and Vice-Presidency both becoming vacant, and a provision that, in the event of the resignation of the President or Vice-President, it shall be in writing.

The manner of counting the electoral vote has thus far been determined by joint resolution of the House of Representatives and the Senate.

Immediately after the election of 1876, a controversy arose as to whether Mr. Tilden or Mr. Hayes had a clear majority of the electoral vote, and when the electoral colleges subsequently met in their respective States, two returns came from several States, and by the counting of either one of those electoral returns, or the rejection of both, the result of the election would be changed. The country was considerably disturbed by the then condition of affairs; grave suspicions were enter-

tained that fraudulent electoral colleges were constituted by violently disregarding or rejecting votes
which should properly have been registered for
the successful candidate, and the country was supposed by many to be upon the eve of another civil
strife as to the Presidential succession, when an
extra-judicial tribunal was organized, known as the
Electoral Commission, composed of five Judges of
the Supreme Court of the United States, five members of the House, and five Senators, from both
parties, fifteen in all, whose determination upon the
question was accepted as final. It is well known, that
by a majority of one vote Mr. Hayes was declared
elected, and duly inaugurated. This condition of
affairs is unlikely ever to happen again, because the
semi-territorial government to which some of the
States which theretofore had been in rebellion
were subjected, created a condition of affairs in
such States favorable to frauds in election returns,
and which made it doubtful for a time whether
the nominal State government was really representative of the people of the State, and the acts of
the government officials were regarded with grave
suspicion by both parties.

The Revised Statutes also provide that the time
for which a President and Vice-President shall be
elected shall in all cases commence on the fourth

day of March next succeeding the day on which
the votes of the electors have been given, and that
that term shall be four years; that the compensation of the President shall be $50,000 a year, and
that of the Vice-President $10,000; the increase of
the President's salary from the amount originally
fixed by the act of 1793 at $25,000, having been
made in March, 1873. There is also a provision
authorizing the appointment, and limiting the expenditure of the President's official household.

The functions of the President are defined in the
second article of the Constitution. He is made
Commander-in-chief of the army and navy of the
United States, and of the militia of the several
States when called into the actual service of the
United States; he has power to grant reprieves
and pardons for offenses against the United States
except in cases of impeachment, and he is authorized to require the opinion in writing of the principal officers in each of the Executive departments
upon any subject relating to the duties of their
respective offices. Power is given him, by and
with the advice and consent of the Senate, to make
treaties, provided two-thirds of the senators concur; with him rests the nomination, and by and
with the advice and consent of the Senate, the
appointment of all ambassadors, all public minis-

4

ters and consuls. He also appoints, subject to confirmation by the Senate, Judges of the Supreme Court and all other officers of the United States the appointment of whom is not otherwise provided for in the Constitution, and which may subsequently be established by law. Power is, however, reserved to Congress by law to vest the appointment of such inferior officers as it may think proper in the President alone, in the courts of law, or in the heads of departments. The President is also empowered to fill all vacancies that may happen during the recess of the Senate, by granting commissions which shall expire at the end of the next session. He is required from time to time to give to Congress information of the state of the Union and to recommend to its consideration such measures as he shall judge necessary and expedient, and he may on extraordinary occasions convene both Houses, or either of them, and in case of disagreement between them as to the time of adjournment he may adjourn them to such time as he may think proper. The President receives ambassadors, diplomatic agents and other public ministers, and is in general terms entrusted with the duty to see that the laws are faithfully executed and to grant commissions to all the officers of the United States. Provision is made for the removal of both the

President and Vice-President and all civil officers of the United States on impeachment for and conviction of treason, bribery, or other high crimes and misdemeanors. He has also the high and important prerogative to veto all legislation of Congress, which veto power is, however, subjected to the condition that in the event of his failure to approve a bill he shall return it with his objection to the House in which it shall have originated, which shall enter the objection at large upon its journal and proceed to reconsider the bill. If, after such reconsideration, two-thirds of the House shall agree to pass the bill, it shall be sent, together with the objections, to the other House, by which it shall likewise be reconsidered, and if approved by two-thirds of that House it shall become a law notwithstanding the Presidential veto. In all such cases the votes of the Houses are determined by yeas and nays, and the names of the persons voting for and against the bill are entered upon the journal of each House. Should the President fail to return the bill, or fail to sign it within ten days after it shall have been presented to him, it becomes a law as though he had signed it, unless Congress by adjournment prevents its return, in which case it does not become a law without the President's signature.

The power to make appointments to office by
and with the advice and consent of the Senate has,
in practice, also largely deviated from the intentions of the draftsmen of the Constitution. By
giving the President this power, it was intended to
place upon him the responsibility of the nomination, and to give the Senate the power to consider
the fitness of the nomination by a canvass of the
merits of the nominee, so as to act as a check upon
the President's personal favoritism, nepotism,
lack of information, or any other influence resulting in an injudicious nomination. When, however,
by the growth of the population and the enormous increase of federal offices consequent upon
such growth, it became practically impossible for the
President to arrive at a judicious conclusion as to
the vast number of appointments which had to be
made with each change of administration. Under
the pernicious doctrine that the prevailing party
had a right to all the federal offices, a habit
at first grew up of asking the advice of the senators of the States in which the officers were to
exercise their functions as to the proper nominee;
and this habit in time grew into a custom, which
gave to the senators, as they insisted, the right
to suggest to the President the names of the
persons who were to exercise federal functions

within the State from which they were commissioned. This became so established a rule of
action on the part of the Presidents, that it became
a matter of custom that when both senators of a
State for which an appointment was made declined to
confirm, the Senate deemed itself bound to reject the
nomination. Therefore, during President Garfield's
administration, the two senators from New York resigned their seats in 1881, because what was termed
" the courtesy of the Senate " had been violated in
their cases, and the Collector of the Port of New
York had been nominated without consultation, and
in disregard of their wishes. An active movement
is now proceeding in the United States to institute
some system of civil service reform which will relieve the President from the necessity of making
nominations to the Senate of a vast number of officers who are periodically to be appointed under
the " spoils " system. From the necessities of the
situation the nominations of inefficient men by the
President is inevitable if he acts entirely upon his
own judgment, in disregard and without previous
consultation with the senators from the States. It
is clearly impossible for him to know much of the
persons thus nominated. He is, therefore, dependent upon the senators of the several States for suggestion and advice as to the nominations, and this

dependence makes of the senators the heads of the great political machines of the States, and they thereby become, instead of the President, the fountains of federal honor and office within their respective States. The civil service reform movement, therefore, in the United States will, if successful, deal a blow at the "spoils" system, which makes each Presidential election a raffle for one hundred thousand offices, and the incumbents a vast horde of hungry office-holders, upon whom assessments for campaign funds can be levied by the party in power, which are promptly paid, because an incumbent knows full well that a refusal to contribute involves danger to him from his own party, and that a change of administration bringing into power the opposition party, will, almost as a matter of course, cause his office to be vacated. This reform is also an attack upon the " courtesy of the Senate," which constitutes senators, instead of mere judges of proper or improper nominations, a cabal to dictate nominations to the President, and in the event of a Presidential refusal, to decline confirmation, irrespective of the merits of the nominees.

Each term of the Presidential office begins on the fourth day of March succeeding the election, and continues for a period of four years. The people of

THE EXECUTIVE POWER. 79

the United States are at liberty to reëlect the incumbent if they see fit : there is no constitutional restriction upon them in regard to the number of times he may be reëlected. But as Washington declined a nomination after his second term had expired, and pointed out, in so declining, the impropriety of repeated elections of the same officer, however popular, it has become part of the unwritten law of the United States that the Presidential term should not be extended beyond eight years.

In case of the removal of the President from office, or of his death, resignation or inability to discharge its powers and duties, it is provided that the same shall devolve upon the Vice-President. And it is further provided that Congress may by law provide for the case of the removal, death, resignation or inability of both President and Vice-President, and declare what officer shall then act as President, and such officer shall act accordingly until the disability be removed or a President be elected. Congress did provide, that in such a case the President of the Senate, or, if there be none, the Speaker of the House of Representatives for the time being, shall act as President until the disability is removed or a President elected ; and in the event of the office of both President and Vice-President becoming vacant, the Secretary of State shall thereupon cause a notification to be made to the Executive of every State, and a new election shall thereupon be ordered.*

There is no provision for succession, in the event of there being no President of the Senate and no Speaker of the House of Representatives. The death of President Garfield, at a time when there was neither President of the Senate nor Speaker of the House of Representatives, created a case when, in the event of the death of President Arthur before the Senate could be convened, no succession for the Presidency had been provided for. It is therefore clear that a further provision must be made by law for such a possible contingency.*

Another question which arose during the prolonged disability of President Garfield, intermediate between his wounding and his death, is one which has never yet received complete and satisfactory solution, and may create trouble unless anticipated by law. The Constitution provides that, in the event of a Presidential disability, the office of President shall devolve upon the Vice-President; but there is no provision that such a devolution of the office

* See Addenda, new law.

shall be simply temporary in character, and that the Vice-President shall resign the same when the disability ceases to exist. The great personal popularity of President Garfield, the hope of speedy recovery from his disability, and the widespread sympathy for his condition, made it inexpedient for the Vice-President to claim the office of President during this inability of the President to perform the duties of his office. But had the Vice-Presidency then been held by a person of less delicacy of sentiment and appreciation of popular opinion, the questions of who should determine when an inability arises, and for what term the Vice-President should hold office in the event of the disability being removed, might have become very serious ones. These recent events, therefore, point to some further amendments of the Revised Statutes in relation to the Presidential office.*

The President is not subject in the exercise of his discretion to any judicial interference. The Supreme Court of the United States cannot compel his signature to any act, nor cause him to refrain from doing any act. There is but one way to reach an abuse of his authority, and that is by impeachment. There is but one example in the history of the United States of an impeachment of

---

* *See* Addenda, new law.

4*

the President, and that is the impeachment of Andrew Johnson.

The House has the sole power of impeachment. The Senate has the sole power to try impeachments. When sitting for that purpose, they are on oath or affirmation. When the President of the United States is tried the Chief Justice of the United States presides, and no conviction can be had without the concurrence of two-thirds of the members present. The English precedents are followed in the trial by impeachment, of the House appointing triers, and the impeached officer having counsel, either assigned to him or appointed by him, to try the cause in his behalf.

Until 1868 the President had the power to create vacancies in the offices of heads of departments and their first assistants, by demanding resignations and filling vacancies temporarily until the Senate's consent could be obtained. In consequence of the conflict which then existed between the Legislative and Executive departments, eventually resulting in the impeachment of President Johnson, an act was passed allowing suspensions but preventing the President from making removals, and from making temporary appointments, except in the cases of death, voluntary resignation, absence or sickness of the chief of any bureau.

Under the implied powers which the President of the United States has received by the general investiture of power as the chief Executive officer of the United States, may be enumerated the following : As Commander-in-Chief of the Army and Navy of the United States, he has power to engage in hostilities, to institute a blockade, and to authorize captures and condemnations on the high seas. He has power to recognize a State Government in so far as to determine whether the government organized in a State is the duly constituted government of that State. He has power to protect aliens, as the care of our foreign relations is committed to him ; to remit forfeitures under his pardoning power ; to order a *nolle prosequi* to be entered at any stage in a criminal proceeding in the name of the United States ; to order a new trial on the sentence of a court martial ; and in time of war to suspend the writ of *habeas corpus* in any district where for the time being the civil authorities are powerless. He is authorized by the Constitution to appoint heads of departments in his official household. This is likewise done by and with the advice and consent of the Senate. This official household constitutes the Cabinet. The term Cabinet is not known to the Constitution of the United States, and has

84 CONSTITUTIONAL HISTORY.

been adopted in American political parlance in imitation of the term for the chiefs of the departments of the English Government. The Executive officers, who are the more immediate advisers of the President, and in the selection of whom greater latitude is allowed by the Senate than in that of any other officer, are the Secretary of State, Secretary of Interior, Secretary of the Treasury, Secretary of War, Secretary of Navy, Postmaster General, and Attorney General.

The Departments respectively under the direction of the secretaries are known as the Department of State, the Department of War, Department of the Treasury, Department of the Navy, Department of the Interior, the Post-office Department, and that under the Attorney General as the Department of Justice. There is also a Department of Agriculture, the head of which is, however, not a Cabinet officer.

The several duties of the Department of State are by law defined to be correspondences, commissions, and instructions to or with public ministers and consuls from the United States; carrying on of negotiations with public ministers of foreign states or princes; receiving memorials or other applications of foreign public ministers or other foreigners, and such other matters respecting foreign affairs as the President of the United States shall assign to the department, and the Secretary shall conduct the business of the department in such manner as the President shall direct.

To the Secretary of State are also entrusted the custody and charge of the seal of the United States and the seal of the Department of State. It is his duty to promulgate the laws ; to publish the same ; to give notice of intended or proposed amendments to the Constitution of the United States ; to give notice of the adoption of constitutional amendments, and to promulgate the same ; to lay before Congress, within ten days after the commencement of each regular session, a statement of the returns of port collectors and of foreign agents, a report of the foreign regulations of commerce and other commercial information, and of consular fees, and a synopsis of such of his communications to and from diplomatic officers as he may deem expedient to give for public information, a full list of all consular offices, &c.

The Department of the Treasury is charged by law with the duty of adjusting all claims and demands whatsoever by the United States or against them ; to keep an account of all appropriations, receipts and expenditures, and make estimates of the expenses of all the departments of

the Government; to keep accounts of all receipts
of internal revenue, and the accounts of all officers
collecting revenue; to keep an account of all expenditures for contingent purposes ; an account of all contingent expenditures for all governmental bureaus ;
and an account of all the funded indebtedness.
The Secretary signs all warrants on the Treasury
of the United States, and is charged with the duty,
from time to time to digest and prepare plans for
the improvement and management of the revenue,
and for the support of the public credit.   It is his
duty to prescribe the forms of keeping and rendering all public accounts and making returns ; he is
charged with the collection of all duties on imports
and tonnage ; and all accounts of the expenditures
of public moneys are to be settled within each fiscal year, except where the distance of the places
where such expenditure is to be made shall make
further time necessary.

It is his duty to interpret the revenue and
custom laws of the country, and to make proper
regulations not inconsistent with law in relation to
such collection.   He is charged with the duty of
preparing proper statistics showing the amounts of
goods that are imported and exported ; and also
what regulations he has made in relation thereto.
He is authorized to receive deposits of gold and

to give certificates therefor, and the coin and currency of the country are placed under his supervision. He is authorized to appoint disbursing
agents; to appoint persons who are authorized to
recover moneys due to the United States, and to
see to it that the revenue laws of the country are
enforced. The Secretary of the Treasury is required to make an annual report to Congress,
which report shall contain, according to the provisions of law, an estimate of the public revenue
and public expenditure for the fiscal year then current; plans for improving and increasing the
revenues from time to time, for the purpose of
giving information to Congress, and adopting
modes of raising moneys requisite to meet the
public expenditures; he is also to report all contracts for the supplies of the service which have
been made by him under his direction during the
year preceding, and also a statement of all expenditures of moneys appropriated for the discharge of
miscellaneous claims not otherwise provided for,
and paid by the Treasury; he is to report to Congress his rules and regulations in relation to the
appraisal of goods imported into the United
States, and to make a report showing the value of
such goods, and how much duty was collected; a
complete statement of the amounts collected from

seamen and the amounts expended for seamen; the amount expended at each Custom-house and the number employed thereat. A Bureau of Statistics is created under his direction and control, which is required to collect statistics of the agricultural, manufacturing, and domestic trade; of the currency and banks of the several States and Territories; and the Secretary is required to accompany his annual statement of public expenditure with reports which may be made to him by the auditors charged with the examination of the accounts of the Department of War and the Department of Navy respectively, showing the application of moneys appropriated for those departments for the respective year. He is required to lay before Congress annually an abstract of the separate amounts of moneys received from internal duties or taxes in each of the respective States and Territories or election districts of the United States. He is also required to cause an annual report of statistics of commerce and navigation to be prepared by the chief of the Bureau of Statistics, to be likewise laid before Congress annually; to report the number of persons employed in the Coast Survey and the business connected therewith, and the amount of compensation of every kind paid therefor. Every quarter he is required

to publish in some newspaper at the seat of
Government a statement of the whole receipts of
such quarter, and the whole expenditures of such
quarter; also showing the amount to the credit of
the Treasury, in the sub-Treasuries, in the different banks, in the Mint, and other depositories; the
amount for which drafts have been given, and
those remaining unpaid; and the balances remaining subject to draft; likewise to note all changes
made in the public depositories, and the reasons
for such change.

The law provides for the appointment of con-
trollers, auditors and treasurers in the department,
and specifies their duties.   It also provides for the
appointment of Registers, Commissioners of Customs, Commissioners of Internal Revenue, Con-
troller of the Currency, and of the Bureau of
Statistics, and Bureau of the Mint.   The heads of
these several departments are appointed by the
President, by and with the advice and consent of
the Senate, but the officers so appointed are placed
under the direction of the Secretary of the
Treasury.

The Department of Justice, at the head of which
stands the Attorney-General of the United States,
consists, in addition to the Attorney-General, of an
Assistant Attorney-General, a Solicitor-General, a

Solicitor of the Treasury, an Assistant Solicitor of the Treasury, a Solicitor of Internal Revenue, a Naval Solicitor, and Examiner of Claims, all of whom are appointed by the President, but are under the direction of the Attorney-General. The Attorney-General is required to give his advice and opinion upon all questions whenever required by the President. No public money is to be expended upon any site or land purchased by the United States for any purpose until the written opinion of the Attorney-General is had in favor of the validity of the title, and the District Attorneys of the United States in the various judicial districts of the United States are required, upon the application of the Attorney-General, to furnish any assistance or information in their power in relation to the title of public property lying within their respective districts.

All the Executive Departments are authorized to ask for advice from the Attorney-General on any question of law upon which the heads of the departments may have doubt. The Attorney-General and Solicitor-General are required to argue suits and writs of error and appeals to the Supreme Court of the United States, and suits in the Court of Claims in which the United States is interested. And the officers of the Department of Justice, under the direction of the Attorney-General, are required to give all opinions and render all services requiring skill of persons learned in the law, necessary to enable the President and heads of Departments, heads of Bureaus, and other officers in the departments to discharge their respective duties. They are required to procure proper evidence for, and to conduct and prosecute all suits and proceedings in the Supreme Court and Court of Claims, in which any officer of the United States is a party or may be interested. General superintendence is given to the Attorney-General over all the United States attorneys and marshals of all districts in the United States as to the manner of the discharge of their respective duties. The Attorney-General is authorized to employ counsel in such cases as in his discretion may require additional counsel.

The Solicitor of the Treasury has a general supervision over the bonds and actions of all persons charged with the collection of taxes and internal duties. He has power to take cognizance of, and to take measures to prevent and detect all frauds or attempted frauds upon the revenue, and to make such rules in relation to the collection of the revenue as in his judgment, and with the approbation of the Attorney-General, he may see fit.

The Attorney-General is required annually to print an edition of such opinions as may be deemed by him worthy of permanent record; and to make annually a report of the conduct of his office and of his subordinates, to Congress.

The Post-office Department consists of the Post-master-General and three Assistant Postmasters-General, appointed by the President. It is the duty of the Postmaster-General to establish and discontinue post-offices; to prescribe the manner of keeping accounts and rendering returns ; to make contracts for postal service ; by and with the consent of the President, to negotiate postal treaties and conventions ; reduce or increase the rate of postage or mail matter conveyed between the United States and foreign countries ; make rules and regulations as to fines, penalties, forfeitures or disabilities in relation to his department. He is required to make an annual report to Congress of all contracts made for carrying the mail within the preceding year; the prices paid, etc., of all land and water mails established or ordered within the preceding year; the names of persons employed to transport it, price paid etc., and all allowances made to contractors within the preceding year in addition to the sum originally stipulated in their respective contracts, and the reasons for the same; to report all the curtailment of expenses effected within the preceding year; to report on the revenues of the department for the preceding year, and the amount actually paid for carrying the mail, and comparing the same with preceding years. The Postmaster is required to report to Congress all contracts made for the carriage of mail matter, and to give a detailed account of the postal business and agencies in foreign countries, which report is first to be submitted to the Secretary of the Treasury, and then printed and submitted to Congress as part of the Treasurer's Report.

The Department of the Navy consists of the Secretary of the Navy and Assistant Secretary of the Navy and a large executive force. The War Department consists of the Secretary of War and a large executive force. It is unnecessary to enter into detail as to the duties and functions of the Naval and War Departments, as the terms indicate what their functions are.

The Department of the Interior is a much more complicated one. The Secretary of the Interior has an Assistant Secretary, appointed by the President. The Secretary of the Interior is charged with the supervision of public business relating to the following subjects: 1. The census;

therefore a Census Bureau with its staff of officers
is under his direction and control. 2. The public
lands, including mines. 3. Indians. 4. All pensions and bounty lands. 5. All patents for inventions. 6. The custody and distribution of all
publications. 7. The Education Department. 8.
The Government Hospital for the Insane. 9. The
Columbia Asylum for the Deaf and Dumb. Under
him, therefore, there is a Commissioner of the
Land Office ; a Commissioner of Indian Affairs ; a
Commissioner of Pensions ; a Commissioner of
Patents, and Assistant Commissioners ; Superintendent of Public Documents, a Bureau of Railroads, Superintendent of Census, Director of Geo-
logical Surveys, and Commissioner of Education.

A supplemental Executive Department was
created in 1862, independent of the other departments, but the head of which is not a member of
the cabinet, called the Department of Agriculture.
This commissioner is charged with the duty of
procuring and preserving all information concerning agriculture which can be obtained by means of
books and correspondence, and by practical and
scientific experiments ; to collect new and valuable seeds and plants, and to test by cultivation the
value of such of them as may require such tests,
and to propagate such as may be worthy of

propagation, and to distribute them among agriculturists. This purchase and distribution of seeds by the department is confined to rare and uncommon ones, or such as can be made more profitable by frequent changes from one part of the country to another, and the purchase for propagation of trees, plants, shrubs, vines, and cuttings, are confined to those which are adapted to general cultivation, and to promote the interests of agriculture and horticulture throughout the United States.

CHAPTER IV.

ONE of the main reasons why the Articles of Confederation failed securely to establish national entity, was because no proper judicial organization existed thereunder to enforce the law; Congress was made the tribunal of last resort in controversies between the States, and the only power given to Congress to create judicial tribunals was to create prize courts.

Alexander Hamilton, in treating of the Judiciary department of the United States and the necessity for its creation, with reference to the power to adjudge acts void which are passed by a coördinate department—the Legislature—says : "The complete independence of the courts of justice is peculiarly essential in a limited Constitution. By a limited Constitution I understand one which contains certain specified exceptions to legislative authority, such for instance, as that it shall pass no bill of attainder, no *ex post facto* law and the

96

like. Limitations of this kind can be preserved in practice in no other way than through the medium of the courts of justice, whose duty it must be to declare all acts contrary to the manifest tenor of the Constitution void; without this all the reservations of particular rights or privileges would amount to nothing. * * * It is urged that the authority which can declare the acts of another void must necessarily be superior to the one whose acts may be declared void. As this doctrine is of great importance in all the American Constitutions, a brief discussion of the ground on which it rests cannot be unacceptable." .

"There is no position which depends on clearer principles than that every act of delegated authority contrary to the tenor of the commission under which it is exercised is void. No legislative act, therefore, contrary to the Constitution can be valid. To deny this would be to affirm that the deputy is greater than his principal; that the servant is above his master; that the representatives of the people are superior to the people themselves; that men acting by virtue of powers may do not only what their powers do not authorize, but what they forbid. If it be said that the legislative body are themselves the constitutional judges of their own powers, and that the construc-

5

tion that they put upon them is conclusive upon the
other departments, it may be answered, that this
cannot be the natural presumption where it is not
to be collected from any particular provision in
the Constitution. It is not otherwise to be supposed that the Constitution could intend to enable
the representatives of the people to substitute their
will to that of their constituents. It is far more
rational to suppose that the courts were designed
to be an intermediate body between the people and
the Legislature, in order, among other things, to
keep the latter within the limits assigned to their
authority. • The interpretation of the laws is the
proper and peculiar province of the courts. A
Constitution is in fact, and must be regarded by
the judges as a fundamental law. It must, therefore, belong to them to ascertain its meaning as
well as the meaning of any particular act proceeding from the legislative body. If there should
happen to be an irreconcilable variance between
the two, that which has the superior obligation
and validity ought to be preferred. In other words,
the Constitution ought to be preferred to the
statute, the intention of the people to the intention of their agents. Nor does the conclusion by
any means suppose a superiority of the judicial
to the legislative power. It only supposes that the

power of the people is superior to both, and that
where the will of the Legislature declared in its
statutes stands in opposition to the will of the
people declared in the Constitution, the judges
ought to be governed by the latter rather than by
the former ; they ought to regulate their decisions
by the fundamental laws rather than by those
which are not fundamental. * * * It can be of
no weight to say that the courts on the pretence
of a repugnancy may substitute their own pleasure
to the constitutional intentions of the Legislature.
This might as well happen in the case of two con-
tradictory statutes, or it might as well happen in
every adjudication upon any single statute. The
courts must declare the sense of the law, and if
they should be disposed to exercise will instead of
judgment, the consequence would equally be the
substitution of their pleasure to that of the legislative body. The observation, if it proved anything,
would prove that there ought to be no judges distinct from that body. If, then, the courts of justice
are to be considered as the bulwarks of a limited
constitution against legislative encroachments,
this consideration will afford a strong argument
for the permanent tenure of judicial officers, since
nothing will contribute so much as this to that independent spirit in the judges which must be

essential to the faithful performance of so arduous a duty."—*Federalist* No. 78.

I have cited the foregoing passage at length because vesting courts with power to declare the acts of the highest law-making power unconstitutional would, at first blush, seem to be dangerous. In the mother country, from which the United States derived its institutions, such a power is not given to the courts. Violent constructions of the meaning of words employed by the Legislature are sometimes resorted to, on the theory that Parliament could not have intended to mean anything repugnant to natural justice ; yet no British Court ever declared an act of Parliament void on the ground of a violation of the English Constitution.

But for the fact that there is a check upon the judges to prevent them from wantonly vetoing legislation by declaring it to be unconstitutional, the judiciary would be the supreme governing power of the land, and that as there is no power superior to the judicial one, to revise their errors of judgment or to make inquiry whether they have reasonably exercised that power or not, it is within the power of the court of last resort of the United States to declare every act unconstitutional, however violent such a declaration may be and thus nullify all legislation. There is, however, in the Constitution of the United

States a check upon this power, lodged in the leg-islative body itself. The power to impeach and to remove for any cause appearing sufficient to two-thirds of the Senate upon presentment by the House, makes all the members of the Supreme Court of the United States subject to removal if they are guilty of a gross violation of the judicial discretion lodged by the Constitution in them. And as the members of the Senate, who are charged with the duty of trying the impeachment are responsible to their States, and the members of the House who make the presentment are in their turn responsible to their constitutents—the people of the States—(by this system of checks and balances thus created by the Constitution for the purpose of preserving each department within its proper sphere) are finally called upon to deter-mine whether their servants have acted within the limits of the powers respectively delegated to them.

The reasoning of Hamilton seems to be conclu-sive—that no written Constitution deputing limited powers can, by any possibility, be enforced against the deputed agents exercising for the time such powers, unless a court of judges, sitting for life or during good behavior, is interposed between the people and their legislative agents, clothed with

the power to declare a final opinion on the constitutionality of the statutes emanating from the
Legislature.   The Constitution of the United
States does not stand alone in that particular. All
the State Constitutions grant to the State Courts
of last resort the power finally to declare upon
the constitutionality of State legislation, and every
statute, therefore, passed in the United States may
be called into question, as to the constitutional
power to enact the same, either before a State or
federal court, or before both.

The judicial power of the United States is
lodged under the Constitution in a Supreme Court
and such inferior tribunals as Congress may from
time to time ordain and establish.

The judges of the Supreme Court and inferior
courts hold their offices during good behavior, and
they are entitled to receive a compensation which,
during their continuance in office, is not permitted
to be diminished.   The judicial power conferred
upon the Supreme Court extends to all cases in
law and in equity arising under the Constitution,
the laws of the United States and treaties made, or
which shall be made, under their authority ; to all
cases affecting ambassadors and other public ministers and consuls; to all cases of admiralty and maritime jurisdiction to which the United States shall

be a party ; to controversies between two or more
States ; between a State and citizens of another
State ; between citizens of different States ; between citizens of the same State claiming
lands under grants of different States ; and
between a State or the citizens thereof and foreign
States, citizens or subjects. By the eleventh
amendment to the Constitution, however, it was
enacted that the judicial power of the United
States is not to be construed to extend to any suits
in law or in equity, commenced or prosecuted
against one of the States by citizens of another
State, or by citizens or subjects of any foreign
State.

It is further provided in the Constitution, that
in all cases affecting ambassadors and other public
ministers, consuls, and cases in which a State shall
be a party, the Supreme Court shall have original
jurisdiction. In all the other cases before mentioned,
the Supreme Court has appellate jurisdiction, both
as to law and fact, with such restrictions and regulations as Congress may make. As the Constitution itself declared wherein the original jurisdiction of the Supreme Court shall consist, Congress
thereafter became powerless to assign original
jurisdiction to that court in cases other than
those specified in the article. A State may bring

an original suit in the Supreme Court against a citizen of another State, but not against one of her own citizens.

Although the Constitution vests the Supreme Court with original jurisdiction in certain cases mentioned, which may not be enlarged by Congress, Congress, nevertheless, may lodge concurrent jurisdiction in some of the inferior courts created by it under the powers conferred by the Constitution.

Under the Constitution, the States are prohibited from doing a number of things, some of which are incompatible with the interests of the Union. There would be no possibility to keep the States within the limitations thus imposed if the States themselves were to be the judges of the extent of such prohibition, or its application to a particular case ; and, therefore, with the Supreme Court of the United States is necessarily lodged the power to correct and prevent infractions thereof. " This body," says Hamilton, " must have either a direct negative on the State laws, or authority in the federal courts to over-rule such as might be a manifest contravention of the articles of the Union. There is no third course that I can imagine. * * * Controversies between the nation and its members or citizens can only be properly referred to national tribunals. Any other plan would be contrary to reason, to precedent, and decorum."

"The peace of the whole," again says Hamilton, "ought not to be left at the disposal of a part. The Union will undoubtedly be answerable to foreign powers for the conduct of its members, and the responsibility for an injury ought ever to be accompanied with the faculty of preventing it. Therefore, the federal judiciary ought to have cognizance of all causes in which the citizens of other countries are concerned. This is not less essential to the preservation of public faith than to the security of public tranquility. The power of determining causes between two States, between one State and the citizens of another, and between the citizens of different States, is perhaps not less essential to the peace of the Union than that which has just been examined. The institution of the Imperial Chamber by Maximillian, towards the close of the fifteenth century, did much to prevent the dissensions and private wars which had theretofore harried Germany. It may be esteemed a basis of the Union, that the citizens of each State shall be entitled to all the privileges and immunities of the citizens of the several States, and if it be a just principle that every Government ought to possess the means of executing its own provisions, by its own authority, it will follow, that in order to the inviolable maintenance of that equality of privileges and immunities to which the citizens of the Union will be entitled the national judiciary ought to preside in all cases in which one State or its citizens are opposed to another State or its citizens."

The jurisdiction conferred in the case of treaties is so necessary a one that it is almost too clear for argument. The cognizance of maritime causes is a necessary part of the power of the National Government as a matter of public peace. It is the only jurisdiction that was conferred by the Articles of Confederation on national courts.

The only case where citizens of the same State can go into the courts of the United States, is where they claim lands under grants of different States.

Shortly after the adoption of the Constitution, the Judiciary Act was passed, constituting national tribunals inferior to the Supreme Court, the powers and duties of which, under judicial interpretation, we propose now to examine.

When the question to which the judicial power of the Federal Government extends under the Constitution forms an ingredient of the original cause, it is in the power of Congress to give the

federal courts jurisdiction of that cause, although
other questions of fact or law may be involved in it.
The other questions may be decided as incidental
to that which gives the jurisdiction. Cases may
arise under the laws of the United States by implication, so that they come under the judicial
power of the Federal Government. It is not unusual for a legislative act to involve consequences
not expressed. Where a defendant seeks protection of the laws of the United States or under the
Constitution in any of the States, it is a case arising under the law, and gives to the United States
courts jurisdiction.

The Constitution not only confers admiralty
jurisdiction upon the courts of the United States,
but as it superadds the word maritime, every latent
doubt is removed thereby as to the extent of the
jurisdiction, and it has, therefore, been held to include all maritime contracts, torts and injuries
which are, in the understanding of the common
law as well as of the admiralty law, maritime
causes. The grant, therefore, of admiralty power
to the federal courts was not intended to be limited
or interpreted by the theory of cases of admiralty
jurisdiction in England when the Constitution was
adopted. The admiralty, therefore, has jurisdiction over maritime contracts, although the power

contemplated begins and ends in the State, and is prescribed only in waters within the State; and the admiralty jurisdiction extends to torts committed on the navigable waters although they are within the body of a county within the State.

As to the original jurisdiction of the Supreme Court of the United States, Congress cannot add to nor diminish that jurisdiction; but in the creation of the inferior federal courts, it may so regulate the jurisdiction conferred by the Constitution as to deprive one court of it, substitute another court, or change the courts upon which jurisdiction has been conferred at its own will; and of course it can modify the practice of the court in any other respect that it may deem conducive to the administration of justice.

It is not competent for the States, by any local legislation, to enlarge or limit, or narrow the admiralty and maritime jurisdiction of the federal courts. In exercising this jurisdiction they are exclusively governed by the legislation of Congress, and in the absence thereof, by the general principles of the maritime law. The State Legislatures have no right to prescribe the rule by which the federal courts shall act, nor the jurisprudence which they shall administer. If any other doctrine were established it would amount to a complete surrender of the jurisdiction of the federal courts, to the fluctuating policy and legislation of the States. If the States have a right to prescribe any rule, they have a right to prescribe all rules, to limit, control, or bar suits in national courts.

In an early case before the Supreme Court of the United States it was claimed that an Indian nation with which the Government had entered into engagements analogous to treaties, was a foreign state in the sense of the Constitution; but this claim was negatived by the court, and the existence of such tribe as an independent power denied. The Indians in that respect form an anomaly in American jurisprudence, because they are neither citizens nor aliens while in their tribal condition. They are under the exclusive jurisdiction of a subdepartment of the Interior Department of United States government, known as the Indian Department, but during a brief period they were under the jurisdiction of the War Department.

There are many cases where the State courts have concurrent jurisdiction with the United States courts, such as where the United States sues, where a State sues a citizen of another State, where a State sues an alien, where a citizen of one State sues another State, where a citizen sues an alien and where an alien sues a citizen. In all such cases, however, it is provided by United States statute, that a removal can be had of such causes either before or after issue joined and before trial, into the United States courts by either party to the record.*

The reader's attention has already been drawn to the Amendment of the Constitution which provides that a State cannot be made a party at the suit of a citizen of its own State or of another State, adopted for the purpose of guarding against the impairment of the dignity of the State by being constantly subjected at the instance of any private individual to being dragged before the Supreme Court of the United States as a delinquent. Although this provision guards a State, as such, from being made a party, nevertheless the construction given by the United States courts to this clause, allows State officers, upon whom rests the duty to perform an act under the direction either of the Constitution of the United States or a statutory law of the United States, to be subjected to mandatory proceedings on the part of the Supreme Court of the United States, compelling them to conform to judgments and decrees, and to perform or not to perform a particular act.

At the time of the formation of the Constitution

---

* *See* Addenda, new law (1888).

considerable criticism was made upon the clause which secured a jury trial in criminal cases alone; but as the common law of England was part of the heritage of the people of the United States, and as a large part of the system of jurisprudence which was thus transferred to the American people from England was that which was administered by chancellors without a jury, it was deemed wise not to interfere with the body of law wherein jury trials were unknown, for which no substitute could readily be found. Besides, as the Constitution of the United States was mainly intended to guard against tyranny, and as the tyrannical powers of government would be exercised not in private personal claims cognisable in equity courts, but through the criminal courts, and might be attempted to be exercised by bills of attainder passed by pliant legislative bodies, the provision preventing the passage of *ex post facto* laws and bills of attainder and securing to every man the right to a trial by jury at the place where the alleged crime was supposed to be committed, was a sufficient safeguard against the tyranny of executive and legislative power. A statute was therefore held to be unconstitutional which provided that a party might be tried by the court without a jury on a charge of libel, although that statute gave him the right to appeal to another court where the charge must be tried by a jury, because the accused was entitled in the first instance to be tried by a jury without having his cause prejudiced by a conviction by a court prior to such trial; and although the statute gave the prisoner power to determine how he should be tried, yet as the constitutional provision was intended not for the protection of one individual, but for the protection of the community, such a waiver of his rights was not conclusive: the courts would look at the record alone, and if the trial was unconstitutional the individual waiver made no difference as to the illegality of the conviction.

No provision in the United States Constitution is perhaps more conservative of individual liberty, or more carefully worded in that particular than that which relates to treason. No case of constructive treason can arise under the plain provision of the Constitution in that particular. No conspiracy against the Government, however clear, unless it consists of the actual levying of war, can be construed to be treason. Even resistance to the execution of the laws of the United States accompanied with force, if such resistance is for a private purpose only, is not treason. To constitute the offence of treason, the resistance must be of a public nature.

Under the section which gives to the citizen of each State the privileges and immunities of the citizens of the several States, it has been held that a citizen of one State cannot claim the right to vote for an election to office in another State in which he is not a citizen under the special laws of that State. Each State has the right to declare who its citizens in a political sense shall be. The meaning of these rights of a citizen of one State in other States has been limited to the right to hold and dispose of real and personal property, to trade, and to transact all the private affairs of life ; but it is held that it was not intended by the Constitution to obliterate the privileges and immunities which arise from citizenship in the several States, nor to interfere with the rights of the States to pass such laws as they may see fit by which they can properly determine whom to admit to the right of suffrage, the time of residence within the State necessary to constitute citizenship, nor to limit the power of the States to subject their citizens, and therefore the citizens of all other States, to certain regulations and limitations as to political rights arising from property or residence considerations. Nor can a citizen of one State claim immunity from the laws to which another State subjects its citizens. The main purpose of this provision is to prevent dis-

criminating legislation against citizens of one by
other States, and to secure for them the equal
protection of the laws of all States. Nor can a
citizen claim protection of the laws of his own State
in another State, because were he permitted to do
so, his rights would be superior in the State of
which he is not a citizen to those which he has
wherein he is a citizen. Another limitation exists,
that the word citizen means citizen of the United
States. If either of the States recognized certain
persons as citizens who are not so recognized by
the United States, such citizens would not have
the immunities and privileges accorded to the
citizens of the United States. If a State were to
recognize as citizens of the State women or minors
who are not admitted to the rights of citizenship
in the United States, they could not claim this
general citizenship by reason of the special law
creating them citizens within the domain of a single
State.

Under the clause of the Constitution of the
United States which gives Congress the power to
dispose of and make all needful rules and regulations respecting the territory belonging to the
United States, a considerable body of legislation
and of judicial decisions has sprung up in relation
to the public lands of the country. At the time of

the adoption of the Constitution a vast body of land was ceded by several States to the general Government. By the Louisiana and Florida purchases, the Texas acquisitions, and subsequently by the purchases from Mexico under the Guadalupe Hidalgo treaty of a large proportion of the present western coast of the United States, and finally by the purchase of Alaska, an enormous territory, covering three and a half million square miles, came into the possesion of the United States to act with as it saw fit. With this domain the Government dealt; first, in selecting vast tracts for the Indian tribes; secondly, in reserving miners' rights; thirdly, in providing homesteads for actual settlers; fourthly, in granting concessions to soldiers in the Indian, Mexican, and Civil wars by way of bounty; fifthly, in gifts to States for educational and other purposes; sixthly, in making enormous grants to railway corporations as inducements to build the trans-continental lines which connect the Pacific with the Atlantic coasts; seventhly, by the sale of the public lands as a source of revenue. Under the homestead laws any person may select one hundred and sixty acres, and after a specified time, if he erects thereon a house and actually tills the soil and gives notice of his intention to occupy the same, he can for a mere nominal payment cov-

ering expense of issue of patent, etc., become the
owner of the land he had in possession.

Under the Florida, Louisiana, and Mexican
purchases the United States was called upon to
deal with grants of great bodies of land which had
been by the Spanish and French Crowns and
Mexican Government ceded to individuals, colonies
and adventurers during the prior occupation of
that territory by these foreign governments.
Under the promise given by the treaties by which
the purchases were made, that full faith and credit
would be given to titles theretofore acquired in
good faith, the United States has issued patents
for vast tracts of those territories to individuals
whose claims of title antedated the cession to the
United States.   An attempt has been made in
recent years to limit the rights acquired under
such patent to eleven square leagues, but such
efforts have been rejected by Congress, on the
ground, that however desirable it may be to prevent the public domain from being monopolized,
good faith demanded and the treaties compelled
respect for such prior titles by immunity from the
claim of the United States to lands thus separated
from the public domain.

Under the provision of the Constitution which
gives to the Constitution of the United States and

the laws of Congress supreme power, only such power is meant which has been specifically or by necessary implication conferred upon Congress by the Constitution. The States are sovereign and independent governments in all matters not delegated to the general Congress. Their power to tax is unrestricted unless they exercise it in such a way as to impede the operation of proper United States legislation or the functions of United States officers. In this power the State is sovereign and supreme, and its wisdom or fairness cannot be inquired into by federal tribunals.

The amendments to the Constitution, with the exception of the last three, are mainly intended to secure personal rights against infringement by the United States Government. Under the first amendment which forbids Congress from passing any law respecting the establishment of religion or prohibiting the free exercise of speech, of the press, or of the people peaceably to assemble, it has been held that Congress has no power to punish individuals for disturbing assemblies of peaceable citizens; that this is the prerogative of the several States, and that it belongs to the preservation of the public peace entrusted to local legislation.

Although the right of the people to keep and bear arms is secured by the Constitution of the

United States, the provision has been held not to prevent the passage of a law to prevent the carrying of concealed weapons.

Under the provision which secures the right of the people against unreasonable searches and seizures, it has been held that those provisions of the United States revenue laws which authorize a revenue officer to issue a summons for the production of books and papers were valid, and that this provision in itself does not prevent the Legislatures of the several States in absence of any State and constitutional inhibition from passing such seizure laws as they see fit.

The provisions securing all persons held to answer for a capital or otherwise infamous crime against conviction except by a presentment or indictment of a grand jury, except in cases arising under the land and naval forces in time of war, or public danger, have been construed not to apply to misdemeanors, and not to apply to trials in a State court for an alleged crime without any previous indictment by a grand jury. And although a man may not be twice put in jeopardy of life or limb for the same offence, nevertheless he may be twice tried for the same crime, if no acquittal or conviction has been had by a prior jury because of a disagreement or mis-trial. In the provision that no man shall be deprived of life, liberty or property without due process of law, process has been held to mean some form of proceeding of a judicial nature known to the common law. Therefore, an order of the President is not due process, nor is a statute which deprives a man of his property by the repeal of a prior grant of land due process. Rights once acquired cannot be divested without a process known to judicial forms, resulting in a trial of some kind.

In the same amendment it is provided that no private property shall be taken for public use without just compensation. This of course implies that no private property shall be taken for private use at all, with or without compensation. Public use, of course, implies all use made necessary by war, in which event property may be taken without compensation; and also for all public purposes, when there is no war, which arise under the exercise of the power of eminent domain. This right need not be exercised directly by the general Congress, but may be deputed to corporations by giving grants of power to them to perform functions public in their character, such as building of roads, bridges, water-ways, &c., and who may be empowered to exercise the right of eminent domain on making compensation in a manner provided by a statute.

No State nor the United States can take property
from individuals for ends which are not public.
Thus it has been held that to exercise the taxing
power in aid of private enterprises, however desirable the encouragement of such enterprises may be
for the general prosperity of the community, is unconstitutional and improper legislation. It is possible that at some future day the Supreme Court
of the United States may reverse its former decisions under the regulating of commerce clause
and, upon the ground just stated, declare protective
tariff legislation under guise of laws for the collection of revenue unconstitutional. No State
can condemn the property of the United States.
.The power in that respect of the Federal Government is exclusive. It can neither be enlarged nor
diminished by a State, nor can any State prescribe
the manner in which it must be exercised, and the
consent of a State can never be a condition precedent to its exercise.

In case of criminal prosecutions the Constitution
limits the power of the courts to trials within the
district where the crime has been committed, gives
to the accused the right to be confronted with the
witnesses against him, secures for him the compulsory process of courts to obtain witnesses in his
favor, and compels the courts to assign counsel for

his defence. Under this provision it has been held by the United States courts, that no persons, except those who are connected with the army or navy, in districts where the courts are open can be charged with crime and tried before a military commission.

One of the most important protections to individual liberty embodied in the Constitution of the United States is in the seventh article of the amendments, which provides that no fact tried by a jury shall be reëxamined by any court in the United States otherwise than according to the rules of common law. This secures citizens of the United States against vexatious proceedings by which they may be again and again harassed on the same subject matter of complaint, after the matter has once been judicially determined. When so judicially determined both the laws of the States and the procedures of the courts of the United States provide for proper appeals by means of which the question of errors may be considered and determined, and thus alone the subject matter of the controversy may be reviewed. When determined, however erroneously, by a court of last resort or by a competent judicial tribunal from whose judgment no appeal has been taken, the judgment is to be considered final, and in the

6

interests of justice not to be shaken nor to be re-examined by any department or any special court or by any other court, as between the same parties.

Trial by jury is so often referred to in the National and State Constitutions that what is a trial by jury has been the subject of judicial examination. It has been held that a decision by a jury in which three-fourths of a jury are permitted to determine, is not such a trial by a jury; and that the only proper judgment known to the Constitution that can be rendered in a trial by a jury, is that which requires unanimity on the part of the jury.

The eighth amendment, which provides that excessive bail shall not be required, nor excessive fines be imposed, nor cruel or unusual punishments be inflicted, has been held to apply only to the imposition of fines and punishments by United States tribunals for offences against the United States, and that it was not intended to protect the citizens of the several States from the penal codes of such States, although the fines or punishments may be considered both excessive and cruel.

The thirteenth, fourteenth, and fifteenth amendments, which were the result of the civil war, had for their objects the abolishing of slavery, the securing to all persons who were citizens of the United States the position of citizens of the States wherein they resided, and to prevent any State from withholding the equal protection of its laws from any of the citizens of the United States by reason of any distinction of race, color, or previous condition of servitude. They also had for their object the repeal of the apportionment of congressional seats which had previously been based upon population unrepresented as citizens; the slaves in the Southern States, counting as part of the population prior to the war for purposes of representation, although treated as chattels for all other purposes, gave to the South an undue proportion of representation as compared with the free white population of the North. These amendments were also intended to prevent persons from becoming officers of the United States, who had actually engaged in rebellion unless the disability was removed. And finally their provisions are clear and unmistakable declarations forever to prevent the questioning of the validity of the public debt of the United States which had been created to suppress the rebellion, and on the other hand forever to prevent the United States from assuming to pay, or the States from ever permitting the payment of, any debt which had been created or incurred in aid of the insurrection or rebellion. Every claim for loss or emancipation of any slaves, or losses by rebels of property, is forever barred by these amendments, and all courts have the duty imposed upon them to declare all such debts, obligations and claims illegal and void. Under the foregoing amendments it has been held that the States are not permitted, under State educational laws, to exclude colored children from equal educational advantages because of color or their African descent, but that separate schools might be maintained wherein such children may be educated apart from the whites.

Under the provision that the rights of the citizens of the United States shall not be denied or abridged by the United States or any State on account of race, color, or previous condition of servitude, it has been held by the Supreme Court of the United States that the right of suffrage is not thereby conferred upon any one ; that it simply prevents the States from giving preference to one citizen of the United States over another on account of race, color, or previous condition of servitude, and that it leaves the States as free as theretofore to regulate the right to vote, but prevents them from making any distinction by reason of race, color, or previous condition.

We have now passed in review the leading articles of the Constitution of the United States, and the main questions that have arisen for judicial determination under them. The apprehension that was originally felt that the Supreme Court of the United States would not faithfully declare the principles of the Constitution, and that it either on the one side would be under the domination of the legislative body, or, on the other, attempt to dominate the Legislature by improperly declaring such measures unconstitutional which could be so declared only by a violent misinterpretation of the fundamental law, has proved unfounded. The duty has thus far been performed with conscientious firmness, and so thoroughly do the people of the United States, including its Legislatures, rely upon the fearless performance of that duty on the part of the courts of last resort, that when an objection is made in a legislative body, that a certain provision in a proposed law is of doubtful constitutionality, the ready answer is made that if it is so the courts will so declare it, and thus eliminate it from the law.

We have seen that the Supreme Court of the United States itself is established by the Constitution. The power to establish inferior tribunals was given to Congress. The Supreme Court having original jurisdiction in two classes of cases only, viz., in cases affecting ambassadors, other public ministers and consuls, and in cases in which the

State is a party, Congress could not vest any portion of the judicial power of the United States in other than the courts ordained and established by itself. The appointment is vested by the Constitution in the President, but the organization of these inferior tribunals was made by the Judiciary Act of 1789. This act repeats the language of the Constitution of the United States in creating the Supreme Court, and extends the power of the court so as to include the right to issue writs of prohibition to the district courts when proceeding as a court of admiralty and maritime jurisdiction, and writs of mandamus in cases warranted by the principles and usages of law to any courts appointed by the authority of the United States or to persons holding office under the authority of the United States, where a State or an ambassador or other public minister, or a consul or vice-consul is a party. It defines the appellate jurisdiction of the Supreme Court to be by appeal, or writ of error from the final judgments of circuit courts or district courts acting as circuit courts ; in civil actions brought there by original process or removed there from the courts of the several States ; in all final judgments in the Circuit Court in civil causes removed there from any district court by appeal or writ of error where the amount in dispute exceeds two thousand dollars; also in cases of equity where the amount in dispute exceeds five thousand dollars; in all prize cases where the matter in dispute exceeds the sum of two thousand dollars, an appeal lies from the judgments of the District Courts. Likewise the Supreme Court is to entertain appeals of prize causes which were depending in the Circuit Courts. It is provided that if the judges are divided in opinion in any Circuit Court, the point shall be certified to the Supreme Court, and its decision or order in the premises shall be remitted back to the Circuit Court and there entered of record. An appeal is provided by the act of 1863 from final judgments or decrees of the District of Columbia to the Supreme Court of the United States. By subsequent legislation, under which the Court of Claims was created, appeals were provided for to the Supreme Court of the United States from decisions of the Court of Claims when such decisions are adverse to the United States in every case, and where adverse to the claimants when the amount in controversy exceeds three thousand dollars. It was further provided by the Judiciary Act that in case of a final judgment or decree in any suit in the highest court of a State in which a decision in the suit could be had, where is drawn in question the validity of a treaty or statute of, or an authority exercised under, the United States, and the decision is against its validity, or where is drawn in question the validity of a statute or an authority exercised under any statute, on the ground of being repugnant to the Constitution, treaties or laws of the United States, and the decision is in favor of its validity, or where any title, right, privilege or immunity is claimed under the Constitution, or any treaty or statute of, or commission held or authority exercised under the United States, and the decision is against the title, right, privilege or immunity, especially a set-off or claim by either party under such Constitution, treaty, statute, commission or authority, in such case the final judgment or decree may be reëxamined, and reversed or affirmed in the Supreme Court of the United States on a writ of error, and the writ shall have the same effect as if the judgment or decree complained of had been rendered or passed upon in a court of the United States, and the proceedings upon the reversal shall be the same except that the Supreme Court may in its discretion proceed to a final decision of the cause and award execution, or remand the same to the court from which it was removed ; and the Supreme Court may reaffirm, reverse, modify or affirm the judgment or decree of such State court, and may award execution or remand the same to the court from which it was removed by the writ.

This was a most important addition to and clear definition of the powers of the Supreme Court, for without it State courts, when once having acquired jurisdiction of a case, the same not having been removed or not being removable under the law to the federal courts, would have had the final power to determine upon the interpretation of an act of Congress or of a treaty, or of the application of the Constitution to any particular case ; and however strenuously a litigant might have invoked the protection of the Constitution of the United States against the wrong which was attempted to be done him, and however correct his views might have been, it would still have been in the power of the court to have denied, as against a statute of the State, any relief, and wilfully to have shut its eyes to the protection which was intended to be given by the Constitution of the United States to the litigant, and its decision would have been final, but for the fact that the Judiciary Act secures to every litigant the right to spread upon the record the questions applicable to his case, arising under the act of Congress or under the Constitution of the United States, and thus open to himself an

6*

appeal to the court of last resort of the United
States. Not only was this provision necessary for
the purpose of securing the supremacy of the Constitution and the acts of Congress thereunder over
the Constitutions and laws of the several States,
but it was also necessary for the purpose of securing uniformity of decisions and of interpretation
of the Constitution of the United States itself.

A vast number of questions have arisen under
this power of appeal to the Supreme Court of the
United States, and the business of that court became
so encumbered by reason of the numerous appeals
from State courts on the mere suggestions on the
record of a United States question, that it became
necessary for the court, somewhat arbitrarily, to
limit the appeals in such cases, and to limit the
inquiry arising from such an appeal from a State
court to the one question, "Is there a United
States question involved, and if so has it been
properly decided by the State courts?" The
Supreme Court of the United States have therefore declared that when an appeal is made from,
or writ of error taken to a court of last resort of
a State, they will not reëxamine as an appellate
court the correctness of the decision of the court
of last resort upon any other point than the constitutional one or one arising under the act of Con-

gress ; so that if they should come to the conclusion
that the case was correctly decided on the constitutional question, however erroneously the decision
may have been arrived at on questions which arose
entirely under the law of the State independent of
the Constitution of the United States and of the
United States laws, they will allow the decision to
stand. This action of the Supreme Court prevents
appeals to the Supreme Court of the United States
being taken by simply suggesting a constitutional
question in order to have the advantage of that
court's reëxamination of the whole record, and
if error be found to send it back to be corrected.

In cases, however, where the State itself is a party
or so directly interested that the bias of the State
court may be supposed to be in favor of the State's
views as against the United States Constitution or
the act of Congress, then the court will look into the
record sufficiently to see whether the decision upon
other points was not merely colorable, and not deem
itself concluded by the facts as found by the court
below ; in other words, whether the appellate jurisdiction of the Supreme Court applies in such a
case or not is not to be determined for the Supreme
Court by the findings of fact on the part of the
lower court which would preclude its jurisdiction,

but the Supreme Court of the United States will itself examine into facts sufficiently to ascertain whether or not its jurisdiction attaches.

The Judiciary Act further provides for writs of *ne exeat* by the Supreme Court and circuit judges, and of writs of injunction by the supreme, circuit and district judges ; a limitation upon the power to issue writs of injunction to State courts except in cases of bankruptcy ; and for the sake of uniformity in the various districts and circuits of the United States, the laws of the several States, except where the Constitution of the United States and statutes of the United States otherwise require, are re- garded as rules of decision at common law in the courts of the United States where they apply ; and a recent Judiciary Act has made even the forms of procedure in common law proceedings of the several State courts in the various districts where the courts sit, the forms of pleading and procedure of the United States courts.

Provision is made to prevent injustice by the dragging of persons out of the district in which they reside, by compelling plaintiffs, residents of the same State, to commence their actions within the district where the defendant resides, and all parties are permitted in the United States courts to manage their own cases personally or by counsel. The

Judiciary Act of 1789 makes ample provision for the issue of writs of *habeas corpus,* empowering and compelling all judges of the United States courts to issue this writ of privilege ; it gives an elaborate and detailed procedure for the return of the writ and the adjudications thereupon, and for appeals to circuit courts and Supreme Court of the United States, and stays all proceedings on the part of the State courts pending the consideration of the *habeas corpus* by the court below and the proceedings on appeal. Except in the Court of Claims the United States cannot involuntarily be made a party in a proceeding at law. The jurisdiction of the Court of Claims, as has been stated, is confined to claims founded upon any law of Congress or upon any regulation of an executive department, or upon any contract express or implied with the Government of the United States, and all claims which may specially be referred to it by either House of Congress ; all set-offs, counterclaims and claims for damages, whether liquidated or unliquidated on the part of the Government of the United States against any persons making claim against the Government in the courts.

By the acts of 1863, 1864, and 1868, the large claims arising from the seizure of cotton in the Southern States towards the close of the rebellion, were specially referred to the Court of Claims for action. The lobbies of the Houses of Congress prior to the organization of the Court of Claims had been so beset by claimants that it was found necessary to organize a special tribunal to take into consideration some of the cases which prior to that time were constantly presented to Congress. As the court, however, is one of limited jurisdiction and as numerous cases of claims against the United States Government arise, of which the court has no jurisdiction, the committees of Congress are still besieged by claimants, and appropriations are annually made by acts based upon reports of committees in cases where such committees sit as a court of judicature determining upon contested claims against the United States. Such a committee lacks the dignity and power of an ordinary court of justice, is subjected to influences which courts of justice are not ordinarily subjected to, and has not the machinery of a trained bar and regular sessions and continuous investigations by means of which the truth is ascertained in courts of justice. Hence meritorious claims are overlooked and meretricious ones are so often paid through the instrumentality of Congress, that the question has recently been considerably agitated whether it would not be wiser to have the sovereignty of the United States Government sufficiently unbend as to allow it to be sued in its own courts in the same manner as a private litigant.*

Both before and shortly after the adoption of the Constitution it was subjected to very severe criticism on the ground that it did not contain a Bill of Rights. A careful examination of the first twelve amendments will show that they were mainly passed to satisfy that objection. The objection that was urged to their adoption was that they were unnecessary; that the Constitution begins with the declaration, "We, the people of the United States, to secure the blessings of liberty to ourselves and our posterity, do ordain' and establish this Constitution for the United States of America;" that as the very purpose of the Constitution was to secure the blessings of liberty this declaration was, as Alexander Hamilton thought, a better recognition of popular rights than that which is contained in the elaborate declaration of rights in every State Constitution. It was, however, thought wiser in order to direct and quicken public opinion as to the rights which were intended to be reserved to the people, and which were not intended to be delegated to the general Congress, that they be in terms so specifically declared that any infraction thereof would be immediately recognized as unconstitutional and void. The first amendment, which related to free-

* *See* Addenda, new law (1887).

dom of religion "was enacted under the solemn consciousness," says Story, "of the dangers from ecclesiastical ambition, the bigotry of spiritual pride, and the intolerance of sects, and it was therefore deemed advisable to exclude from the national Government all power to act upon the subject. One of the reasons, too, for the necessity and wisdom of this course was the fact of the different religious complications of the majorities in different States. In some of the States the Catholics predominated; in others, Episcopalians; in others, Presbyterians; in others, Quakers; and any recognition on the part of the Government of any religion, except in the vaguest possible sort of way, would have given rise to considerable amount of jealousy and bickering."

The same amendment contains the security for freedom of the press and of speech. It is necessary to say that this security was not intended to give to any citizen an absolute right to speak or write or print whatever he saw fit without personal responsibility to the person aggrieved thereby. Every man was intended to have the right to speak and the right to print his opinions upon any subject whatever, without any prior restraint by way of censorship; but if he injure any other person in his rights of person, property or reputation, he is subject to civil and criminal prosecution for such injury precisely as he would be for any other injury to person or property. "Without such limitation," says Story, "it might become the scourge of the republic." The question how far the Government has the right to interfere with the press under the security thus afforded, and where licentiousness begins and liberty ends, is one which has often been mooted, but has not yet found a satisfactory solution. There is, however, much force in the contention that if the Government is to determine at any time what is liberty and what is license, then the constitutional provision is but a tissue of empty words, because every government, however autocratic, admits of certain strictures. The question is simply as to where the line should be drawn. The sounder doctrine in the United States now seems to be this: that the Government cannot exercise a restraint upon publications; in other words, no censorship of the press can be exercised under the constitutional guaranty that men may speak and write freely what they please; and however dangerous and bad the doctrine may be which is being advocated or promulgated by the press, it is not within the power of the Government to prevent its publication. On the other hand if the press attacks private rights, calumniates individual char-

acter, or destroys domestic peace, it is responsible
to the individual aggrieved both by criminal indictment for libel and by private prosecution for
libel for the injury thus sustained. And the equity
courts have power to restrain the intended publication of articles if they are injurious to private
rights, and are not merely the discussion of a
public question. Whether the United States Government can be forced to carry through the mails
literature which is confessedly immoral, is a question which has not yet received final adjudication.
Upon the instigation of the New York Society for
the Suppression of Vice, the object of which is
mainly directed against immoral publications, the
United States Government has refused to carry certain libidinous and clearly immoral sheets. This
refusal is of course destructive of the business of
the publications, and as the refusal was generally
accompanied by declining to redeliver the sheets
in question, it practically amounted to a confiscation of private property. In the lower courts this
course on the part of the Government has been
held to be constitutional and proper, as it was in
part the exercise of police surveillance and supervision, and no man's right to speak or write what
he pleased was impaired by the refusal of the Government to carry such writings. The argument,

however, against this position is that as the general
Government through its revenue laws maintains a
postal department to which all are supposed equally to contribute, to deny the facility of the postal
department is to impose in fact a punishment for a
particular writing, and is thus an impairment of
the freedom to publish, which was intended to be
secured by the Constitution. The question will
probably receive final adjudication by the Supreme
Court before long. During the war of the rebellion, 1861–1865, several of the metropolitan papers
were imposed upon by a forged proclamation of
President Lincoln calling for an additional draft of
four hundred thousand men, to repair the disasters
to the Union arms. This pretended proclamation
greatly intensified the feeling of despondency that
had already taken possession of the people in the
North at that particular juncture of the war. The
newspapers publishing the proclamation were or-
gans of the Democratic party, and were therefore
subjects of suspicion on the part of the general Government. They were suspended by military orders,
and a military force took possession of their premises and stopped for a short time the publication
of these journals. The question of the right or
authority of the Government in time of war so to
suspend a paper was never judicially raised. The

order suspending them was recalled on the discovery by the Executive Department of the Government that the mistake was an innocent one and that it was not intended wilfully to embarrass the Government in its military operations, but was wholly the consequence of an imposition. Under the authority of the case known as the Milligan case, decided in 1866, we are bound to assume that the Supreme Court of the United States would have declared such a suspension illegal and unwarranted by the Constitution at any point where the civil tribunals were in full force, even in time of war. At the theatre of war, of course, a different rule prevails ; but because a nation is at war every part thereof is not necessarily under the domination of the drum-head court-martial.

The right of the people peaceably to assemble and petition the Government for the redress of grievances is one which was borrowed from the Declaration and Bill of Rights in England, with very little change in phraseology. No judicial opinions have ever been given upon this clause, because the right has never been denied.

The right of the States to have a militia, and the right of the people to keep and bear arms, are subjects of the succeeding amendment. These are substantially in the Bill of Rights of 1689. That this provision simply means arms necessary for the militia and not to secure to each man the right to keep a private arsenal, goes without saying. That no soldier shall in time of peace be quartered in any house without the consent of the owner was to prevent the billeting of soldiers in time of peace upon the people. This amendment has in practice been found to be unnecessary. The army of the United States in time of peace is so small and the public property of the United States so vast that there is no necessity ever to billet soldiers upon the inhabitants. The right of the people to be secure in their persons, houses, papers and effects against unreasonable searches and seizures, and to prevent such searches and seizures, except upon due warrant issued by a court of justice, is one which would seem to be essential for the preservation of personal liberty, and has been twice assailed in the United States, once under the Alien and Sedition laws during the administration of Jefferson, and the second time during the war of the rebellion by the State and War Departments. In both cases the Executive Departments sought refuge under the principle of *salus populi suprema lex ;* that the country was in peril and that it was necessary to disregard a single constitutional provision for the purpose of saving the whole structure.

The revenue laws of the United States contain many clauses of questionable authority by which revenue officers are entitled to search and seize books and papers of merchants and private citizens, and the question is not yet fully determined whether such inquisitorial proceedings and seizures are not, both in spirit and in letter, repugnant to this provision of the Constitution.

That excessive bail shall not be required, nor excessive fines imposed, nor cruel and unusual punishments inflicted, is again a transcript of a clause of the Bill of Rights of the Revolution of 1688. This clause operates as a restriction upon the powers of the United States courts alone, and not upon the State courts.

The various amendments have from time to time been the subject of judicial decision, but the most important of the amendments are the last two of the first eleven, which are to the effect that the enumeration in the Constitution of certain rights shall not be construed to deny or disparage others retained by the people. Were it not for this clause it might have been argued with considerable plausibility, that as the people saw fit, by amendments, to incorporate into the Constitution, a Bill of Rights, whatever they failed to preserve or mention they ceased to have. This provision was made to guard against the evil suggested in the *Federalist* when it gave a reason why the Constitution had not given a Bill of Rights, because the reservation of powers without a Bill of Rights was larger than the reservation of powers with a Bill of Rights.

The next and last amendment of the first eleven is that the powers not delegated to the United States by the Constitution, nor prohibited to it by the Constitution, are reserved to the States respectively or to the people. This is a rule of interpretation of the Constitution which probably would have been followed by the courts without this express declaration. The Constitution is an instrument declaring limited and enumerated powers, and, therefore, whatever power is not given is withheld; but the declaration has been productive of much good, and took the matter of whether the United States is a government of merely delegated powers out of the range of controversy.

One great step in advance, however, must here be noted between the old Articles of Confederation and the Constitution of the United States, inasmuch as here the expression is "the powers not delegated to the United States by the Constitution," and in the Articles of Confederation it was "powers not *expressly* delegated or prohibited." Therefore, as a large proportion of the powers exercised by Congress arises from powers which it derives by necessary implication from the powers expressly conferred, the United States government differs in that respect from the Government under the Articles of Confederation, inasmuch as that had no power which had not been specially conferred, and therefore had no powers by implication. Hence it was crippled at every turn because the organic law which constituted it did not in express terms confer the right to pass a particular bill.

CHAPTER V.

THE foregoing chapters give a succinct statement of the provisions of the Constitution and
of the leading questions that have been decided
under that instrument. An understanding, however, of · the institutional history of the United
States would be incomplete if the political and
constitutional questions entering into politics from
the time of the adoption of the Constitution down
to the present day were not sketched, in however
superficial and rapid a form. The political divisions of parties in the United States unquestionably
exerted a very strong influence upon judicial decisions and the interpretation of the provisions of
the Constitution of the United States. There is an
unconscious influence exercised by public opinion
upon the minds of those who are called upon to
decide finally constitutional questions, which is
neither corrupt nor sinister, but which causes a
written constitution to approximate more closely

7   145

to an unwritten one, like that of England, by making the written word bend and yield to the necessities of the hour, as a large and influential majority
may determine, and that without constitutional
amendment. The limits of this book do not permit so analytical a survey of the whole field as to
show in detail the influence and pressure of public
opinion upon the Supreme Court of the United
States and the gradual yielding of the court to the
pressure of that opinion, or the influence of the
opinions held by the members of the court on political subjects upon their decisions as a court.
The reader must make those applications for himself when the story of the political parties in the
United States shall have been told.

It will be remembered that the Constitution came
into existence under an almost irresistible pressure
of necessity either to disestablish the Government
of the United States and to leave each State free as
an independent sovereignty to make such alliances
as it might see fit—because the Articles of Confederation proved but a rope of sand—or to organize a
Government clothed with sufficient power to enforce
obedience to its laws ; with power to assess and collect revenue, with power to make war, treaties of
peace and foreign alliances, and having both towards
the States and as against foreign nations all the attri-

butes of sovereignty. The jealousy of the States, however, which caused the principal difficulty under the Articles of Confederation, and the ambition of local State leaders who were apprehensive that the formation of the Constitution of the United States would be destructive of their influence, and who therefore opposed the Constitution even after its adoption, survived sufficiently to cause within an early period thereafter a renewal of hostility to the pact, no longer in the form of open opposition to the Union, but under the form of urging a strict and limited construction of the powers conferred upon the federal Government, and to put forth an exaggerated claim of sovereignty for the component States of the Union.

Under the Constitution of the United States Washington was unanimously elected first President, and he so continued for the period of eight years, and probably would have continued to hold the office during the period of his life, if he had not voluntarily seen fit to withdraw at the end of his second term, presumably for the purpose of •creating an example to limit the Presidential term, so that thereafter there should be a sufficiently frequent change of the Executive head of the Government to prevent future elections from being mere idle forms, and also to prevent a consolidation of power in the hands of the Executive, which long continuance in office would inevitably bring about.

During Washington's administration differences of opinion were held largely in abeyance. The commanding personal dignity of Washington and the complete confidence reposed in him by the body of the people, his unimpeachable personal character and his remarkable good sense and moderation, gave to the country during such first eight years that peace, quiet, and freedom from political agitation which were above all things needful for the purpose of establishing the Government, rehabilitating its financial condition which had become almost hopeless under the Confederation, placing foreign relations upon a sound footing, and allowing the people of the United States and its Government a tranquil growth unharassed by internal conflict.

The adoption of the Constitution itself was of course accompanied with considerable opposition. But ten States had adopted the Constitution at the time of the inauguration of the Government, and in some of the States the Constitution was adopted by but slight majorities. There were naturally, therefore, after the Constitution, as well as before, two parties—Federalist and Anti-Federalist—the lines of which were, on the whole, retained after the Government was inaugurated. The Anti-Federalist party claimed, after the Constitution was adopted, as strong a loyalty to the government as the Federalist party itself, but the form of opposition it then adopted was to limit the general Government to the strict letter of its powers.

The first Congress met in the City of New York. The first questions that engrossed its attention after the adoption of the Constitution were the organization of the Judiciary, the revenue duties on imports and exports, as a system of taxation for the replenishment of the Treasury to carry on the necessary purposes of government. The discussion in Congress on the tariff laws shows that at the very outset the question of using the tariff as a means of protecting " infant " manufactures was one which entered into the method of formulating the legislation as part of the system. Fitzsimmons, of Pennsylvania, was mainly the author of the first tariff list. James Madison, although he owned himself, as he said in the debate, " the friend of a very free system of commerce, and that if industry and labor are left to take their own course, they will generally be directed to those objects which are most productive, and that, in a manner more conservative and direct than the wisdom of the most enlightened Legislature could point out," nevertheless conceded (a concession which, by the light since thrown upon these questions by scientific research, appears to have been an error) that as to the navigation element of the tariff, if American citizens were left without restraint, and the law made no discrimination between vessels owned by citizens and those owned by foreigners, while other nations made such discrimination, such a policy would go to exclude American shipping from foreign ports. He conceded the necessity that every nation should have in itself the means of defence, and that in the period antedating the Constitution, establishments had grown up under the powers which those States had of regulating trade, which ought not to be allowed to perish in consequence of recent alterations, and as he was the leader of the House, his surrender to the idea of making protection an incidental consideration in the raising of the revenue of the United States engrafted that system upon the legislation of the country. A discrimination was imposed in favor of teas imported in American bottoms ; a tonnage duty was imposed, discriminating in favor of American products; a discriminating duty on spirits was passed in favor of nations having commercial treaties with the United States. In the first Congress the slavery question made its earliest appearance in the shape of a proposition, emanating from Mr. Parker, of Virginia, to insert a clause, imposing a duty of ten dollars on every slave imported, with a view of discouraging the slave trade. The motion was not agreed to, but the discussion which it raised, in which Madison took an important part, is interesting, as showing that at that time many of the Southern States were anxious to limit the growth of the slave power, and looked forward to the period when slavery might become entirely obliterated. The same Congress passed a Navigation law for the registering of American vessels ; created a Coast Survey; organized Departments ; and placed the power of appointment and removal in the hands of the President. The power of removal by the President was strongly opposed, and the measure conferring it passed the Senate only by the casting vote of the Vice-President, Mr. Adams. The discussions which preceded and accompanied the adoption of the Constitution by the various States, so unmistakably demonstrated the apprehensions of great masses of the people, that the Constitution was not sufficiently guarded by the declaration of the rights of the people, which were to be free from any possible impairment at the hands of authority, that Mr. Madison at once proposed amendments to lay those fears at rest, and the amendments which have been the subject of consideration in the last chapter, were the result of this action. Jefferson's objections to the Constitution as it stood in 1789, were mainly met by the amendments, except the one in reference to which he was extremely strenuous, that the Executive shall not be reëligible to office. The important subject of the national debt was laid over until the following session for the purpose of receiving the report of the Secretary of the Treasury upon a plan for its liquidation. On the subject of the public lands nothing was done except to effect the passage of an act for the government of the Northwest territory. The most stormy debate of the session was upon the question of the permanent seat of the federal Government. The Southern members wanted a site on the Potomac; Pennsylvania wanted a return to Philadelphia, which had been the seat of the Continental Congress. The House agreed, as a matter of compromise, to fix the seat of Government on the Susquehanna. The bill came back from the Senate so altered as to substitute for the Susquehanna the district ten miles square, adjoining Philadelphia. The House agreed to this, with a slight amendment which made it necessary to have the bill go back to the Senate; but by that time the dissatisfaction of the Southern members had made itself so apparent that it was deemed wiser to lay the whole matter over to the following session.

The only important administrative question that characterized the first year of Washington's administration in addition to the mere selection of persons to fill the various offices, was the making of treaties with the Indian nations ; and as along the whole western frontier the Indian affairs were in a most unsettled state, it was necessary to take immediate measures to prevent a general outbreak among the Indians against the new Government. Washington appointed commissioners to treat with them, and these commissioners confirmed some of the old Indian treaties that had been made by the various States, and promised the Indians immunity from taxation and forcible prevention of settlers from trespassing upon their lands.

At the opening of the following session Alexander Hamilton, the Secretary of the Treasury, reported the debt due to the Court of France and to private individuals and foreign nations, something below twelve million dollars, and the domestic debt at $42,500,000. The highest possible tone was adopted by Hamilton as to the obligation of the United States for the payment of the debt and the expediency of doing so, and not to lend ear to the suggestions which were made to scale

7*

the debt because of the depreciated prices at which the then holders had bought up its evidences on speculation. The State debts arising out of the war, which were practically repudiated, made another addition of $26,000,000. He proposed the funding of the debt at six per cent., and to receive in payment of the new bonds the evidences of the old debt, and to create a sinking fund from post-office proceeds for the gradual extinction of the new debt. The Continental paper money, which amounted nominally to $200,000,000, had by the Continental Congress itself been reduced by a system of scaling at the rate of one for forty. There were $78,000,000 of the Continental paper money yet outstanding, and it was intended not to disturb that reduction, but to accept the Continental paper money upon the basis of two and one-half cents on the dollar. It was finally agreed that the Government should pay the holders of the certificates of the United States the face thereof, and the question arose on the assumption of the State debts. This led to an extremely acrimonious debate, arising from the fact that some of the States had largely provided for the expenses of the war by taxation, while others ran recklessly into debt, and it was evidently unfair to the inhabitants of the States who had borne the burden of taxation during the war for the purpose of preventing the accumulation of a debt, that they should be now called upon to pay the interest and eventually the principal of bonds representing the reckless issues of bills of credit by sister States, and thus to tax themselves for the freedom from taxation which their neighbors had enjoyed.

The plan of Hamilton finally prevailed on a very close vote. During the second year of the Union under the Constitution a bill was passed to locate the seat of Government for ten years at Philadelphia, and thereafter permanently on the Potomac. This measure was passed only by combining therewith the assumption of the State debts, as a compromise measure. During the third year of Washington's administration a division arose in the Cabinet, which subsequently resulted in a party division on the bill to incorporate the Bank of the United States. Jefferson and Madison were of the conviction that it was an unconstitutional measure and had a tendency to corrupt the powers of government. Hamilton and Knox, members of the Cabinet, gave their written opinions in favor of the President signing the bill. Randolph was also opposed to it. It is fair to say, however, that the Republican party, which subsequently became the Democratic-Republican, and later the Democratic party, drew considerable accession of strength from the Federalist party in process of time, because the loyalty of the Republican party to the Constitution since its adoption could scarcely be questioned. Opposition to the Constitution itself had well-nigh died out. There was room and reason, however, for the existence of a party of strict constructionists of the powers conferred, actuated by a strong determination to confine in every possible way the Federal party within the limits of federal power and to assert the local rights of States as to all matters not conferred by the Constitution to federal control. The firm conviction had taken root in the minds of many able men in the United States, of whom Jefferson was the leader, that State organizations were the only means by which the liberty of the citizen could be preserved, and that a nation of the territorial extent and diversity of interests of the United States would in time become a centralized power sufficiently strong to crush out individual liberty unless there existed in the form of States *quasi* independent governments — as *imperia in imperio* sufficiently powerful to. oppose a barrier against any encroachment of the central Government.

During the administration of Washington, the divergence of the ideas represented by Thomas Jefferson and those represented by Alexander

Hamilton, became more and more marked, so that on December 31, 1793, Jefferson felt constrained to retire from Washington's Cabinet. During part of the time of Washington's administration, the relations towards both France and England had become critical, but Washington's tact overcame the difficulties ; and the causes of irritation, although not entirely removed, were for the time being suppressed. Washington refusing to be a candidate for a third term, caused the election, in 1796, of John Adams and Thomas Jefferson as respectively President and Vice-President of the United States. It will be remembered that the election was then held before the new amendment took effect under the original clause of the Constitution, by which both great parties in the United States were substantially represented in the offices respectively of President and Vice-President ; because under the original clause he who had the largest number of votes became President, and the one next in number became Vice-President. Therefore, Adams, representing the Federalist party, became President of the United States, and Thomas Jefferson, who was then the leader of the Republican party, became the Vice-President. Madison, who had heretofore acted between the two parties, became at that time, with Jefferson, one of the leaders of the Republican party. During Adams' administration the party lines became more closely drawn, and there was considerable accession of strength to the Republican party as measure after measure was introduced and debated, which seemed to indicate a centralization of political power. Another of the reasons why the Republican party grew in strength about that period, was, that there were incessant petitions for the abolition of slavery introduced in Congress, and whilst Congress protested in several instances that it had no right to interfere with domestic slavery in the United States, the Southern and Middle States felt that their safety against the ultimate interference in that particular by the United States Government rested upon the general acceptance of the States rights doctrine insisted upon by the Republican leaders.

During the first year of Adams' administration (1797) affairs with France became complicated by reason of the war then waging between France and England, in which France insisted that America, her former ally, should, if not openly aid the French republic, at least take a position of armed neutrality as against England. The decrees of the French republic which injuriously affected American commerce led to a rupture of diplomatic relations, and caused, in the following year, the passage of the Alien and Sedition laws, the Alien law empowering the President to expel such persons as he might find who were plotting against the public peace, and the Sedition act being designed to restrict the freedom of speech and liberty of the press. The passage of these measures by the Federal party added to its unpopularity. The desire on the part of the people of the United States to preserve peace, caused them to look with grave suspicion upon the active preparations which were then made for war. In the year 1800 a condition of irritation, almost of war, already existed between France and the United States. But with the dissolution of the French Directory in 1799, and the accession of Napoleon as First Consul of the French republic, a treaty was soon concluded. The year 1800 also witnessed the first caucus nomination for Presidential candidates in the United States under the Constitution. In 1800 an election took place for President of the United States, to take the place of Adams. When the electoral votes were counted, in February of the following year, it was found that no election had taken place, as Aaron Burr and Thomas Jefferson had an equal number of votes, and the choice under the Constitution devolved on the House of Representatives, which, on the thirty-sixth ballot, elected Mr. Jefferson President.

A breach had taken place between the two great leaders of the Federal party, Adams and Hamilton, immediately prior to the election of Jefferson, which weakened the Federal party considerably, and caused the success of the Republicans. During this contest between Jefferson and Burr for the Presidency, each one having had seventy-three votes in the Electoral College, Hamilton cast his influence in favor of Jefferson and led to his election. This and subsequent acrimonious contests between Hamilton and Burr, caused the unfortunate duel between them in 1804, which cost Hamilton his life.

The dangers to the country which this struggle for the Presidency disclosed, led to the adoption of the twelfth amendment, by which the President and Vice-President are voted for by the Electoral College separately on distinct lists, and each independently of the other.

Jefferson introduced, when Congress met after his election, the innovation to send a message to Congress instead of opening Congress in person. It savored too much of British forms for the President to open Congress in person, and hence the Republican party, to show its contempt for monarchical institutions, adopted, through the instrumentality of Jefferson, the form which has since been followed by every President of the United

States, of not meeting Congress in person, but of sending messages, as from time to time his views to Congress are to be expressed. The leading incident of Jefferson's first few years of administration was the purchase of Louisiana from Napoleon for $15,000,000. Louisiana as then ceded was a territory out of which ten States (inclusive of what is now known as Louisiana), three Territories, and a large part of two other States have since been carved.

Jefferson continued in office during two terms, at the end of which the electoral votes were cast for James 'Madison and George Clinton. This was again a Republican triumph. As early as 1805 the Federal party was reduced to seven senators and twenty-five members of the House. The parties divided on the Embargo Act. Feelings which subsequently developed into a war with Great Britain, arising from the impressment of American seamen and interference with American ships, were awaking. It was claimed that in the war between England and France, almost six thousand American seamen had been impressed into the British navy. The embargo was intended as an act of retaliation against both England and France for the mischievous effect upon American commerce of the Milan-Berlin decrees and the British Orders in Council.

During the administration of Madison war was declared against England on the 18th of June, 1812, which lasted until December 24th, 1814, when a treaty of peace was signed at Ghent, although the actual hostilities continued until February, 1815, when the news of the signing of a treaty first reached America.

During the war the Federal party fell into utter confusion and disgrace in consequence of its opposition to the war and because of the call of the convention known as the Hartford Convention, in which some of the New England federalists strongly announced, through their representatives there, the theory of secession, if the war should be prosecuted much longer, as it was claimed that the war was destructive of the interests of the Eastern States, while it but remotely affected the Middle and Western States. The successful termination of the war strengthened the Republican, or Republican-Democratic party, as it was then called, to such a degree that it dominated in almost every State in the Union. The result of the war was the swelling of the debt to more than $127,000,000, but the moral results from it were on the whole beneficial, because the gallantry with which the navy was handled, and the victory at New Orleans, won under General Jackson on the American side, gave to the American people a degree of self-reliance which largely developed the growth of a spirit of national feeling in the United States.

The charter of the Bank of the United States having expired in 1811, it was reorganized in 1816, with a capital of $35,000,000. Within a comparatively short period the method of its administration produced a speculative era which brought in its train a financial crisis and distress.

The main political questions which agitated the people of the United States during the period of Madison's administration concerning the relations of the United States with England were war or anti-war before the war broke out, and a vigorous prosecution of the war or a discontinuance of it whilst it was in operation. It was during the latter part of this period that Webster made his first appearance in the Congress of the United States, and commanded immediate attention by his eloquence and talent for debate.

At the close of Madison's administration the thirteen States of the Union had already grown into nineteen, the population of 4,000,000 had grown to almost 10,000,000, and the House of Representatives had grown to a body of 213 members.

In 1816 James Monroe, the Republican-Democratic candidate, was elected President. The second

year of Monroe's administration witnessed the commencement of the struggle on the slavery question
between the Northern and the Southern States,
which culminated in the War of the Rebellion in
1861. On the bill to authorize the people of the
Territory of Missouri to form a constitution and
State government, and for its admission into the
Union, Mr. Talmage, of New York, offered the following proviso : " Provided that the further introduction of slavery or involuntary servitude be prohibited, except for the punishment of crimes whereof
the party shall have been convicted, and that all
children born within said State after the admission
thereof into the Union shall be free at the age of
25 years." This raised a storm, which was only
quieted for a time in the year following by the
Missouri Compromise. This came about by an
attempt to pass the bills to admit Missouri and
Maine as States together, in one bill, restricting
slavery in them. The measure which was passed
eventually was the prohibition of slavery from the
rest of the Louisiana accession north of the 36° 30'
north latitude. During this year Florida was ceded
by Spain, and the eastern boundary of Mexico was
fixed at the Sabine River, thus transferring Texas,
which was debatable ground as to whether or not
it came to the United States with the Louisiana

purchase, to Spanish rule as part of the nego-
tiation which resulted in the Florida purchase.
The actual exchange of ratifications, however, did
not take place until 1821. In 1821 Monroe entered
upon his second term. During that year the Missouri struggle came up again on the application of
Missouri for admission, after the passage by her of
a State Constitution. During that year Henry
Clay, by reason of his great services as pacificator
between the North and the South, became a recognized leader in American politics.

The message of Monroe to Congress in 1823
announced for the first time the doctrine of opposition on the part of the United States to intervention on the part of European governments
in the affairs of states and governments other than
the United States on the North American continent, claiming a sort of protectorate in that
particular for the United States, at least in so far
as to insist against non-intervention of European
powers in the affairs of governments on the North
American continent. This doctrine has become
known as the "Monroe doctrine," and was expressed in these terms: "We owe it, therefore, to
candor and to amicable relations existing between
the United States and those powers (the European
powers) to declare that we shall consider any

attempt on their part to extend their system to any portion of this hemisphere as dangerous to our peace and safety. With the existing colonies or dependencies of any European power we have not interfered, but with the Governments which have declared their independence, we have, on great consideration, and on just principles, acknowledged, we could not view any interposition for the purpose of oppressing them or controlling in any other manner their destiny as any other than an unfriendly disposition towards the United States." This was called out by what was supposed to be the design of the Holy Alliance to extend a fostering care over the young American republics of Spanish origin of a wolfish character.

The year 1824 witnessed the first sectional struggle upon the tariff question, the North and Middle States voting in favour of a protective tariff, the South voting solidly against it.

At the end of Monroe's administration the public debt had been reduced from $123,000,000 to $90,000,000, and the country was in a state of remarkable prosperity.

In the autumn of 1825 John Quincy Adams, a Republican, was elected President of the United States by the House of Representatives, in consequence of a failure to elect by the Electoral College. John C. Calhoun was elected Vice-President.

An attempt was made during the early years of President Adams' administration to amend the Constitution as to the mode of electing the President of the United States by having him elected directly by the people in Congressional districts. Although the proposition met with approval in both branches of the Federal Legislature, it failed to obtain the necessary two-thirds vote in both branches, and therefore no further steps were taken.

In February, 1826, the republics of South America made a proposition to the United States to deliberate with them upon measures for common advantage, at a Congress to be held at Panama. This led to serious opposition on the part of the South, for the reason that as some of the South American republics had recognized the equality of the negro by admitting him to citizenship, it was, as they claimed, an indirect way of recognizing negroes as citizens. The debate upon this proposition intensified the feeling in Congress on the slavery question, and was the clearest possible demonstration that the Missouri Compromise, which was intended forever to allay all bitterness upon this subject, fell short of what was expected from it. The feeling of mutual distrust between the Northern and Southern States was still further increased by the tariff legislation of 1828. The duties were made higher, and the people of South Carolina petitioned their Legislature "to save them if possible from the conjoint grasp of usurpation and poverty." They declared that the citizens of South Carolina would be condemned to work as tributaries of the Northern and Middle sections of the Union under such tariff legislation. The Legislature of Georgia protested against the tariff act in 1829, and the Legislature of South Carolina during the same year made a solemn protest against the same measure.

Andrew Jackson was elected President of the United States in 1828, with Calhoun again as Vice-President during his first term, and Martin Van Buren as Vice-President during his second term. General Jackson in his inaugural address stated that the popular sentiment declared in a manner too legible to be overlooked, the task of reform to be the duty of the administration. This, as interpreted in practice, meant that he was to remove the office-holders of the former administration, and during the first year of his administration he made upwards of seven hundred removals from office on political grounds, without including subordinate clerks, whereas during the forty years preceding there had been but sixty-four removals. This system of wholesale removal, not on the ground of the unfitness of the occupant for the position, but because his views were not entirely in harmony with the administration, on matters which but remotely, if at all, affected the duties of his office, inaugurated the "spoils" system in American politics. Subsequently upon every change of Presidential incumbents, by the election of chiefs of party differing from the party then in power, a decapitation of public officials took place, so that it became an accepted principle as to tenure of office in the United States, that appointments were for the four years only during which the President was elected, and whether the appointment was to continue thereafter depended entirely upon the accident whether there would either be a subsequent term for the same Presidential incumbent, or whether the same party would remain in power, and therefore the same influences which caused the appointment could be kept at work to continue the incumbent in his position.

In his very first message to Congress General Jackson recommended an amendment to the Constitution, giving to the people the direct election

8

of the President. No steps, however, were taken by Congress to submit that question for ratification to the people.

The nullification doctrines, by which is meant the doctrine of the right of the States to refuse obedience to laws of the United States when they are supposed to be inimical to their interests, were openly avowed by some of the Southern States, notably South Carolina, and by the then Vice-President of the United States. Mr. Calhoun was the recognized chief of the party of nullification, and gave to it whatever intellectual impulse and theoretical basis it had. The feeling between President Jackson and the Vice-President upon this subject became so marked, that in March, 1831, the entire Cabinet, with the exception of the Postmaster-General, resigned.

The charter of the United States Bank once more expiring by limitation, the President of the United States took a determined stand against its renewal. In his annual message, he said: "Nothing has occurred to lessen in any degree the dangers which many of our citizens apprehend from that institution as at present organized." 1831 also witnessed the organization of the Mormon settlement at Kirtland, and also in Missouri.

During the session of 1832 the Senate and House

of Representatives passed a bill to re-charter the
bank of the United States, but the President vetoed
it, and the vote of two-thirds of both branches
could not be obtained to pass the act over the
President's veto.

In November of the same year, South Carolina
passed an act to nullify the tariff bill of Congress on
the ground that it was an unconstitutional measure,
and in December of the same year, the President
issued a proclamation to warn the citizens of South
Carolina from engaging in acts of resistance, sent
troops to Charleston under General Scott to enforce
the laws; and stated in his declaration that if South
Carolina could nullify the revenue laws of the
United States, every other State could do so, and
therefore no revenue could by any possibility be
collected, as all imposts must be equal. In January
following, President Jackson published his nullification message, and there was danger of an immediate conflict between the State of South Carolina and the United States Government, which
was avoided by a compromise on a modification
of the tariff of 1828; the duties were annually
to be reduced one-tenth for seven years, at the
end of which time all of the excess of the duties
above twenty per cent. should be equally divided
into two parts, and one part struck off at the

end of one year and the other at the end of the following year ; so that at the end of nine years all
duties should be reduced to twenty per cent. on
value.   It was declared that this act was to be permanent.   The bill passed both Houses, and allayed
the discontent, and prevented at that time the necessity for resort to arms.

During the recess of Congress, after his inauguration for the second time in 1833, Jackson removed
the deposits from the United States Bank.   This
caused the bank, as a matter of retaliation, to contract its loans, which in turn, with other causes,
produced a commercial crisis, and great financial
distress, which continued down to 1838.   In the
interval, the United States Bank suspended payment, and finally, became insolvent.

During Jackson's administration there were
three parties in the United States : the Democratic, of
which Jackson was at the head ; the Anti Masonic,
and the National Republican.

The old Republican party had before that time
changed its name to the Democratic party, and was
technically known as the Democratic-Republican
party, by which name it has preserved its organization down to the present time.

Martin Van Buren became the nominee of the
Democratic party towards the end of the Jackson

administration, and then for the first time the Whig party made its appearance as an offshoot of the National Republican party—the name Whig, for the last named party, appeared for the first time in an election in 1834.

During the administration of Jackson the United States debt was substantially extinguished. When his administration commenced the public debt amounted to $58,500,000, and when it ended it amounted to but $291,089. The debt was not wholly extinguished, simply because the bonds were not handed in for payment. The exports of the United States had risen from $72,000,000 to $128,000,000, at the end of his administration, and the imports from $74,000,000 to $190,000,000.

The division of parties at this time arose mainly from the difference of construction of the powers of the United States Government, and was in another form the continuation of the struggle which commenced before the Constitution of the United States was framed, between the powers of the States and of the United States, and after it was adopted the contest continued upon the construction to be given to the Constitution of the United States. It will be remembered that at the time of the formation of the Constitution a large proportion of the leading and influential citizens of the country were opposed to the merging of the State sovereignties into that of the United States under the form in which this was accomplished by the Constitution of the United States. After the Constitution was adopted and the power of the United States grew both at home and abroad, and the prosperity of the community developed, this form of opposition was entirely extinguished, but was transmitted into a strict construction of the Constitutional powers granted. When the Republican party, however, came into power, the Federalists or Loose Constructionists, for the purpose of limiting the power of their opponents, found themselves in a position to be compelled to adopt almost wholly the language of their former opponents, and thus strangely enough became the Strict Constructionists, in the earlier period of the Republican success under Jefferson to the extent that in the Hartford Convention they asserted in as radical a form as was subsequently asserted by some of the Southern States, the right of the States to nullify Congressional legislation if they deemed it unconstitutional. The success of the war of 1812 caused the Federalist party so utterly to fall into disgrace that it became extinguished as a party organization. The desire to use the credit of the United States for purposes of internal improvement, and the growing influence of

the manufacturing classes, caused a new organization—the Whig organization—to arise, which again
in its tenets and its tendencies resembled the Federal party. They claimed the right to use the funds
of the Union for purposes of internal improvements,
and to have the United States subscribe or loan its
credit for the purpose of internal improvements in
various States, and to use the revenue system of
the United States for the purpose of encouraging
domestic manufactures, to grant subsidies and to
build up manufacturing industries of the nation at
the expense of the commercial and agricultural interests.

At the time of the inauguration of Martin Van
Buren as President of the United States, the contest which theretofore had been carried on between
Congress and the President, by the passage of bills
favoring internal improvements, but which were
vetoed by the President, continued, so that at the
time of the opening of the 13th administration the
lines between the Whigs and Democrats were
closely drawn upon those questions. Van Buren's
administration began under circumstances of extreme
financial distress. Excessive issues of paper money
had caused reckless speculation and raised the
prices of lands far beyond their actual value, and
the sudden calling in of loans in the spring of 1837

resulted in a suspension of specie payments by the banks which precipitated a commercial and financial panic of the utmost severity. The President then for the first time recommended a plan of sub-treasury deposits, for the purpose of preventing at any future time a further copartnership between the Government and the banks, and to have for the Government substantially its own depository and disbursing agents throughout the United States. In 1840, by a small majority, this independent treasury scheme became successful ; but indications were already but too abundant that the Whig party, making capital of the financial and commercial distresses of the Van Buren administration, and attributing it largely to the fact that the Government refused to lend its aid to internal improvements, and that it had bankrupted the banks in consequence of the organization of the independent treasury plan, was gaining ground in the United States, and would probably obtain control of the Government at the next Presidential election. In 1839 the Abolitionist, or Anti-Slavery party, made, for the first time, Presidential nominations. At the Presidential election in November the Whig electors were elected throughout the United States, except in two Northern and five Southern States. In these the Democratic electors were chosen. The nominees of the Whig party, Gen. Harrison and John Tyler, were elected respectively President and Vice-President of the United States. Just one month after his inauguration, President Harrison died. This was the first time that a President died in office, and the Vice-President, John Tyler, under the Constitution became the chief Executive officer for the unexpired term. Mr. Tyler was known at the time of the election not to be strongly in sympathy with the Whig party, and he was placed upon the ticket as a matter of concession to the Southern element and with the view of catching Democratic votes. The breach between him and the party that elected him was precipitated almost immediately after his accession to the Presidential chair, by his veto of the bill to incorporate the fiscal bank of the United States.

The Whig party had succeeded in the presidential election, upon the platform of the reëstablishment of a national bank and its promise to pass internal improvement bills. The veto of the bill caused a conference between the President and the leaders of the House and of the Senate, to bring about an agreement as to a bill that he would consent to. Such a bill was drawn, and it was claimed that it received the approval of the President; but after its passage he vetoed it, in consequence of which his

8*

whole Cabinet, with the exception of Mr. Webster, resigned. The President was then thrown entirely into the hands of the Democratic party, and the Whigs who had the majority in Congress, regarded him as an antagonistic and democratic President.

The northeastern boundary controversy, which was at that time one of the questions in dispute between America and Great Britain, was adjusted between Lord Ashburton and Webster by the treaty known as the Ashburton treaty, in 1842.

During the years 1843 and 1844 the annexation of Texas became an important party question. The South, apprehensive of the development of population in the northwestern territory and the rapid formation of free States, which threatened to endanger the system of slavery, determined with the aid of the President to extend its territory in the southwest and to annex Texas —out of which many States could be carved—to the United States. Texas had been in part settled by adventurers from the States. Its original Spanish population was largely merged by intermarriage with Americans, and many of the Mexicans were driven back toward the Rio Grande. On the 2d of March, 1845, the bill to annex Texas was finally passed. Florida was also admitted as a State, thus adding to the slave power.

In November, 1844, James K. Polk was elected President of the United States, he being a Democratic candidate, and George M. Dallas Vice-President. The newly-elected President, on taking his seat, committed himself fully to the policy of Tyler with reference to Texas, and immediately ordered possession to be taken of the territory by the troops of the United States. General Taylor took command, and pushed its occupation almost to the Rio Grande. Without any formal declaration of war, a conflict was precipitated between the Mexican troops and the American troops, and in the midst of the excitement arising from the news of this clash of arms between the Mexican troops and the United States army, in which the army of the United States proved successful, Congress declared that a state of war existed between the United States and Mexico, and was called upon to make the necessary appropriation for carrying it on with effect. The army of occupation was then superseded by an army under General Scott, to take possession of the City of Mexico itself, and after a series of uninterrupted victories, Mexico was captured and peace dictated. A treaty was formed between the Mexican Congress and the American Commissioners, by which the independence of Texas was recognized and its annexation to the United States confirmed. This extended the territory of the United States on the southwest to the Rio Grande River from El Paso to its mouth. In addition to this, the territory of New Mexico and Upper California was ceded. For this cession of additional territory the United States paid Mexico $15,000,000, and assumed the payment of some $3,500,000 due to Mexico from certain citizens of the United States. By a subsequent purchase, for $10,000,000 more, known as the Gadsden purchase, an additional territory was acquired.

During the period of the war with Mexico for the acquisition of Texas, the Anti-Slavery party, in consequence of the aggressive spirit shown by the South, and the determination to extend the slavery territory, became more and more formidable, and on the debate on the Wilmot proviso—a provision to prohibit slavery from all territory to be acquired from Mexico—it was apparent that a considerable accession of strength to the anti-slavery element had already been made among the United States representatives.

The tariff struggles, the war with Mexico, and the question of the limitation of slavery in the newly acquired territory, in all of which the South prevailed, were the main political questions which divided parties during the Polk administration. In 1846, the Oregon question was settled by a treaty with England, by which the boundary line was fixed at 49° north latitude, instead of 54° 40′, as originally claimed by the United States. In 1848, the Democratic party nominated Lewis Cass for President, and Benj. F. Butler for Vice-President. The Whig national convention nominated as the candidate for President Gen. Zachary Taylor, who divided the honors of the brilliant success of the Mexican war with Gen. Scott, and Millard Fillmore, as candidate for Vice-President. The parties, as declared in their platforms at that time, divided on the free trade and protection question, the Democratic party insisting that no more revenue should be raised than is required to defray the necessary expenses of the Government ; that justice and sound policy forbade the federal Government to foster one branch of industry to the detriment of another, and that Congress had no power under the Constitution to interfere with or control the question of slavery ; on the other hand, the Whig party, at a ratification meeting held in Philadelphia, claimed as a part of its fundamental principles, no extension of slave territory by conquest; protection to American industry, and the loan of the credit of the United States for the purpose of internal improvements. An offshoot of the Democratic party, known

as the Free Soil party, at the same time nominated
Martin Van Buren as President, and Gen. Dodge of
Wisconsin as Vice-President.   Gen. Dodge declining Charles F. Adams was selected in his place.
Its division from the Democratic party arose mainly
on the question of extension of slavery to the territories ; they agreed with the Whigs upon the
question of river and harbor improvements, that
they were objects of national concern, and that it was
the duty of Congress, in the exercise of its constitutional power, to provide therefor.   In this tri-
angular fight, the Whigs succeeded in electing
their candidates, and consequently Gen. Taylor, of
Louisiana, and Millard Fillmore, of New York,
were respectively inaugurated on the 4th of March
1849, President and Vice-President of the United
States.

The total population of the United States at that
time was a little upwards of 23,000,000.   The acquisition of new territory by the United States Government reopened the old Missouri Compromise question, and it was resolved, mainly through the
instrumentality of the Southern leaders that the
territories should themselves determine whether
or not they should recognize slavery or prohibit it
within their own borders, in the event of their
becoming States.   This right was known as " squat-

ter sovereignty." The newly arrived immigrant in any territory, usually occupying lands of the United States which by improvements became his own under the laws of the United States, was known as a "squatter." The South calculated upon the superior activity of its own people, and somewhat upon their aggressiveness, to hold in awe and check the more peaceably inclined settlers from the Eastern States and from Europe, and that by the terrorism that thus could be exercised they could secure a large proportion not only of new States closely contiguous to the territory of the old slave States, but also invade some of the Northwestern territory, and thus prevent the power of free States from spreading in that direction. The first shock of disappointment to this calculation came through the finding of gold in California. This caused a migration from the Eastern States to the Pacific coast of so many strong and fearless men that, within the very territory that the Southern leaders supposed to be their own, and which would have been devoted to slavery by law under the old Missouri Compromise had it not been repealed by the votes of the Southern Congressmen, the establishment of slavery was utterly outvoted and routed. California made application as a free State, by a majority so overwhelming that its admission in 1850 could not be rejected by the then pro-slavery

Congress of the United States. However, the Southern feeling of disappointment at the result of this mistaken calculation, together with the suspicion that it had been largely due to the rapid accession of strength of the Anti-slavery party both in numbers and in influence, caused another compromise bill to be passed in the interest of slavery, by which it was agreed to form the Territories of Utah and New Mexico without any reference to slavery, to admit California as a free State, and to pay Texas $10,000,000 for the surrender of its claims to the Territory of New Mexico. A most stringent bill was also passed to return fugitives from justice and persons escaping from the service of their masters. The slavery question entered upon a new phase on the introduction of a bill to organize the Territory of Nebraska in February, 1853. During the few years intervening from 1850 to 1853 great bitterness arose in some of the Northern States on the subject of the Fugitive Slave bill. The provisions of the bill gave to United States commissioners the power, without judge or jury, to return fugitives from justice, and prohibited State courts from issuing writs of *habeas corpus* for the purpose of testing the question of the right to the return of the claimed fugitive, denying to the States the right to try the title of the master to the slave. Some of the States refused to enforce the law, notably Massachusetts, and even passed laws to prohibit its enforcement. When the political parties met in 1852 the question of slavery was the main one before them. Both the Whig and Democratic parties vied with each other in assurances to protect slavery within the States, the Democratic party declaring that Congress had no power under the Constitution to control this "domestic institution" of the Southern States, and that all the efforts of the Abolitionists to induce Congress to interfere with questions of slavery had a tendency to diminish the happiness of the people and endanger the stability and permanency of the Union, and they pledged themselves to abide by and faithfully execute the acts known as the Compromise measure settled by Congress, and more especially the Fugitive Slave act. The Whig convention declared that the series of acts of the Thirty-second Congress, known as the Fugitive Slave law, are received and acquiesced in by the Whig party in the United States as a settlement in principle and substance of the dangerous and exciting questions which they embrace, and they promised that so far as they were concerned they would maintain them and insist upon the strict enforcement thereof. Therefore, upon the main question of slavery, the Demo-

cratic and Whig parties, the two leading parties, expressed almost in the same terms their
determination to carry out faithfully the Compromise measures of 1850, and to enforce the
Fugitive Slave law. The only protest of any
national party against this subserviency to the
slave power came from the Free Soil Democracy,
which nominated Mr. Hale, of New Hampshire, and
Mr. Julian, of Indiana, respectively for President
and Vice-President, and in their platform declared
that the Fugitive Slave laws were repugnant to the
Constitution, to the spirit of Christianity, and to the
sentiment of the civilized world. They insisted that
no permanent settlement of the slavery question
could be looked for except in the practical recognition of the truth that slavery is sectional and freedom
national. The Democratic party, in 1852, succeeded in electing its President by an overwhelming majority, and Franklin Pierce and William R.
King, the nominees of that party, were inaugurated on March 4th, 1853, respectively as President and Vice-President of the United States.

During the early part of President Pierce's
administration, the organization of Kansas and
Nebraska as Territories was the all-absorbing subject of discussion. The proximity of Missouri to
both of those territories, Missouri being a slave

State, made the Southern people feel themselves secure that they could control the organization of the Territories if to the Territories were left the determination of the question of slavery or not within their limits, and a large number of pretended settlers, known as border ruffians, immediately migrated from Missouri into Kansas and Nebraska, and organized a territorial government in favor of•slavery.

The bill abrogating the Missouri Compromise of 1820, known as the Kansas-Nebraska bill, was passed in May, 1854, and for several years the so-called "Kansas war" was carried on between the partisans of slavery and anti-slavery—a war not merely in name, but which involved considerable bloodshed.   Congress recognized the pro-slavery territorial constitution, known as the Leavenworth Constitution, and the Governors who were appointed by President Pierce were appointed with the view to influence these Territories to carry out the pro-slavery programme by the adoption of pro-slavery Constitutions for their admission as States.

During 1854 the claim was made that the Compromise bill of 1850 had abolished the compromise of 1820, and that therefore the new States to be admitted north of the Missouri line could be invaded by the slave power as well as those south of the Missouri line.   The debates during Pierce's admin-

istration in Congress resulted in a division between
Northern and Southern Whigs, the Northern Whigs
calling themselves anti-Nebraska men. The Northern Democrats were evenly divided on the Kansas-
Nebraska measure, and the Southern Democrats
acted as a unit. During the same period a new
party came into existence, known as the Know-
Nothings, which was subsequently called the
American party. As that name indicates, it was
opposed to elevating to office any but natural born
American citizens, or those who had lived long
in the country. It was strongly anti-Catholic in
feeling. For a short time it became a national
party, and in 1855 carried nine of the State elections,
and in 1856 nominated Presidential candidates. In
1856, the anti-Nebraska party adopted the name of
the Republican party. It was largely composed of
the elements of the Whig party. Almost the whole
of the Northern Whig element entered into it, and
it obtained considerable accession of strength from
the Democratic party, as it was the only formidable
organization which resisted at that time the demands of the slave power as to the spread of slavery into the new Territories.

The conflict in Kansas created a very considerable
amount of bitter feeling throughout the United
States, more especially in the Eastern States, where-

in the cry of "bleeding Kansas" caused a large amount of money to be collected, which was expended in arms, and sent to the settlers of Kansas and Nebraska. The Territory of Kansas was divided into a pro-slavery and a free State division, and on the 5th of September, 1855, a convention at Topeka repudiated all that had been done in favor of slavery, claimed that it was the act and deed of Missourians alone, and determined to form a State government in the interest of freedom. In 1856 the free State settlers elected State officers under the Topeka Constitution. President Pierce, however, recognized the pro-slavery Legislature, and placed United States troops under the orders of the Governor to enforce the pro-slavery laws of the territory.

During the discussions on the Kansas question in Congress Senator Sumner, the leading Senator from Massachusetts, made a speech which was deemed personally offensive to Senator Butler, of South Carolina, and a representative by the name of Brooks, also from South Carolina, struck Senator Sumner with a cane, whilst he was seated in his chair in the Senate, with such violence that the Senator suffered several years from the effects of the blow. This incident naturally increased the bitterness between the two sections.

Pending the struggle in Kansas a new election

for President of the United States was held, under
which again the Democratic party was successful.
James Buchanan, of Pennsylvania, and John C.
Breckenridge, of Kentucky, were respectively
elected President and Vice-President of the United
States, and took their oaths of office on the 4th of
March, 1857. Within a few days after the election
of President Buchanan, the Supreme Court of the
United States, in the Dred Scott case, decided that
negroes had no other rights or privileges but such
as the political power of the government might
choose to grant to them, and that Congress had
no more right to prohibit the carrying of slaves
into any State or Territory than it had to prohibit
the carrying of horses or other property, whose
secured possession was guaranteed by the Constitution. The dissenting justices, on the other hand,
claimed that it was only by State laws that the
negro was made property, and that by the law of
nature and of nations, and even by the Constitution of the United States, there was no recognition
of the slave as property ; that it was only by virtue of municipal law, the authority of which was
confined to the territorial boundary of the State,
that any human being could be regarded as
property, and the rights of the owner were limited
to the territory where this special kind of property

was recognized. This decision startled the Northern people of the United States, and a renewed
effort was made to wrest Kansas and Nebraska from
the slave power. The South knew that if in this
struggle Kansas and Nebraska were taken from
them, their hopes successfully to compete against
the Northern States, and to maintain the slave
power, rested either on the acquisition of Cuba by
the Union as a territory out of which to form new
States, the annexation of part of Mexico, or the
whole of it, so as to carve out new slave States, or,
on secession from the Union, and the organization
of an independent government in which slavery
could be secured from every possible attack.

The Kansas struggle lasted until after the election of Mr. Lincoln as President of the United
States. Two constitutions had been passed in
Kansas, one known as the Lecompton Constitution,
with slavery, which claimed to have 6,000 majority;
but the free State settlers refused to vote on the
ground that they were not permitted to vote against
the Constitution, the only form of ballot being one
either for the Constitution with slavery or the same
Constitution without slavery. The President of the
Senate insisted upon the admission of Kansas as a
slave State. The House was willing to admit Kansas with the proviso that the Constitution should

again be submitted to the popular vote. No agreement was arrived at, and some time in 1859 a new Constitution was submitted to the people in Kansas known as the Wyandotte Constitution, which prohibited slavery, and received a majority of 4,000 in its favor.

The Kansas struggle, lasting as it did through the whole of Buchanan's administration, caused party lines to divide sharply in 1860 upon the question of slavery. All other questions were merged in that all-important one. The Southern States, although they had control of the General Government, felt themselves beaten at every point by the growth of a popular sentiment against slavery which proved superior to their astuteness as politicians, and superior to the influence exercised by the more militant character of their population, aided by threats of secession and war in the event of the failure on the part of the North completely to submit to their dictates. Although they succeeded in forcing measures through Congress, they were visibly gradually losing strength. The Democratic party met in Charleston, South Carolina, on the 23d of April, 1860, and divided there into two wings. At this distance of time the difference between the two wings of the Democratic party on the slavery question does not seem to have been a very serious one. The Southern wing affirmed its confidence in the correctness of the Dred Scott decision, and in terms said that neither Congress nor the Territorial Legislatures had a right to prohibit slavery in [the Territories. The Douglas Democrats simply refused to admit the conclusion, although they asserted the premises of the Dred Scott decision, said that it was just and final, and that they would abide by it. The Douglas platform was adopted, and many of the Southern delegations then withdrew. The Democratic convention, after the withdrawal of the delegations, nominated Stephen A. Douglas for President and H. V. Johnson for Vice-President. The seceding delegates nominated J. C. Breckenridge, of Kentucky, and Joseph Lane, of Oregon. A Constitutional Union party—a new name for the former American party—nominated John Bell and Edward Everett. At the election in November every Northern State, with the exception of New Jersey, elected Republican electors, and thus secured the election of Lincoln as President of the United States upon a platform declaring that freedom was the normal condition of the Territories, which Congress was bound to preserve and defend. Immediately after the election of Lincoln was placed beyond doubt, the South Carolina Legislature, in 1860, called a State Convention, which passed almost

9

unanimously an ordinance of secession, and appointed commissioners to treat with the other slave States for a withdrawal from the Union, and to treat with the United States Government for a division of the national property and of the public debt. By the end of February, 1861, Florida, Mississippi, Louisiana and Texas, as well as Georgia and Alabama, had likewise passed ordinances of secession. Tennessee, North Carolina, Arkansas, Kentucky and Missouri were still wavering and awaiting the current of events. President Buchanan, when Congress met, detailed the condition of affairs in the South, denied the right of secession, but expressed himself as powerless to prevent the passage of the resolutions, and intimated doubts as to the power of Congress to make war upon the States. The session was mainly occupied with attempts at compromise. The Crittenden Compromise was one which was most before Congress, and had the greatest chance of success. The main provisions of the bill were that slavery should be prohibited north of parallel 36° 30', recognized and never interfered with by Congress south of that line, and that the Federal Government should pay for all slaves rescued from officers after arrest. These provisions were intended to be made part of the Constitution of the United States, and were never

to be altered or amended by the Union as it existed. The Republicans in Congress refused to vote
for this measure, and the Southern members therefore refused to entertain it. In February, 1861, a
Peace Congress was convened at the request of the
Virginia Legislature, and met at Washington. It
adopted and reported a number of resolutions for
congressional action, all of which Congress refused to entertain. An amendment to the Constitution, however, was recommended by Congress,
which forbade Congress ever to interfere with
slavery in the States. Meanwhile a convention of
delegates from the seceding States was called, which
met at Montgomery, and organized the Government
which was known during the war as the Confederate States of America. It in many respects copied
the Constitution of the United States; it in words
recognized slavery; it extended the term of the
President's office; it prohibited tariffs for any purposes other than revenue. Jefferson Davis and
Alexander H. Stephens were chosen President and
Vice-President. A Cabinet was appointed, Departments were organized, and immediate preparation
was made to carry on war.

As a sufficient number of Southern delegates had
now withdrawn to give to the Republicans an undoubted majority in both Houses of Congress,

Kansas was admitted immediately with a free Constitution ; Nevada, Colorado, and Dakotah were organized as Territories, a new tariff law was passed, mainly in the interest of the Eastern States and Pennsylvania, as the opposition of the free-trade Southern members being withdrawn, all organized opposition to a protective tariff was for the time being at an end.

This brings us to the era of the administration of Mr. Lincoln and the breaking out of the war. President Lincoln was inaugurated on the 4th of March, 1861. His inaugural message expressed a determination to relieve Fort Sumter, and asserted in unambiguous terms the right of the Union to prevent its own destruction. The attempt to resupply Fort Sumter in Charleston harbor precipitated an attack on April 13th, 1861, by South Carolina, which inaugurated the Civil War. Fort Sumter surrendered on the 14th of April, and on the 15th the President issued his first call for troops, which was immediately responded to by the Northern States. An insignificant remnant of the Democratic party remained true, after hostilities actually began, to the idea that secession was a constitutional right, and that there was no power in the United States Government to coerce a State. Within a fortnight after the breaking out of the war, Virginia, North Carolina, Tennessee and Arkansas threw in their fortunes with the South; Delaware, Maryland, Kentucky and Missouri, remained, with small majorities, loyal to the Union.

Early during the war the question of the status of the slave became a very important one. Gen. Fremont, having control of the Missouri department, proposed to free the slaves of Missouri; but his order to that effect was overruled by the President. Gen. Butler was more successful by a happy euphemism in declaring the slaves to be contraband of war, wherein he had the support of the Secretary of War.

In September, 1862, President Lincoln issued a proclamation that in the event of the rebels refusing to return to their allegiance by the 1st of January, 1863, he would then issue an emancipation proclamation. Accordingly, on the 1st of January, 1863, during a period of extreme depression and doubt as to the ultimate success of the Union arms in suppressing the rebellion, the Federal armies having met in 1862 with many serious reverses, the proclamation was issued by which the slaves in the States then in rebellion were declared to be free. The slaves held in States not in rebellion were not affected by this proclamation, an amendment to the Constitution being necessary to accomplish that result as to the " property " of loyal citizens in those States. The emancipation proclamation, after declaring the districts within which it was to be operative, was couched in a spirit of humanity to prevent an insurrection of slaves by enjoining them "to abstain from all violence, unless in necessary self-defence," and promised them that "such as were fitted would be taken into the armed service of the United States, to garrison forts, stations, and other places, and to man vessels of all sorts in said service."

The difficulty in creating the necessary loans, in the early period of the war, and a fear to dampen the ardor of the North by burdensome taxation, caused the passage of a Legal Tender bill, by which the currency of the United States had an enforced circulation—a measure of doubtful constitutionality, but which, as the Supreme Court of the United States subsequently declared, was a justifiable exercise of the war power.* A national banking system was created, by which the banks were required to invest their capital representing circulation in United States loans, so that a large amount of the United States Government bonds was compulsorily absorbed in that manner.

During the four years that the war lasted, two States were admitted into the Union : West Virginia,

* See Addenda and note on page 43.

carved out of Virginia proper, and Nevada. In 1864 the Fugitive Slave law was repealed. Attempts were made in February, 1865, by the President to make peace with the Southern States on the condition of their return to the Union. Although no authorized version of the negotiations has ever been given to the public, it was conceded that with the exceptions of consent to the abolition of slavery, and submission to the authority of the Union on the part of the South, every condition that the Southern States could ask would be submitted to by the North, involving possibly the adoption of the Southern debt and the reimbursement to the Southern slaveholder for slaves lost. But the Southern leaders madly rejected all propositions.

The war at that time, in consequence of Sherman's march through the Southern States, and the pressure upon Gen. Lee's army exercised by Gen. Grant's forces, was rapidly drawing to a close in favor of the Union.

Lincoln was in 1864 reëlected President of the United States, and inaugurated on the 4th of March, 1865.

In April, 1865, the surrender of General Lee, followed quickly by the surrender of General Johnson, practically ended the war. On April 14 President Lincoln was assassinated at a theatre in Washington, and Andrew Johnson, who had been elected as Vice-President, became, on the 15th of April, the President of the United States. This unfortunate assassination of a President in whose wisdom and moderation the people of the United States had very great confidence, added materially to the difficulty of dealing with the Southern States then lately in rebellion. To admit them as States in the full possession of their sovereignty, with the negroes disfranchised, although liberated, was to place the negroes once more in the power of their former owners, and therefore to some degree a violation of the implied pledge given by the United States to the negro race, both by the emancipation proclamation and by the use of thousands of able-bodied negroes in the army and navy, that the promise of freedom should be followed by protecting them from oppression thereafter. In any event, the Government was called upon to exercise a guardianship to prevent their reënslavement or such deprivation of political rights as would amount to a perpetual condition of servitude of the race. On the other hand, the United States Constitution had made no provision for the condition of affairs which the war had brought about. To extend the right of suffrage at once, without a period of education intervening, to the lowest type of a laboring population, made by the system of slavery an entirely irresponsible class of human beings, was full of danger to all vested property interests and to civilization itself in the States where they preponderated. The right of suffrage was always regulated by the States themselves ; the States, as sovereigns, had a right to the organization of their own governmental functions without interference by the federal power except that general provision which made it the duty of the national Government to see to it that the form of government adopted by the States was republican in character. For the purpose of exercising a guardianship over the negroes, and to prevent their being unjustly or harshly dealt with by the Southerners who were formerly slaveholders, the Freedmen's Bureau was organized immediately after the close of the war, with agents in every Southern State, for the purpose of adjudicating upon the rights of the negroes and to prevent their being wronged.

President Johnson, who had spent his adult life in a slave State, and who was a strict constructionist of the Constitution, refused to recognize the methods of reconstruction which Congress saw fit to adopt; he appointed provisional Governors for the States lately in rebellion, and declared his pur-

9*

pose that their terms of office should endure only until a permanent government could be organized. The passage of the Freedmen's Bureau bill, which was vetoed by the President, and of the Civil Rights bill, which was also vetoed, but both of which were nevertheless enacted by the congressional overriding of the vetoes, created an antagonism between the Republican majority in the legislative body and the President, which soon ripened into an open rupture.

The fourteenth amendment was adopted by both houses in June, 1865. The Civil Rights bill declared freedmen citizens of the United States. The reasons against this declaration were sound and cogent, because it admitted to the rights of citizenship a large number of persons whose prior condition of servitude and enforced labor made them extremely dangerous citizens. As the right to vote implies not only the right of the voter to protect himself against the aggression of others, but also involves the power, through the instrumentality of taxation, which is placed in the officers elected by the voters, to confiscate the property of others, it was apprehended by many that demagogues and adventurers would win the freedmen, by illusory promises of personal benefits, to give them their votes, and that, by the creation of public debts and the exercise of the power of taxation, they would mercilessly confiscate the property of citizens subjected to their sway.

Another Freedmen's Bureau bill passed both houses in the summer of 1866. This was also vetoed by the President, but finally passed over the veto and became a law. When Congress met in December, 1866, the conflict between the Legislative department of the Government and the Executive became so acrimonious, measures passed by Congress were so constantly vetoed by the President, that a determination was formed on the part of Congress to remove the President by impeachment.

In January, 1867, a bill was passed which took from the President the power to proclaim a general amnesty. The Army appropriation bill contained a provision by which the President was virtually divested of his command of the army, by making it imperative that all his orders should be given to the General of the army who could not be removed without the previous approval of the Senate. The General of the army at that time was General Grant, who was relied upon as antagonistic to President Johnson and loyal to Congress.

Nebraska was admitted that year as a State. A new bill was passed to provide governments for the States which lately had been in insurrection. The

States were divided into military districts, each under the government of a General. This military government was to continue until a State Convention chosen by all those who had previously been declared by Congress to be citizens, and therefore negroes included, should form a State government, and ratify the fourteenth amendment. The ratification, therefore, of the fourteenth amendment was a compulsory process, and can scarcely be deemed the voluntary act of the States which had previously been in rebellion.

The Tenure of Office bill, passed over a veto, took from the President the power of removal without the consent of the Senate, but enabled him to suspend until the Senate could act, and declared it to be a high misdemeanor to make any such removal except with the consent of the Senate.

During the summer following this Congress, Edwin M. Stanton, who had been Secretary of War, was asked by the President to resign. Stanton refused to resign. He was thereupon suspended under the provisions of the Tenure of Office bill, and Gen. Grant was appointed Secretary of War *ad interim*. On the 14th of January, 1863, the Senate refused to agree to Stanton's removal. Gen. Grant vacated the office, and Stanton was reinstated. The President thereupon again removed Stanton and appointed Gen. Thomas in his place. Thomas accepted, but Stanton refused to quit. Both the Senate and House being in session, and the President having clearly violated the provisions of the Tenure of Office bill, the House resolved to impeach him before the Senate on this and other but less tenable grounds, and on the 5th of March the trial of the impeachment was begun. This was the first and only impeachment of a President of the United States under the power granted by the Constitution. In the Senate the vote stood 35 for conviction and 19 for acquittal. The requisite two-thirds majority, therefore, not having been obtained, a verdict for acquittal was entered, and the impeachment trial fell through.

The political contest for the Presidency turned mainly upon the reconstruction legislation. Grant and Colfax were nominated by the Republicans in 1868 ; Seymour and Blair by the Democrats. The election resulted overwhelmingly in favor of the Republican party. On the 20th of February following the fifteenth amendment to the Constitution, guaranteeing the right of suffrage without regard to race, color, or previous condition of servitude, was adopted by Congress. On the following 4th of March Grant and Colfax were sworn into office.

During President Grant's first term of office the reconstruction of the Southern States proceeded rapidly under the plan laid down by Congress. The greatest part of the time of Congress was taken up in legislation to secure to the negroes their rights, armed conflicts having taken place at various parts of the Southern States between negroes and whites, arising from the enforced equality of the former and the inveterate prejudices of the latter against their recognition as citizens, and to the unfortunate selections of Governors and legislators in the reconstructed States, by which men known as " carpet-baggers," adventurers from the Northern States, went to the South for the purpose of securing office, and, in the troubled condition of affairs, foisted themselves into positions of importance and trust, which they vilely and outrageously abused. As under the amendments to the Constitution the debts of the States in rebellion incurred for the purposes of the war, and the whole of the Confederate national debt were irrevocably repudiated and extinguished, the States were at the time of the reorganization free from all debts, except such as had been created anterior to the rebellion. This offered in the creation of new public debts a great quarry for plunder to the legislative and executive officers who had, during this period, become possessed of political power; and debts were created in a most reckless manner ; bonds were issued amounting to

many millions of dollars, for which the States never
received any return, and the proceeds of which
were in the main embezzled and wasted. This
condition of affairs created a righteous, but for the
time being helpless, indignation, on the part of the
Southern propertied classes, as these Governors
and legislators not only rested their tenure to offices
upon the votes of the most ignorant and depraved
part of the population of the Southern States, but
also had at their beck and call the army of the
United States to enforce obedience as against citizens who had a stake in the community, and who
were compelled quietly to submit to seeing part of
their property confiscated by the taxing power, and
the remainder mortgaged by the debt-creating
power.

The settlement by arbitration of the claims of
the United States against England for the depre-
dations committed during the civil war by the
Alabama and other Confederate cruisers fitted out
in English ports, was the most important step of
the Grant administration as to foreign policy.

The incidents connected with Gen. Grant's first
administration, of corruption on the part of the
office-holders in the Southern States, and the class
of people to whom he gave his confidence in the
Northern States, created considerable reaction
against the plan of Congressional reconstruction

as practically carried out, and divided the Republican party into two divisions. Horace Greeley, the editor of the *Tribune*, was at the head of the wing against the administration party, and Gen. Grant remained the representative of the bulk of the Republican party. In 1872 the Republican party renominated Grant for President, and Wilson for Vice-President; and the Liberal Republicans nominated Horace Greeley, of New York, for President, and B. Gratz Brown, of Missouri, for Vice-President. The Democratic party, at a subsequent convention, adopted the Liberal Republican candidates; but the election resulted overwhelmingly in favor of the Republicans, and President Grant's second term of office began.

One of the instruments of oppression that had been devised with much ingenuity for the purpose of perpetuating the power of the adventurers who succeeded in obtaining control of the Government in the Southern States was what was called a Returning Board, a commission which was originally appointed by the Governors of the States with or without the consent of the Legislative department, which had the power to perpetuate its own existence by filling by coöptation vacancies in its own board, and which had the power to reject the votes of whole districts where, according to the finding of the commission, intimidation had been exercised. This power substantially gave to these Returning Boards the determination of an election; however large the majority adverse to their party might be in certain districts, the vote could be wholly rejected on the mere ground of intimidation, of which they themselves were to be the judges.

During Gen. Grant's second term of office, the question of the resumption of specie payments and the payment of the national debt in gold became the source of most of the conflicts in Congress. The veto by Gen. Grant of a currency bill by which an attempt was made on the part of a majority in Congress to increase the irredeemable currency of the United States, marked the turn of the tide toward correct principles of finance, and gave a strong impetus to a regression to a sound basis for the national currency by its eventual redemption in coin, and of a full and complete recognition, not in words only, of the right of the public creditor to payment in specie. During the war the currency of the United States fell, as calculated in specie, to about thirty-six cents on the dollar—gold stood at one time at 280. At the time of the suppression of the rebellion the premium on gold had fallen to below 30. As gold commanded an increasing premium, commodities and land had a proportionate nominal increased valuation, and many mortgages on Western lands were easily paid off in depreciated paper which could not have been so readily discharged in coin. Under this fictitious prosperity, a return to specie payments, accompanied by a return to normal prices, seemed like a wide-spread calamity, and many an inhabitant of the United States sincerely thought that an irredeemable currency was the source of prosperity, and a return to specie payments the sacrifice of real benefits to a sentimental sense of honor in favor of the public creditor.

It was not perceived that considerable of an inflation would be caused by the return to specie payments, as $250,000,000 in coin which were hoarded were added to the circulation. The notion that a return to specie payments would cause financial distress was shared by so large a proportion of the people, that it became questionable whether within any reasonable period the United States notes would be exchangeable for coin. It was only through the persistent efforts of political economists that one constituency after another was won over to sound financial views, and interference with the law fixing the day for a resumption of specie payments was prevented.

The crisis of 1873, followed by a period of extreme

depression of values in 1874, 1875, 1876, added very considerably to the so-called Greenback or Inflationist influence, and was an additional cause in delaying a return to specie payments. Congress had declared in 1875 that on the 1st of January, 1879, the resumption of specie payments should take place, and on the day appointed the result was achieved. This happy result was aided by fortune more than by the wisdom of the politicians, the country having in 1877 experienced, by reason of an extraordinarily good crop and a failure of the European crop, a revival of industry, followed in 1878 by a further increase of national wealth by another extraordinarily good crop and another failure of crops in Europe. These two events turned the tide of gold in the direction of the United States, producing the double effect of both increasing the facilities of the United States Government to resume, and greatly reducing the ranks of the adversaries to resumption.

In 1876 the democrats nominated Samuel J. Tilden, of New York, and the Republicans Rutherford B. Hayes, of Ohio, for the office of President of the United States. The election of 1876—Colorado and Nebraska having in the interim become States in the Union—required for a choice 185 electoral votes. Mr. Tilden had 184 unquestioned electoral votes. Mr. Hayes had 165 unquestioned

electoral votes.   Thus Mr. Tilden required but one
vote to constitute him President, and Mr. Hayes
twenty.   The votes that were questioned were one
from Oregon, the Governor of which certified to
one Democratic and two Republican electors
arising from a disqualification on the part of one of
the electors, although unquestionably the disquali-
fied elector had been elected; seven from South
Carolina, as to the vote of which there was at first
a very considerable amount of doubt, and was made
the subject matter of litigation within the State,
the vote, however, was certified for the Republican
electors; four from Florida, and eight from Louisiana.   The popular majority in Louisiana and
Florida was undoubtedly in favor of the Democratic electors.   It was only through the instrumentality of the machinery known as the Returning Board that the vote could be changed into a
Republican legal majority.   The Returning Board
of Louisiana was composed of men whose former
conduct had already been discredited by a Republican Congress under an investigation carried on by
a Republican committee.   The electoral vote of
Florida was declared by the State authorities themselves to have been illegally cast for the Republicans, and the State, by the only means in its
power, deliberately recalled the vote of the State

before the vote was counted, and also duly commissioned Democratic electors, whose votes were cast in favor of Mr. Tilden.

In Louisiana the manipulations of the Returning Board form one of the most humiliating chapters of fraud in American politics; the certification in favor of the Louisiana Republican electors, though regular in form, was created by an instrumentality which, if generally adopted throughout the United States, would make a farce of popular elections. Although these manipulations of results gave a colorable right, before the vote was declared, to Mr. Hayes as the elected President of the United States, yet Mr. Tilden, who had unquestionably received by far the greater popular vote, would, in the absence of any Returning Board machinery, have undoubtedly been declared the President of the United States. In this situation, both parties claiming the Presidency, it was apprehended that another civil war might result if no means were found by which this condition of affairs, unprovided for by the Constitution, could be temporarily dealt with. The Constitution gives to the President of the Senate the right to receive the electoral votes and to open them, and that then they shall be counted in the presence of the Senate and House. Prior legislation had formulated the manner in which this proceeding should be conducted. The

House was Democratic, the Senate was Republican. The House, therefore, would inevitably refuse to count the Presidential votes in the manner in which the Senate would count them, would reject the Republican votes of Louisiana and Florida, and the one vote from Oregon, and would either declare Mr. Tilden elected President of the United States by counting the rival certificates from such States, or declare that no election had taken place and proceed to elect under its constitutional right, which would have resulted in Mr. Tilden's election. At this juncture of affairs a compromise was made between the parties by the passage of what is known as the Electoral Commission act, by which five Senators, five Representatives, and five Justices of the Supreme Court of the United States were constituted a court to whom all the votes upon which the two houses could not agree were to be referred, the decision of which was to be final, unless overruled by both houses. This commission stood in all its determinations eight to seven, there being eight Republicans and seven Democrats, and thus counted in Hayes and Wheeler as President and Vice-President of the United States by determining all the disputed questions in favor of the Republican party. The attitude of both political parties during this contest must have appeared to the cynical observer

as a strange exhibition of the slight hold that principles have upon political parties under the pressure
of personal ambition and party dictation. The Republican party was compelled, from the necessity of
the situation during the war, to construe the Constitution in the most liberal spirit and in the loosest
possible way to meet the stretches of power necessary to bring the States in rebellion, by means
of an armed force, back to the Union; to deny the
rights of States against the rights of the United
States, and to limit the State power to the narrow-
est compass. The Democratic party, on the other
hand, was, from its position on the slavery question
before the war, from its position of quiet antagonism
during the war, its position in opposition to the reconstruction legislation of the United States Government during Republican administration subsequent to the war, driven to take a position as advocate of extreme State rights doctrines. In the
contest, however, before the Electoral Commission
the parties suddenly changed positions on what was
supposed to be an ingrained difference of party
policy between them. The Republicans became
the most strict constructionists of the Constitution
as to State rights. They claimed that the official
return of a sovereignty of the magnitude of a State,
however brought about, could not be inquired into

by the limited and circumscribed sovereignty of the
United States Government; and even when the
State of Florida solemnly protested that its return
had been fraudulently obtained, the members of
that party declined to review the decision of the
State when it once had been solemnly asserted.
The Democrats, on the other hand, claimed the
right, on the part of the Government of the United
States, upon so vital a question as the election of a
President of the United States, to inquire how the
State's return was made up, and to take cognizance
of frauds which were practiced in the election, which
substantially nullified and vitiated the State's action,
and to reform such if it be in conformity with justice.

The decision of the Electoral Commission was
generally acquiesced in for the sake of peace. The
compromise was deemed final, and Rutherford B.
Hayes and William A. Wheeler were duly inaugurated President and Vice President of the United States.

The Hayes administration fell within a period of
political tranquillity, and it was also distinguished
by the high personal character of the Cabinet appointments. It received very general support, and
that administration very largely reaped the advantage arising from an era of unexampled and
unparalleled prosperity on which the United
States then entered by reason of the extraor-

dinary developments of the Northwest and of the mining regions of Colorado, Arizona, Nevada, Utah and Wyoming. During this administration there was an immense increase of exports, in part caused by the failure of the crops in Europe and by the developments which had been made in the railways of the country in increasing the facilities and cheapening the cost of transportation. Resumption was accomplished, and although Congress framed some injudicious legislation in favor of the remonetization of silver at a rate below its market value, as a sop to the heresies of Greenbackers, and as a bounty to owners of silver mines, yet on the whole the administration of Mr. Hayes, and the congressional legislation of that period, produced an advancement of the public credit, a decrease of public burdens, and set a term to and ended the wasteful, wicked, and corrupt administration of the Southern States by the carpet-bag governments.

The election of 1880, wherein the standard-bearer of the Democratic party was Gen. Hancock, and of the Republican party Gen. Garfield, resulted in the elevation of Gen. Garfield to the Presidential chair, by the determining vote of the State of New York. The platform of the Republican party in 1880 committed that party to the protective tariff which from 1860 on, was the continuous fiscal policy of the

10

United States Government. The Democratic party, on the other hand, had adopted a plank in favor of a tariff for revenue only. The chances of the campaign were decidedly in favor of the Democratic party. The suspicion that a wrong had been done in the elevation of President Hayes, still lingered in the minds of the people sufficiently to lead many republicans to desire a rectification of that wrong, by the election of a Democratic President in 1880. Late in the campaign, the Republicans issued a series of violently aggressive attacks on the free-trade plank of the Democratic party, by which it was attempted to be shown that the prosperity of the United States was largely due to the protective policy; that the manufacturing industries would be utterly crushed in the event of the Democrats prevailing, and that the laborer would be deprived of his hire and his family of bread, if the free-trade policy were to be inaugurated as against the protective policy which it was claimed had produced within the twenty years then last past such wonderful results in developing the prosperity of the nation. The Democratic party, instead of boldly combatting these utterly unfounded assertions, had become demoralized by the twenty years' exclusion from power, and was so false to principles, and so anxious to succeed that the sacrifice of all the ballast in the way of principle it still had in the hold of its ship, was determined upon by its then leaders. This caused its standard-bearer to issue a letter at a moment of panic saying that he was personally in favor of protection, whatever the platform might say, and caused the Democratic speakers to hasten to explain away what they supposed to be a damaging element of their platform, though the real element of their strength—the revenue reform plank—and to outbid the Republicans for support as a protectionist party. This act lost them votes from Republican free-traders, who were willing to vote for the Democratic ticket, and gained them no adherents from the Republican ranks. A vulgar forgery of a letter was issued by the party against Garfield, attempting to convict him of a policy favoring Chinese immigration. To add to the Democratic calamity, the Democratic party had allowed its organization in the city of New York, where its strength was greatest, to fall into the hands of "bosses" and juntas of politicians who were at all times willing to sacrifice for the sure gains of the local offices the larger and more problematical results of a national victory, and as the State and Municipal elections are held simultaneously with the national election in the State of New York, a small change of votes caused by these

sinister and personal interests, was sufficient to
give by a small majority the thirty-five electoral
votes of the State of New York to the Republicans instead of to the Democrats, for whom in the
computations theretofore made it had generally
been counted. The result was the election of Mr.
Garfield as President of the United States, whose
term of office, beginning on the 4th of March, 1881,
came to a termination by a mortal wound inflicted
July 2d at the hands of a malignant assassin, death
ensuing on the 19th day of September, 1881. Thereupon Chester A. Arthur, who had been elected Vice-
President upon the same ticket with Mr. Garfield,
became the President of the United States.

With the settlement of the slavery question, reconstruction, and return to specie payments, the
Republican party finished its work. It lives now
on the record of its past history. The Democratic
party, except as to the free-trade principle, to which
it can scarcely be said to be faithful, has now no
distinctive principle from the Republican party. It
still insists in its platforms upon State rights, but
as such rights are not really assailed, it can scarcely
be deemed a vital question in American politics.
Indeed the caucus system, thirst for office and
popularity, have so demoralized both great political parties, that their dissolution is a mere ques-

tion of time.   Upon causes deeper than any which
the present leaders of these parties are likely to
forecast or anticipate, will depend the reorganization of American political parties upon political
issues of the future, involving principles asserted
on the one side, and denied by the other.

CHAPTER VI.

IT is, of course, impossible to foretell with accuracy the changes time may bring forth, which will materially modify and affect the organic law of the United States. Whatever development the United States, in the near future, may experience will necessarily come from within and not from outward pressure. Unlike the nations of Europe, the United States has no neighbor sufficiently powerful to affect its policy or to modify its constitution. It requires no standing army; and so long as England performs the police duties of the seas, it requires but little of a navy. It has no occasion to fear any serious foreign intervention, and it is therefore left freer than any other nation within the period of modern civilization to pursue its own development. In that respect its position is *sui generis ;* nothing resembling it as a national power has ever appeared on the face of the earth, except the condition of savage

222

tribes and insular nations, not brought within the influence of civilization, as to the severance of political interests from that of all other peoples. The good that is within it can, therefore, come to its ripest development: the evil that it contains, unless corrected, will bring its direst sinister consequences. The influence of foreign nations upon it are entirely of an industrial, intellectual, and commercial character.

A combination of circumstances beginning with the war of 1861, intensified by the extension of the means of intercommunication between the States by the railway and the telegraph, in conjunction with the natural and artificial waterways of the country, has made of the United States a solidified nation, within the generation last past, to an extent that was not anticipated by its founders, a consolidation much more complete than the theory of American institutions would seem to justify. State lines exist and will continue to exist for all purposes of penal and municipal law, except in so far as they may, as already shown in these pages, be overridden by the paramount law of the Union. Yet the traveler who starts in a railway train at Boston and remains in the same palace car until he arrives at San Francisco, travels through twelves States and Territories without noticing any State line, and rapidly comes to regard the whole domain as his one country. The tendency of the times is necessarily to weaken the power of the State on the allegiance of the individual, and to lead to a greater and greater consolidation and unity of interest of the whole United States. This tendency is still further accelerated by the inability on the part of the individual States to deal with the economic and social questions which necessarily arise from the extension of the means of intercommunication between the States, and the necessity for the existence of a general power to deal with them. Already the States have felt and have, to a considerable degree, acknowledged their inability to deal with the railway and the telegraph question. The decisions of the Supreme Court in recent years, recognizing the inability on the part of the States to deal with these questions, have considerably extended the jurisdiction of this court over transportation routes lying partly within one State and partly within another, or upon a river running through two or more States. In the so-called Granger cases the Supreme Court has asserted jurisdiction in cases of all inter-State commerce in which goods or passengers are taken from one State beyond its own borders within the domain of another. This tendency will continue to consolidate the power of the United States upon all indus-

trial and commercial matters as to which the States
have a common interest, and for the purpose of putting that question at rest so that the United States
may deal with that subject precisely as it deals with
the subject of bankruptcy, a constitutional amendment will, in all probability, be adopted and acted
upon, granting to the United States Government in
express terms that which it already claims to have
by implication, so that it may deal fearlessly and
effectively with the important problems that arise
from the organization of great monopoly interests
which are incident to modern methods of the transportation of goods and passengers.

With the exception of the Pacific railways, all
the railway corporations of the United States were
chartered by the States, and though many of them
have thousands of miles of line traversing many
States, they claim their powers under the separate
charters of the different States through which the
lines run, and are in theory only amenable to the
States covered by their lines of rails. Inequalities
of rates, however, creating unjust discriminations
between individuals of different States, and exercising a function analogous to that of taxing arbitrarily and without control, have and do create a
power within the nation so great that it threatens
sooner or later emphatically to dispute with the

10*

authorities of the United States whether the railway or the governmental power is the greater. The State political machinery has to a very considerable degree already succumbed to the exercise of this power, and therefore to make head against it it will be found necessary to clothe the general Government with sufficient attributes of sovereignty to deal with the subject adequately.

That this necessity runs counter to a very correct theory of decentralization, and that the liberty of the individual is endangered by all centralization of power, is a truth to which thoughtful students of political history cannot shut their eyes. But precisely as in Germany a false decentralization of power had to be succeeded by a nation having centralized national power, with the view to intelligent and proper decentralization; so in time it may be necessary in many particulars to disregard State lines and the localizing of power resulting from such State lines, for the purpose of more intelligent and more effectual decentralization in those particulars wherein it is beneficial, and also to secure centralization in those matters wherein decentralization involves danger to the commonwealth.

The development of the taxing power arising from the war quadrupling the number of office-holders in the United States within the period from

1860 to 1870, and increasing as it did the ordinary expenditures of the United States Government, independently of interest on the public debt, from $60,000,000 in 1860 to $220,000,000 in 1867, has in itself aggravated certain evils which only were easy to be borne at a period of time when the United States had a debt of $64,000,000, representing per capita $1.91 in 1860, instead of a debt of $3,000,-000,000 in 1865, with a per capita charge of $78.25.

From the time of Jackson's administration appointments went by favor, not by merit, and that which was favor originally, degenerated into a claim of right dependent upon political activity in favor of the successful candidate. Appointments were made to high offices not because A. B. was specially qualified for the office, but because A. B. was a skillful or efficient worker in the campaign which preceded the successful election of the incumbent. This system not only fills the public offices of the United States with inefficient and corrupt officials in high station, and keeps out of political life the capable men, who are disinclined to perform party work as a condition precedent to accession to office, but it also created the same system under those officials as to all their subordinates; and as from the Presidential office down to the lowest political official, tenure of office is dependent upon the continuation of the administration, at every recurring election these officials strive by personal activity at the polls, and in the organization of the machinery of elections and nominations, to continue in power the political party to which they belong, so as to preserve their personal incumbency of the office, and they were to a very large degree, and still are, regularly assessed to pay the political expenses of a campaign. Millions of dollars are thus raised, in the *interim*, from office-holders in the United States at every recurring Presidential election, or even local elections, which may have a remote effect upon the Presidential elections, to pay the expenses of campaigns and to create a " corruption fund " for the purposes of the party to which these office-holders respectively belong. So intolerable has this abuse become that for some years tentative efforts have been made, even by administrations, to correct some of the more flagrant evils of this system, and during the administration of General Grant a Civil Service Commission was organized to deal with the subject. The influence of party, however, was too powerful for any permanent success during General Grant's presidency, and the Civil Service Commission came to an end.

As President Hayes was elected upon a platform

which pledged his administration, in the event of his success at the polls, to the inauguration of a system of civil service, steps were inaugurated shortly after the 4th of March, 1877, to create a system of promotions by merit and permanence in the tenure of office. The contest, however, of the politicians against it, and the somewhat half-hearted manner in which the system was pressed by the administration itself, prevented any great progress being made in that reform during the administration of President Hayes.

The Republican party again pledged itself to civil service reform in the platform of the convention which nominated Mr. Garfield, and although during the early period after his inauguration much of the time of the administration was taken up by personal wrangles between senators and the President on the question of the exercise of the Presidential prerogative of appointments to office without dictation from senators, which operated to prevent any considerable progress being made in the introduction of a harmonious system of civil service, yet from the character of President Garfield it was a reasonable assumption that during his administration some decided step in advance would be taken looking toward the practical introduction of this reform.

The Democratic party discovered that during the contest for the Presidency it was confronted by a vast army of office-holders, contributing a vast fund, through assessments on their salaries, to the sinews of war of their adversaries, to prevent the accession of Democrats to power. Such assessments were paid because the office-holders knew that their official existence would be terminated in the event of a change of administration under the domination of an adverse party. This fact brought about a conversion of the Democratic party in favor of some reform of the civil service which would take that important element of opposition out of future contests to prevent its accession to power, so that in the United States both political parties are now pledged to the introduction of civil service reform, and a bill introduced by Senator Pendleton, a life-long Democrat, which secures fixity of tenure in all the lower grade of offices, is in a fair way to become a law; and there is but little doubt that within a few years the public service of the United States will be brought more in harmony with the condition of public service in other civilized countries.

The evil of the abominable "spoils" system in the United States is not so much in the incompetency of the officers—as the American's adaptiveness enables him quickly to learn the routine duties of an office—nor in the waste of public moneys (because in a community so rich in productive power as that of the United States the amount which wastefulness can take from it, is a burden easy to be borne); but in the fact that the "spoils" system demoralizes both parties, and makes contests, which should be for principle, mainly for plunder, and induces parties, in the hope of an accession of strength sufficient to obtain political power, not only to lower but absolutely to abandon their principles, and to make their platforms conform to what they suppose will more rapidly win popular success, and thus makes of the quadrennial presidential contests, mere scrambles for office.

Important as it is to secure a reform in the civil service of the United States, that alone, however, even if successful, would not result in any improvement of a very permanent character in the conditions of the party systems of the United States. The causes which make parties permanent institutions in the machinery of government in constitutional monarchies, having like England large bodies of persons who are either placed in positions of exceptional advantage, like that of the hereditary legislators of England, or permanent disadvantage like the classes not admitted to the suffrage, are such that there will necessarily, so long as this condition of affairs exists, be a party seeking to diminish the power of those exceptionally well placed and to increase the political powers of those who are not admitted to the suffrage. This permanent cause for party existence does not prevail in the United States. And yet party lines are drawn as sharply in the United States as they are anywhere, and the tyranny of party is in many respects greater than anywhere else, because the caucus system has permeated it to the uttermost degree and created an autocracy of party managers, the hold of which will not be entirely shaken off— indeed, but slightly loosened—by the introduction of the civil service reform.

That party management in the United States becomes more unscrupulous than it does elsewhere arises in part from the fact that in the United States there is no large leisure class of cultured men who, from a sense of duty or because of their large financial or property stake in the community, devote themselves to its political government. The absence of such a class and the intensity of occupation in industrial employments of the community at large, place the management of party in the hands of briefless lawyers and unsuccessful people in other avocations of life, who, having

been, as a general rule, eliminated downward from
other occupations, devote themselves wholly to political intrigue and the perfecting of the political machinery. As office, and speculation upon the money
expenditures arising from the pursuit of office by
others, through party machinery, are their main objects, there results in time a domination of a class
of politicians, to whom the principles of the party
are mere cries to catch votes, and who doff and
don those principles as it suits their convenience
or their expectations of gain. That both political
parties' contain among their leaders men of a
higher order of intellect, and that even the political machinery cannot get on without men of that
stamp, to whom they are compelled to give honors
and office, is unquestionably true. The character-
ization of the average politician applies more
especially to the people who have control of the
machinery of politics in the large centres of population. This evil condition is promoted and is
enabled to work its worst results by the system of
representation now prevalent, with few exceptions,
wherever representative institutions prevail, viz. :
that of giving to majorities only in circumscribed
election districts the right to representation, instead
of, as far as possible, by some system of minority
or totality representation, aiming at a representa-

tion of the whole community. The hold that the party managers have upon the voters, who would otherwise rebel against their tyranny, is that if the voter fails to vote for the candidate they submit, he either is compelled to throw away his vote on one who has no chance of success, or directly or indirectly to aid the promotion to office of some one nominated by a party machinery equally odious and representing the other side in politics. If, on the other hand, in the election of representatives, small bodies of voters could detach themselves from the main body, and by affiliation with other similarly detached bodies of voters within the State, succeed in representing one or more electoral quotas, as, for instance, in the State of New York, with its twelve hundred thousand voters, having thirty-three Members of Congress to elect, could thus secure one-thirty-third of the voting power of the State, these combined detachments could elect a representative, independent of party, and in this way every important phase of popular opinion could seek and find its own representation. Parties then would represent principles, and they then would not be the mere banner or shibboleth of party, hauled down and replaced as it suits its convenience, and the individual voter would become comparatively independent of party dictation. This would act as a solvent of political parties as at present constituted; would retain what in them is useful and good, and would utterly prevent the evil effects of the caucus system. This reform once introduced, would fructify into inestimable political blessings to the country, as it would make a political career independent of an accidental majority in a district, and secure for that career an entirely different class of statesmen and politicians than party machinery now brings to the front. The civil service reform confessedly will act only upon the minor offices within the United States. This reform of minority representation would be operative for good in a change in the character of the nominees for every important elective office where there are more than two persons to be elected, and would totally alter the character of political parties as at present mischievously constituted.

Another subject which will presently engage the attention of the American people is one which, since 1860, has been driven to the background, that of liberalizing its navigation laws and its system of tariff duties. The rate of taxation in the United States both as to internal revenue and the admission of foreign goods is as yet, it may be said, upon a war footing. When the Southern delegates to Congress withdrew in 1861, the opportunity was immediately seized upon by the protectionists to inaugurate a protective system on the pretence that the Government required an enormous amount of revenue to carry on the war, and that to increase the tariff would increase the revenue, as well as indirectly afford protection to a larger number of home industries. The long-continued adhesion of the Southern States to a system of free trade put for the time being every advocate of free trade in the North, during the progress of the war, in a false position, because it appeared as though he were in favor of the South in advocating free-trade theories. The fictitious prosperity created by the paper currency issued during the war, disguised for the time being the evil influence of a protective tariff. After the close of the war the paramount questions which engrossed the attention of the nation were necessarily those relating to the reconstruction of the Government of the Southern States, and the return to specie payments; subsequently the depression caused by a return to specie payments enabled the advocates of a high tariff to attribute the evils which came synchronously with contraction, to contraction alone. After specie payment was resumed an immediate impetus was given to the prosperity of the country by a combination of causes of which the return to a sound financial basis was but a part.

Successive good crops, the great tide of immigration, and the development of the mining industries of the Western territory as well as the opening up of vast tracts of virgin agricultural lands in the Northwest, together contributed since 1876 to enhance the prosperity of the United States beyond all precedent. This again concealed from the people the evil effects of the tariff legislation, and enabled the tariff advocates to claim for their vicious system the prosperity which came despite their system.

In one respect alone is the evil effect of restriction so visible that it cannot be attributed to any other cause, unaccompanied as it is by any misleading element of prosperity on the other hand, which counteracts it; and that is, in the complete prostration of the shipping interests of the United States, and the almost total extinction of its commercial steam marine engaged in foreign trade.

The beginning of a change in the restrictive legislation of the United States will probably first be made herein. The navigation laws will be made more liberal; an American register will be able to be obtained for ships built in foreign jurisdictions, as an effort must soon be made to bring back to the United States part of the carrying trade which its navigation laws have utterly destroyed. An overflowing treasury will be another reason for revising the tariff. The plea of necessity for higher rates of duty, false as it is because the experience of England and France under the Cobden-Chevalier treaty showed conclusively that the lowering of rates of duty increased the revenue, has also fallen away. A dangerous move, however, in opposition to free trade is already making itself apparent in an agitation for the removal of the internal revenues of the country, which yield a very considerable proportion of the annual income, in the expectation that the removal of these internal revenue duties will compel the maintenance of a high tariff. One of the first steps in that direction had already been made under the plea of a free breakfast table, by which the duty on tea and coffee was lowered, and by putting on the free list a large number of articles which the United States do not at all produce.

Could the Democratic party, which is the traditional party of free trade, be relied upon to be true to its principles upon that subject, it would be reasonable to believe that the very next Congress would succeed in producing considerable reform in that particular; but the result of the recent Presidential election in which the Democratic party as the campaign was drawing to a close, became panic stricken by reason of the attack upon its revenue reform plank in its platform, has so demoralized many of the so-called leaders of the party, that already indications are abundant that some of the Western leaders of that party will in the future Congress be out-and-out protectionists, and attempt to outbid the Republican party in the claim for popular confidence on the ground of willingness to afford protection to home industry as against foreign competition. A reorganization of parties will in all probability result from that question, after both great party organizations shall have been shattered by it; and that reorganization could best be brought about by a previous introduction of the system of minority representation, which would assist in the detachment of great bodies of voters from party affiliations.

One of the problems which, though locally confined to the Pacific coast, is one with which the Union as a whole is called upon to deal, is what is known as the Chinese question. Considerable numbers of Celestials have been attracted to California and the Pacific States generally, and have there proved themselves to be very formidable competitors to American labor, as the wants of the Chinaman are simpler than those of the European and American, and his industry is more continuous and machine-like than that of his rivals. This has created a prejudice against his labor to that degree, that the

Constitution of the State of California has been amended to prevent corporations from employing Chinese labor, and the politics of the Pacific States is largely influenced by that question.

As a mere branch of the protective system, the political economist must of course deny to the agitation against the Chinaman all validity; but there is one argument which is advanced in favor of the exclusion of the Chinaman which has force, and to which the free-trade argument is no answer. The Chinaman refuses to become part of the body politic; no matter how long his residence, he does not become a citizen : he expects to be interred in his country; he lives in separate quarters ; and a considerable addition to that population creates a class of people who are not citizens, and who have no permanent interest in the welfare of the community in which they reside. That such a class, if sufficiently numerous, may become a dangerous one to the civilization of a community, is unquestionably true. That to a large degree, however, his seggregation from the rest of the community is due to prejudice against him, and that in time he may become by social recognition, intermarriage, and citizenship, when that prejudice subsides, a valuable part of the body politic, is likewise true; but this process is necessarily so slow that the unchecked emigration from that vast and teeming hive of humanity, the Celestial empire, will produce much disturbance in the political and social condition of some of our far Western States. This question has already received partial attention by legislation by the Congress of the United States which must rely for justification upon a basis quite other than the false and delusive one of protection to American labor which such legislation is supposed to afford.

A rapid decrease of the public debt takes the question of the payment of the bondholder in any but the best of faith out of the domain of political questions. But there still remains a monetary question which has been unfortunately muddled in the United States by demagoguery. The ratio of silver to gold having been fixed too low by the currency laws anterior to the war, silver was practically driven out of circulation, gold upon that ratio being the cheaper metal. In 1873 Congress demonetized silver for all large payments. Subsequently the rapid decline of silver in the markets of the world, due, in great part, to the demonetization of silver by Germany and the discovery of enormous silver-bearing lodes in the Rocky Mountains, caused a fear amongst silver producers that unless America remonetized silver, silver would fall to such an extent as to seriously impair the value

11

of silver mines. The original dollar was 416 grains standard. Its weight was changed in 1837 to 412½, and its fineness changed to 900 from 892. This coinage of 412½ grains was revived in 1878 in what was known as the Bland Silver Bill, and it was made a legal tender for all debts, public and private, notwithstanding the fact that in recent years the value of silver had sunk so low that the value of the bullion in the dollar of 412½ grains was less than eighty-one cents. The amount required to be coined under the bill is $2,000,000 per month. Thus far no inconvenience has resulted from this coinage, because a considerable part of it has been absorbed by the necessity for small change. A trade dollar also was issued for purposes of Eastern trade of 420 grains, but this is not a legal-tender dollar. A large accumulation of the standard silver dollars is now in the vaults of the treasury, and if no amendment is made to the law as to the rate of coinage, the question will soon be upon the United States whether they desire to have an exclusive silver coinage of a depreciated character, as under the inevitable effects of what is known as the Gresham law, the cheaper currency will drive out the dearer. That this effect would be counteracted by a simultaneous remonetization of silver by the European governments which have heretofore demonetized it, thus creating, for the time being, a strong demand for silver, is doubtless true ; but as the result of recent conferences on that subject gives us no hope in that direction, the United States Government will either have to demonetize silver or raise the number of grains in the silver dollar to a par with gold values, or in the future demonetize gold, and have its currency in a depreciated condition as compared with the actual values of the metal. The question in the United States is more complicated and taken out of the domain of pure theoretical and philosophical discussion on its merits, as to whether a bi-metallic or a mono-metallic currency is better for a community, by the fact that the persons who were afflicted with the greenback mania have become imbued with the idea that, as greenbacks have now become equivalent to gold, their hope of prosperity lies in a depreciated silver currency. It is a curious illustration of how fast a hold the *post hoc ergo propter hoc* error takes upon a community. As the inhabitants of the Northwestern States during a period of rapid issues of irredeemable paper money were enabled to pay off their debts, and were prosperous in so doing, in a currency which incidently depreciated rapidly, many of them concluded that the depreciation was the source of their prosperity, and that therefore any currency that depreciates is useful to them.

In the early period of the war—when the Confederate forces prevailed over the Union armies—the organization of the national banks was devised as a means compulsorily to float the public debt and to create a large home market for United States bonds. The State bank systems, which theretofore existed for furnishing a currency for the people of the United States, were, for good or ill, dependent entirely upon the legislation and the enforcement of the laws in the various States of the Union. The facilities for counterfeiting these issues, as they were by no means uniform in device, were abundant, and the danger of being imposed upon by counterfeit and badly secured bills was very great. These causes produced a constant fluctuation in the value of such currency, and at any moment of financial depression or crisis the currencies of the different States became of different values, and great losses were entailed upon the holders by reason of such fluctuations. The Government issues of paper money, together with the issues of the national banks, based upon deposit of United States bonds, gave a uniform character and value to the currency of the United States. This convenience is so great that the national banking system, although opposed with considerable vigor at first, has been accepted in the United States as a remedy for an evil much greater than that which it in its turn has brought about. There is, therefore, no probability of any concerted action against the national banks, and the system, with some slight modifications, is likely to be as permanent as the national debt. This system has also set at rest the question of the recharter of a United States bank. There is occasional and fitful opposition to the issues of the national banks, on the ground that the Government, by a direct issue of the notes represented by the national bank currency, would save the interest represented by such issue. The objection, however, on the other hand, to give the Government absolute control of the issue of the currency, and the sinister influence that it may thereby exercise upon the money market, is of so much more serious moment than the one of mere loss of interest, that thoughtful people have, on the whole, acquiesced in and deemed it preferable to maintain the system of national banks, rather than to place the monopoly of currency issue entirely in the hands of the Government; and as hitherto no loss has been entailed upon the holders of national bank notes, as actual issues of notes are always secured, whatever fate may betide the bank in its discount and deposit department, the well-grounded objection that existed against the State issues, which caused monstrous losses to holders by failures of banks to redeem, does not prevail against the United States banks. However, if the present rate of extinction of the national debt continues, in less than ten years some other basis than United States bonds must be provided for a uniform currency.

During the war large portions of the public domain were granted to private corporations to assist them in building the Pacific railroads. This was followed by great grants to railway corporations to assist in building railways but remotely connected with the Pacific system. However justifiable the motive originally was to grant the aid of public lands as an encouragement to the building of these great arteries of commerce, yet the aggregate public property thus given away became so great and the monopoly in public lands threatened to become so formidable, that a public opinion has been evoked in the United States that the public domain left under the control of the Government shall be used entirely for the purposes of the settlers, and not be thus given away. It is estimated that the domain given to the North Pacific Railway and branches is equal in territory to that of the whole of France. The increased value of the public domain of the United States will in itself be a check against extravagant concessions of land in that manner, and an intelligent public opinion has been created to prevent wastefulness hereafter.

The advancing wealth of the nation resulting in a growing importance of governmental functions in different departments of the United States Government, which are respectively under the direction of one of the Cabinet officers, and the desirability that these departments should be subjected to the constant criticism of the Legislative branch of the Government, have caused an earnest agitation in favor of giving to Cabinet officers seats in the House of Representatives, with a power to debate without voting on the result; so that in the United States, as in England, interpellations may be made respecting the conduct of any one of the important departments of Government, and an answer elicited on the spot. At the beginning of the American Government these Cabinet officers were personal advisers of the President, were appointed by him, and were responsible to him alone. The fact is now, however, recognized (more especially with reference to the Treasury) that the annual reports or budgets give insufficient information, and that during the course of the year too much opportunity is afforded for sinister influences to accomplish ends having relation to stock-jobbing and the obtaining of private information of intentions on the part of the Treasury as to policy, sale of bonds, etc., a remedy for this would be found if the Secretary of the Treasury were personally responsible to Congress. The further advantage expected to be derived from having the Cabinet or Ministry connected with the popular branch of the legislative body is that in that way some more direct responsibility will attach for the legislation of the Congressional session to the Government in power. One of the serious defects of all American legislation is the almost entire absence of responsibility connected with legislation. The party having a majority has no organized Ministry charged with the duty of forwarding and formulating the public legislation of the session, and however faulty and slipshod, and even mischievous, the Congressional or State legislative law-making may prove during the course of the year, the party having a numerical majority in the legislative body is not responsible because there is no Ministry as part of the law-making power which proposes and promotes legislation. Laws are proposed by individual members upon their own responsibility, and are passed in a hap-hazard and slipshod sort of way. A further argument in favor of the reform is that to compel, on the floor of the House, an explanation of the conduct of the department, does certainly apply the corrective of publicity to all jobbery and peculation. The objection, that the selection of persons to fill executive departments should be made with reference to executive and not oratorical abilities, and that such a change might compel appointments with the view to capacity readily to explain conduct, instead of fitness for administrative work, has but little validity, as a very short experience teaches the average American to talk clearly and glibly on the subject he has in hand.

The evil of including improper items in a bill making appropriations for the indispensable objects of government, thus morally obstructing a veto, caused, in several of the States, a constitutional amendment to be adopted enabling the Governors to veto special items of the supply or appropriation bills, and to approve the remainder. The clearly extravagant character of the River and Harbor Bill of 1882 has awakened public attention to this subject, and will, doubtless, at an early day, cause an Amendment to the Constitution of the United States to be adopted, which will clothe the President with a like power.

11*

CHAPTER VII.

THE Federal power being one of delegated powers, the States are, in all matters not so delegated, the sole sovereignties. The State Constitutions map out the organization of the State Governments, limit their powers, and are in many respects more important conservators of the liberty of the citizen than the Federal Constitution itself; for the reason that the powers not surrendered to the Government of the United States are much more extensive and much more immediately related to the rights of the individual, and therefore affect him more closely than the powers delegated to the Federal Government. In all their functions and domestic relations, their amenability to deprivation of life or liberty by the criminal law, in the assertion or denial of rights through the civil administration of justice, the State, with but few exceptions, has absolute control over the life, liberty, and happiness of its citizens. This book, therefore, would

250

be incomplete if it did not give some account of the changes which have taken place in recent years in most of the State Constitutions, showing by means of these organic laws the course of governmental development.

During the Revolutionary War most of the original thirteen States adopted State Constitutions, many of which were redrafted shortly after the war; and before the formation of the Constitution of the United states, all the original States had written Constitutions. Every State, on its admission to the Union, submits its Constitution to Congress, so as to give assurance thereby that it has, as required by the United States Constitution, adopted a republican form of government. These Constitutions all contain elaborate declarations of the rights of citizens which are not to be subjected to legislative or judicial interference, and are thereby reserved from the interposition of Government. These declarations of rights also contain carefully worded provisions securing the right to the writ of habeas corpus, of jury trial, and of exemption of private property from seizure for public purposes except on due compensation being made. They set forth how such compensation shall be ascertained; insist upon guarantees of freedom of speech and of the press ; secure the right of petition and the right of citizens to vote at all elections, and require that all officers shall either be elected directly by the people or appointed by some authority elected by the people.

Since the War of the Rebellion the Southern States, in which slavery had theretofore existed, amended their Constitutions, by forever abolishing slavery and every form of human servitude.

The State Constitutions all divide the functions of government into Legislative, Judicial, and Executive, specify the manner in which the Legislature shall be elected, and set forth the powers of the Executive; organize the Judicial system; declare the manner of the appointment of the Judges, and confer upon them their respective jurisdictions. There is much uniformity in these particulars in the State Constitutions. The legislative power is generally vested in a legislative body composed of a Senate and an Assembly. The Senate is a small elective body, each member of which is elected for a longer period of years and from a larger district than the more numerous and popular legislative body, which changes generally from year to year.

Each State has its Governor, elected for terms of from one to four years; some have Lieutenant-Governors and other elective executive officers. In

States where such public works exist, canal commissioners or superintendents of public works are
either elected or appointed under constitutional provisions. State engineers and surveyors exist in most
States, also state prison inspectors and other public boards to take charge of public works. Universally, municipal organizations are created, county
organizations are established, and a system of decentralization of power is adopted for the purpose
of securing local self-government within the domain
of the State. Provisions are contained in many of
these constitutions upon the subject of taxation, so
as to secure uniformity and equality therein, and
prevent the growth of public debts by throwing
safeguards around the creation thereof.

There are provisions in relation to the militia
Most of the Constitutions now contain special articles on the subject of bribery and official corruption, and all contain provisions as to methods of
amendment. In some of the States the Constitution is limited as to duration to a number of years
only, and State conventions are required to be called
from time to time for the purpose of suggesting
amendments.

Some of the original Constitutions of the States
required voting to be *viva voce*, and it was only in
imitation of the Constitution of the State of New

York of 1777, that voting by ballot was generally introduced.

In some of the earlier Constitutions of the States a property qualification was required for the enjoyment of full citizenship, but this qualification has almost wholly been swept away. In the Constitution of the State of Massachusetts there is a provision that the voter shall be able to read the Constitution in the English language, and write his name, and by an amendment to its Constitution in 1863, two years' residence in addition to the time necessary to qualify him to become a citizen of the United States, is necessary before he can be a citizen of Massachusetts.

Under the Constitutions anterior to 1848 many of the officers now elected were appointed by the Governors. Notably so was this the case as to judicial positions. The Constitution of 1846 of the State of New York, which, as to this change was the pioneer State of the Union, was drafted by men who were imbued with a spirit of radical democracy and who looked with suspicion upon all executive power. The Constitution thus framed therefore stripped the Executive office of many of the functions that it theretofore had and added enormously to the number of persons to be elected by the people, including even Judges of courts of record. This change, for reform it can scarcely be called, was adopted in other States, and it is only in recent years that the wisdom of the change has been questioned and some modifications made in the original provision of the New York Constitution of 1846, and those of other States. It was found that electing Judges for so short a period of years as that provided for in the Constitution of 1846 of the State of New York resulted in obtaining in many instances, as Judges, mere politicians of a low order. It therefore became necessary either to return to the appointing power, or to make the tenure longer and the salary larger, so as to make the Judge, at least for a considerable period of time, independent of the favor of political parties. By amendments of 1869 the Judicial system in New York was recast ; the Judges of the higher courts were elected for a period of fourteen years instead of six, as theretofore, and public opinion was brought to bear upon the question of their remuneration, so that the salary of a Judge of the higher courts was made to approximate a little more closely to what could be earned by a lawyer in active practice. The opinion of the Bar, as expressed by organized bodies of lawyers, has been, however, almost uniformly in favor of a return to the system of appointment by the Executive : as the people as a whole, under existing American political conditions, are scarcely the proper custodians of the power wisely to select from among the Bar, the men who are best qualified for judicial functions, and the methods resorted to in order to secure nomination for judicial offices are oftentimes in themselves so demoralizing that it degrades the office in popular esteem, even if the selection by the people on the whole were as wise as that which could be made by the chief executive officer of the State, acting under a sense of his responsibility to the people for making a proper selection. The appointment to vacancies in judicial offices of course must still remain with the Executive, but such appointments are generally limited until either the next succeeding general election or the election following the next succeeding general election.

A firm conviction that decentralization of power was necessary to insure honesty in the administration of public affairs, injected into almost all of these Constitutions the requirement that municipal bodies shall elect their own officers, and that no one shall hold office within the municipality unless elected directly by the people in the locality or appointed by an elected authority therein. This has so multiplied elective officers within the State

that at a general election the voter is bewildered
with the number of people he is called upon to vote
for. He finds it, therefore, more and more difficult to determine upon the fitness of candidates,
and is thus put at the mercy of political wire pul-
lers and leaders who make the selection for him
and call upon him to vote aye or nay between two
or at most three candidates for the same office.
This difficulty has not yet met with an intelligent
solution at the hands of the American people.

Before the adoption of the Constitution of
1846 in the State of New York, and which is here
taken as an example of the leading State Constitutions, because, as before stated, the amendments
made by that Constitution were extensively followed
in other States, a great source of evil was that the
railway, banking, and insurance corporations created so formidable a lobby to secure special legislation and privileges for the benefit of such corporations, that it was deemed expedient to cause general
laws to be passed for their government, and to restrain the Legislature thereafter from passing special laws upon the same subjects. As, however, the
Legislature was permitted to pass special laws in
all cases whenever in its own opinion such legislation was necessary, the restriction, except as to
banks and insurance companies, was not a very

efficient one. This question of special legislation is one which has not been wisely dealt with by the people of the United States, who, in their attempt to reform the evil arising from the lobby interested in pressing for and securing such special legislation, have fallen into a worse evil.

By a constitutional amendment adopted in the State of New York in 1874, the Legislature of the State is prohibited from passing special laws in a large number of enumerated cases which had theretofore been the lobbyist's most lucrative field of practice, and produced the greatest amount of corruption. This amendment has been followed in other States. Albeit in Missouri and Pennsylvania, constitutional amendments of the same character had been adopted even prior to the one of New York. It was supposed that thereby a blow would be struck at corrupt legislation, and that the Legislature would be free to pass general laws upon these matters and be thereafter absolved from all further concern in relation to the subject. It was not then seen that the most dangerous form of special legislation is that which comes under the guise of a general law, or as an amendment to the general law, and that after special legislation is forbidden, any person desiring special privileges or legislation to meet a particular case, could just as well influence the Legislature to amend the general law to meet the case, thereby securing a special privilege, as to cause a special law to be passed. In that manner one law after another has been placed, since 1875, upon the statute book of the State of New York and other States which followed the lead of New York, having their origin in personal interests only, and designed to meet special cases, eventually destroying whatever harmonious legislation there is in the general body of the law. This evil is more insidious and in its effects much more dangerous than the one which it was intended to remedy, and is one especially mischievous in the United States, because, as already shown, there is no body of permanent legislators standing guard over the laws of the State, and no responsible ministry having charge of public legislation and responsible for it. There is not even party responsibility in relation to such laws, which are passed or neglected under the pressure of private interests or in the absence of any such pressure fail. It would have been very much wiser to have methodized legislation; to have separated, as the English Parliament has done, public or general legislation from all legislation which is private or local in character ; to require notice of application for private or local acts before the convening of the legislative body ;

to treat them not as laws, but rather in the nature of judicial determinations on the part of the Legislature after a trial upon their merits at which witnesses are examined and a trained Bar may exert its talents for or against the bill, and secure its proper amendment. This would convert the lobby into a parliamentary bar ; would bring into the sunlight of publicity all schemes, be they of a sinister or beneficial character, affecting private individuals, corporations or localities, by requiring application for such special legislation to be filed before the opening of the session, and due notice of trial to be given by advertisement, etc., thus giving to the community security that such legislation cannot be smuggled through at the latter end of the session, and enabling all opponents to be heard upon the merits as to the impropriety of such measures.

This division of private from local laws would tend also to elevate the character of public legislation ; would prevent public or general laws from being used as mere instruments of private gain, and effectually extirpate the evil which was intended to be removed—a corrupt lobby seeking to gain an advantage from the community by the secret or corrupt passage of improper private and local bills.

The almost unlimited power of municipalities

and counties to create debts for their own purpose or in aid of public works, led to a very formidable evil between 1850 and 1870 by the rolling up of enormous local public debts in aid of railway corporations. While in many instances this aid was perhaps necessary and judicious, yet it led to so much corruption and abuse throughout the States, and became so burdensome upon the localities, which frequently after the aid was voted failed to get the public improvement for the purposes for which they created the debt and imposed taxes upon themselves, that in almost every State in the Union limitations were put upon the lending of the public credit or voting aid to railway corporations by counties and cities. And in many States such aid is now entirely prohibited.

The abuses incident to the distribution of public funds in aid of charities connected with religious establishments, where any particular religious denomination prevailed, as particularly in the city of New York, became of so grave a character that a constitutional amendment was adopted, and in many other States followed, by which cities were prohibited from granting any such aid to religious institutions. Exemptions from taxation have been a fruitful source of mischief in many States ; institutions of a charitable and religious nature have en-

joyed such exemption on the ground that imposing taxation upon the values of their property
would be onerous in the extreme, it being dedicated
in a certain sense to public use, but it was soon
found that many of these institutions had exceptional advantages for property not actually used for
charitable or religious purposes, and such property
while held by them was free from the burdens imposed upon the taxpayers of the State.   This
led to amendments of some of the State Constitutions limiting such exemptions to the building
and land only upon which is erected such charitable
or religious institution, and to no other lands
whatever.

The evils of corporate management have caused
several of the States to provide as a remedy a system of minority representation in the election of
their Boards of Direction as to all corporations
thereafter to be organized ; both Pennsylvania and
Missouri have engrafted such provisions upon their
Constitutions.   Illinois in the selection of the Legislature, and Pennsylvania in the election of Judges
of the Supreme Court, are the only States which
adopted minority representation for public offices.
In Illinois minority representation is secured in
all legislative districts by the provision that,
in all elections of representatives, each qualified

voter may cast as many votes for one candidate as there are representatives to be elected, or may distribute the same or equal parts thereof among the candidates as he may see fit. This secures, in a very limited way, cumulative voting and therefore minority representation.

In some of the States the agitation for women's rights has resulted in securing for married women by constitutional provisions or legislation an undisturbed enjoyment of property rights. In none of the States, however, as yet have women become full citizens.*

A fruitful source of recent constitutional amendments throughout the States has been the growing power of the railroad corporations. In almost all the Western States elaborate provisions are contained in the State Constitutions by recent amendments by which railways are declared to be public highways. The Legislature is required to pass laws limiting the amount of charges; the railway is constitutionally inhibited from discriminating in charges or facilities in transportation, or making any discrimination between transportation companies or individuals, either by way of abatement, drawback or otherwise, and also from making any preference in furnishing cars or motive power between different individuals, and a new set of

---

* *See* Addenda.

officers, known as Railway Commissioners, have
been called into existence. In the State of New
York no constitutional changes were made, but the
Legislature of 1882 passed a Railroad Commission
Act, and the Governor, in 1883, appointed the
board thereunder.

In some of the States the evil of constant alterations in the law and the uncertainties created thereby
have been sought to be prevented by constitutional changes making the sessions of the Legislature biennial instead of annual. This change appears to be a very short-sighted remedial measure
for an undoubted evil. In the States having biennial
Legislatures, great inconvenience at times results
from the impossibility of promptly convening the
Legislature for the purpose of passing a law of pressing necessity. No greater attention is thereby given
to the quality of laws passed; as many bad laws
can be enacted in a short session of one Legislature as in two sessions of consecutive Legislatures.
The true corrective of this evil is the one already
referred to of properly methodizing legislation, and
dividing public from private acts, creating also some
degree of responsibility for public acts by having
a council of revision or some public body to whom
the public acts are to be referred, and which shall
report upon the same as an Advisory Board to the

legislative bodies. Of course, the main evil of bad legislation arises from the fact that the legislators are not qualified for their work. Annual elections of large legislative bodies from the body of the people or the members of political caucuses, small pay for the time given to the public during that period, and the unfortunate American political conditions arising from the domination of the "boss" and caucus systems, bring as a general rule together in the legislative halls of the various States of the Union a body of men but little qualified for the most important work that can be entrusted to human hands—that of legislating wisely and well for their fellow-men. This evil will find its remedy in the United States only after a considerable period of time. One of the conditions of its correction is, as already observed, to dissolve political parties as at present constituted, by minority representation, and to introduce a thorough system of civil service reform.

The development of individual wealth will also in time come to the aid of the people of the United States; as through it they will possess a body of men so emancipated from all necessity of looking after their personal interests, that they can devote their whole time to the public service.

The change from annual to biennial sessions of

12

the Legislature seems to be as inadequate for the purpose of curing the evils of. bad legislation as would be the conduct of a man at the head of a large industrial establishment, who, finding that in consequence of its mismanagement by his super-intendents he runs behindhand year after year, determines to work but half time as a corrective, instead.of changing his managers and changing his methods. He may not (if he is doomed to run be-hindhand) get himself into the bankruptcy courts by working half time quite as fast as by working full time; but it clearly would be better for him either to shut up shop entirely, or to reform his methods of doing business. If biennial Legislatures are a remedy, not to have the Legislatures meet at all would be still a better one ; but this mistaken measure will continue to be adopted precisely as the limitation upon bad special legislation has run its course until the evils occasioned by the supposed change or reform will bring the people of the United States to a realizing sense of the fact that they have gone for relief in the wrong direction.

The great evil in connection with State institu-tions is that which arises from the difficulty in dealing with municipalities so as to leave them on the one hand the power to govern themselves, and yet on the other to restrict a tendency which in all

American cities has developed itself to an alarming degree, of unlimited debt-creating power and methods of unwise taxation.

Within the twenty years from 1860 to 1880, the debts of the cities of the Union rose from about $100,000,000 to $682,000,000. From 1860 to 1875, the increase of debt in eleven cities was 270.9 per cent. ; increase of taxation, 362.2 per cent. ; whereas the increase in taxable valuation was but 156.9 per cent., and the increase in population but 70 per cent.

A large part of this increase of city indebtedness is doubtless due to the fact that in a concentrated community wherein the vast expenditures involved in city administration are to be made, such expenditures in themselves exercise a corrupting influence upon political elections, and create a numerous body of voters who, by reason of such interest in city expenditures, vote for and maintain in office persons pledged to increase them, or in any event not to reduce them. Political parties find in the salaries of city officials and the numerous indirect advantages arising from the contracts to be awarded by the city for all the purposes of city administration, such as water supply, street cleaning, sewerage, lighting, etc., opening of streets and highways, an enormous fund to perpetuate their power and to

supply them with the necessary means to manipulate
the results of the ballot box; but the evil is not due
wholly to city administrators alone. The members
of the Legislatures of the various States have found
in the offices of a great city, subject to their sway,
abundant opportunities for placing friends in office
and also to secure personal advantages of a more
lucrative character.

Before the charter amendments of 1871 for the
city of New York, the annual tax levy of that city,
—appropriations for the various purposes and objects of the city government—was prepared by the
Legislature in the same manner as the supply bill
for the State; and the corruptions incident to the
items which found place in such tax levy were
greater at that period than have prevailed since
the city government had power from that time on
to determine upon the amount of tax to be raised
and the purposes for which it was to be expended,
without having recourse to State legislation. Numerous commissions for special municipal purposes
were appointed by the Legislature, having independent powers to create debt without any vote of the
city or any part of its inhabitants, and thus not only
was the amount annually to be levied by tax heavily
increased by legislative interference, but also the
permanent debt was largely increased, frequently

without the consent and at all times without the power of the city to prevent such imposition.

Therefore, while it is true that the city administration, when left to itself under the peculiar circumstances of a large tax-eating class in every city in the Union having voting power, is likely to run into excesses of debt and extravagant administration, recourse to the Legislature and leaving the city powerless to administer its own affairs, has been shown by past experience to result in even worse effects than decentralization of power leads to. This condition of affairs has led to an investigation of the question to what extent city administration is part of the government of the nation, and whether or not it is not largely the mere administration of private property upon a coöperative plan. Certainly many of the functions of the city government, such as lighting, paving, and laying out of streets, and the supply of water, are not truly governmental functions, but private services, which are performed under governmental forms for the owners of real estate who would themselves provide such service in the absence of any government taking it in charge. Various efforts have been made, therefore, to create somewhere in the city administration a veto power, lodged in the hands of tax and rent payers, upon such expenditures without thereby limiting the suffrage as to any general governmental city functions. Thus far these efforts have not only proved unavailing, but have cast some degree of odium upon their advocates as being supposed to be adverse to the fundamental principles upon which the institution of American governments are based. That this charge against them is not true does not seem much to affect the question, because large bodies of people do not closely analyze, and it requires some intellectual effort to appreciate the difference between a city administration and the general Government. That the tax-eaters should not have absolute control over the taxes to be expended by the tax-payers would appear to be an entirely axiomatic truth in political philosophy. That the population of cities will increase, and that the pressure of competition will necessarily add largely to the proletariat class when any check comes to the prosperity of the people, would also appear to be almost as self-evident. Sooner or later, therefore, the people of the United States will either have to adopt some method of city administration not copied from the administrative forms of the United States or the States, by which such a regulation of the suffrage shall take place that those who have a permanent stake in the community shall, upon all expenditures involving large amounts in cities, have some voice in determining the amount and purposes of such expenditures ; or fairly and freely recourse must be had to a system of minority representation to secure this result. Indeed the adoption of the latter reform would, without resort to any limitation of suffrage, in itself, check the extravagant, corrupt and useless expenditures in cities; but in the absence of the introduction of any such system, the problem is becoming a very serious one as to how, with the growth of a pauper element, property rights in cities can be protected from confiscation at the hands of the non-producing classes. That the suffrage is a spear as well as a shield is a fact which many writers on suffrage leave out of sight; that it not only protects the holder of the vote from aggression, from which point of view it is unobjectionable, but also enables him to aggress upon the rights of others by means of the taxing power, is a fact to which more and more weight must be given as population increases and the suffrage is extended.

Some of the evils incident to city government in the United States are remediable by other means. One of the fruitful sources of evil influences exercised upon municipal administrations arises from a false distribution of power in the city governments. Departments which should be under some central authority and responsible to it, the members of which should be removable by the Mayor at will, who in turn is responsible for the good government of the city to its inhabitants, have become independent bodies having debt-creating power without central control.

The city council chamber, even when not stripped of all responsible legislative functions, as has been notably the case in the city of New York, is called into being under a faulty system. Small districts are created for the election of members of the Board of Aldermen, and frequently a provision is made by which minorities and majorities in the districts have equal representation, so that either small politicans come to the surface in consequence of the small district, or caucus nominations are equivalent to an election, and the election becomes a mere form. This has at times been called minority representation, but it is not so in any proper sense, as it is mere party representation, and not representation of the people.

Attempts have been made in some of the Constitutions of the States, by limiting the ratio of assessment, to check extravagance, but this has proved quite futile as a remedy, because the law is evaded by increasing the assessment so as to keep within the ratio, so that in some of the cities where such a limitation has prevailed the assessed value of property is largely in excess of its actual value, and the ratio of taxation takes a considerable proportion of the actual rental value of real property.

The laws in relation to cities are so constantly changed by the political parties in power within the State, so as to increase patronage in favor of the party in power, and to decrease it as against the adverse party, by either change of officials in office or a transfer of large powers from one department to another, that the Chief Justice of the State of New York in 1875, in a judicial opinion stated that "it is clearly unsafe for any one to speak confidently of the exact condition of the law in respect to public improvements in the cities of New York and Brooklyn. The enactments with reference thereto have been modified, superseded and repealed so often and to such an extent that it is difficult to ascertain just what statutes are in force at any particular time." This grave condition of affairs has led many of the States to appoint bodies of men especially commissioned to inquire into the causes of these evils, and to suggest remedies. New York, Pennsylvania and New Jersey have received reports from the commissions thus appointed, but the remedies proposed threatened so seriously to impair both the power and the

12*   .

patronage of the politicians that they failed of acceptance.

It will be found that the main remedy for almost all the evils of administrative machinery of American cities will be, in the adoption of a constitutional limitation upon the power to create indebtedness, and in a constitutional inhibition upon the Legislature to interfere with the city's administration unless such legislation is demanded by the inhabitants of the city in some formal manner. Further remedies will be found in the remodeling of city charters so as to centre responsibility in the Mayor and the Board of Aldermen, and to subordinate all executive heads of departments to the Mayor and to the legislative department of the city; in the adoption of some system of minority representation, upon a scale sufficiently adequate to create a balance of power within party lines, so that groups of taxpayers may, independent of party dictation, inject representatives of property interests into the local legislative body; in the holding of municipal elections at a different time from State or National elections, and finally in the growth of a conviction in the community which will in time lead them to regard municipal offices as business trusts having no relation to party divisions on political questions, and to repudiate as an unwarranted intrusion the claim of party managers to make nominations for such offices.

ADDENDA.

BEFORE treating of constitutional developments since the publication of the work in 1882, a few subordinate corrections are made in these addenda, necessitated by the intervening legislation which has made a change in the conditions described in the text.

On page 30, reference is made to the Apportionment Act of 1872, which fixed the number of the members of the House of Representatives at 292. By the Apportionment Act of 1882 (Chapter 20 of the Laws of the 47th Congress, passed February 25th, 1882), enacted as the result of the census of 1880, the number of representatives having a voting capacity is increased to 325 ; adding to this membership eight delegates from the Territories, who, however, cannot vote, the House consists in all of 333 members.

On page 43, it is stated that inasmuch as the issue of legal tender notes was based, by the prior decisions of the Supreme Court of the United States, upon the exercise of the war power, there was no ground for apprehension that any addition would be made to the legal tender note issues of the United States in times of peace, and the author expressed the hope that the prior decisions would be permitted to stand as the final expression of the opinion of the Court of last resort of the United States upon that question. That Court, however, in the case of Juilliard vs. Greenman, 110 U. S., 421, decided, March 3d, 1884, that Congress had constitutional power, in times of peace as well as of war, to make the treasury notes of the United States a legal tender in payment of private debts, and that it was authorized to reissue the legal tender notes, which had been practically redeemed under authority of law by the Treasury Department. Justice Gray, in giving the opinion that the power to issue paper money was one of the attributes of sovereignty which appertains to all governments in time of peace as well as of war, felt justified in coming to the conclusion that no such limitation as was put by prior decisions upon this power of the national government was warranted.

This decision is somewhat out of harmony with all the prior decisions of the Court, which conceded that the power to coin money did not include the power to stamp pieces of paper, and which recognized the principle that the government of the United States was one of delegated authority, had no attributes of sovereignty inherent in itself, and that its powers were only such as were specifically delegated (or such as arose from necessary implication as being impliedly delegated) for the purpose of carrying into effect the express powers conferred upon Congress by the Constitution. In the language of Chief Justice Marshall, aptly quoted by Justice Field in his dissenting opinion, the implied powers of the United States are such that they must be appropriate and plainly adapted to the end, not prohibited by, and consistent with, the letter and spirit of the Constitution.

———

On page 44, which states the number of Judges assigned, under the judiciary laws of the United States, to each district, attention should be called to the Act of the 49th Congress, passed March 3d. 1887, which created an additional Circuit Judgeship for the Second Judicial District, which embraces New York City, to meet the necessities arising from the growth of business in that district.

———

On page 54, in commenting upon the Granger decisions, in which the Supreme Court of the United States upheld the right of the States to subject railway corporations chartered by them to restrictions and limitations which had not been originally incorporated into the acts organizing them, it is proper now to refer to the limitation imposed by the decisions more recently rendered by the Supreme Court in the cases of the Wabash Railway Company vs. Illinois, 118 U. S., 557 (1886), and the Western

Union Telegraph Company vs. Pendleton, 122 U. S., 347 (1887), in which it was held that this exercise of power by the States was limited to matters of strictly local concern and did not extend to interstate commerce or transactions.

———

The whole subject matter of the counting of the Presidential vote, as detailed on page 66 of the book, is now regulated by a new statute known as " An Act to fix the day for the meeting of the electors of President and Vice-President, and to provide for and regulate the counting of the votes for President and Vice-President, and the decision of questions arising thereon," being Chapter 90 of the laws of the 49th Congress, passed February 3d, 1887. This statute removes from the domain of discussion the method of procedure relating to the count of the Presidential vote, and makes impossible, so long as it is in force, the vicious, and in many respects dangerous procedure and revolutionary claims put forth in the Tilden-Hayes controversy.

The subject of the Presidential succession is likewise governed by a new law, passed January 19, 1886, being Chapter 4 of the laws of the 49th Congress.

All that portion of the book between pages 66 and 72 must be read in the light of these new statutory enactments, which remove two great perils, and supply important omissions in the law regarding both the Presidential succession and the method of counting the electoral votes that have been cast; thus excluding them from the domain of politics.

The Presidential Succession Bill, in substance, provides, that in case of removal, death, resignation or inability of both the President and Vice-President of the United States, the Secretary of State; or in case of his removal, death, resignation or inability, the Secretary of the Treasury; or in the event of there being no Secretary of the Treasury, by his removal, death, resignation or inability, then the Attorney-General;—and thus on, under like conditions, successively, the various members of the cabinet, in the following order : the Postmaster-General, the Secretary of the Navy, the Secretary of the Interior;—shall act as President until the disability of the President or Vice-President is removed

or a President shall be elected. It is further provided that if
Congress is not in session, nor in due course of law is to convene
within 20 days, and the power of exercising the Presidential
office shall have devolved upon the person thus named in the
act, he shall issue a proclamation, giving 20 days notice of meeting of Congress, and that thereupon a new election shall be ordered for a President. The officers so respectively named, to-
wit, the members of the cabinet must, as a condition precedent
to exercising the Presidential office, themselves have been duly
confirmed and must themselves be eligible to the office of President under the Constitution, and not be under impeachment.

The " Act to fix the day for the meeting of the electors of
President and Vice-President and to provide for and regulate the
counting of the votes, and the decision of the questions arising
thereon," provides that the electors shall meet on the second
Monday of January next following their appointment, and that
the determination of the State authorities under law promulgated
within six days of the meeting of the electors shall be conclusive
as to the counting of the electoral vote and the ascertainment of
the electors appointed by such State. It is made by this Act the
duty of the Executive of each State to communicate, under the
seal of its official Secretary, a certificate of the electors appointed,
giving their names and the canvass of the votes cast for each
person, and to deliver to the electors a like certificate in tripli-
cate, which shall be transmitted to the Secretary of State of the
United States, who is required to publish such certificate and
transmit copies thereof to each house of Congress at its first
meeting.

Congress is required to convene on the second Wednesday of
February in the year following the Presidential election; two
tellers are to be appointed by each House, to whom shall be
handed all certificates, and documents purporting to be certificates, after they shall have been opened by the President of the
Senate, who is to act as the presiding officer at the joint meeting
of the Houses. The House meeting in joint session, the tellers
are to arrange the certificates alphabetically as to the States and
read them. They are called upon to compute all the votes and
declare the result to the President of the Senate, whose duty it

is then to announce the result, and such announcement is made by law a sufficient declaration of the election. All this is done in presence of both Houses.

Upon the reading of any certificate the Presiding officer shall call for objections, if any. Every objection is required to be stated in writing, which shall contain a clear and concise note of the objection, without argument, and be signed by at least one Senator and one member of the House. After such objection is made, the Senate withdraws, and each House considers the objection separately.

In case of a single return from a State, concurrent action by both Houses is required to reject such return. If more than one return or papers purporting to be returns are made, then the dangerous conditions which existed during the Hayes-Tilden controversy of 1877 are provided against as follows :

1st. If there are two or more returns and there has been an executive determination within the meaning of the first section of the Act, within six days of the meeting of the electoral college, such return only shall be counted.

2d. In case of a return, however, involving a doubt which of two or more of the State authorities, after a conflict within the State, is lawfully authorized to determime what electors have been appointed, then only such votes of electors shall be counted as the Houses, acting *separately*, shall concurrently decide are supported by lawful authority.

3d. If there have been two or more returns and there has been no decision by any State court which return is the lawful one, then only the votes are to be counted which the two Houses concurrently shall decide to be those of the lawful electors, unless the Houses acting separately shall concurrently decide such votes not to be the lawful votes. But if the two Houses shall disagree in respect to the counting of such votes, then, and in that event, the votes which shall have been certified by the Executive of the State under the seal thereof shall be counted.

4th. The count is ordered to be suspended until the objection to each State vote has been disposed of in the order in which the objections are made.

5th. The President of the Senate is made the presiding officer, and no debate is allowed in joint session except the motion to withdraw for separate action.

When the Houses separate to act upon the objection, debate is limited to five minute speeches, and each member is permitted to speak but once upon the question, and the main question must be put at the end of two hours after the action is taken in each House.

Elaborate arrangement is made by the Act as to the seats of members of the two Houses for the joint session.

The appointment of officers and their relative precedence in authority are also provided for.

The taking of any recess is forbidden unless a question arises as to the count, and then a recess is not allowed beyond the following morning, except in the case of an intervening Sunday. If the joint session has lasted more than five days then all further recess of any kind is forbidden until the count is completed.

The legislation against Chinese immigration, and the mischiefs which it is supposed the unlimited influx of the inhabitants of the Celestial Empire will work to the industrial and social welfare of the people of the United States, resulted in a treaty with the Chinese Empire, promulgated on the 5th of October, 1881, authorizing the Government of the United States to impose such restrictions as it might see fit upon immigration from that country. This was followed by the law of May 6th, 1882, which suspends for the period of ten years the right of Chinese laborers to immigrate into the United States. By a special provision, travellers and merchants from China who come here with their families and servants for temporary sojourn, and also persons who come here for purposes of study, are exempted from the operation of the Act. This Act was amended and made more stringent by Chapter 220 of the laws of the 48th Congress, passed July 5th, 1884, and the machinery was provided not only to ascertain the purpose for which Chinamen came, but also to secure their return to China in case of any attempted violation of the law.

The practice of European governments to send paupers into this country was met by a law of the same Congress, which prevented such undesirable immigrants from landing, and provided a method for their return to the country from which they were sent, in the event of their coming here in defiance of the law.

By chapter 164 of the laws of the 48th Congress, passed February 26th, 1885, an Act was passed to prohibit the importation of foreigners under contract to perform labor in the United States. This Act was the result of labor agitation against the importation of skilled foreign labor at lower prices than those which were maintained in the United States through the instrumentality of labor unions. It was amended February 26th, 1885, and a method was provided for the return of such persons who on a contract previously entered into came into the United States to perform labor therein. The Act as amended excepts professional actors, artists, lecturers and singers, and persons employed strictly as domestic servants ; and does not operate to prevent the importation of skilled workmen in any new industry established in this country, if such workmen cannot otherwise be obtained.

This Act also provides that it shall not be construed to prohibit any individual from assisting any member of his family or any relative or personal friend to emigrate from any foreign country to the United States for the purpose of settlement here. The law will require further amendment for the purpose of excluding all professional employment from its operation, inasmuch as it is its purpose merely to prohibit mechanics or laborers from being contracted for in European countries to perform service in the United States. An amendment was made by Chapter 220 of the laws of the 49th Congress, passed February 23d, 1887, which prohibits the landing of such persons as were imported in contravention of the law, and provides a method for their return.

The decision of the Supreme Court of the United States which held that the imposition by the State of New York of a tax of fifty cents upon the landing of every immigrant passenger, for the purpose of maintaining a highly useful organization, known as the Emigration Commission, to be an unconstitutional exercise of State legislative power, resulted in the passage of a law by

Congress imposing the same tax as a federal impost and applying the fund thus created for the maintenance of such State Commissions in the States where the immigrants are landed.

———

Chapter 353 of the laws of the 49th Congress, passed March 3d, 1887, repealed the tenure of office bill, which during the bitter contest between Congress and President Johnson in 1867 was enacted for the purpose of tying President Johnson's hands in the removal of executive officers who had previously been confirmed by the Senate, and the provisions of which were subsequently incorporated into the Revised Statutes of the United States. By this repeal, except in so far as the civil service laws may affect his power of appointment and removal, the President is left as free to appoint and remove as he had been before the passage of the tenure of office bill during President Johnson's administration.

———

By Chapter 340 of the laws of the 49th Congress, passed March 3d, 1887, a new departure was made in the legislation of the United States, in prohibiting aliens from acquiring thereafter ownership of lands in the Territories of the United States and in the District of Columbia, and in limiting the amount of land which may be held by corporations. The provisions of the Act prohibit all persons not citizens of the United States or who have not lawfully declared their intention to become such citizens, or any corporation not created under the laws of a State or of the United States, to own or hold any real estate or any interest therein in any of the Territories of the United States or in the District of Columbia except such as may be acquired by inheritance or in good faith in the ordinary course of justice, in the collection of debts, etc. An exception is made in favor of the subjects of those countries that have by treaty acquired the right for their citizens to hold or dispose of lands in the United States. It further provides that no corporation or association more than twenty per cent. of whose stock is owned by persons, corporations or associations not citizens of the United States, shall thereafter acquire or hold any real estate in any of the Territories of the United States or in the District of Columbia. It is further provided that no corporation other than those organized for the construction of railways, canals and turnpikes, shall thereafter acquire, hold or own more than five thousand acres of land in any of the Territories of the United States. Any property conveyed in contravention of the Act escheats to the United States upon appropriate proceedings by the Attorney-General.

This Act has been construed by the Attorney-General of the United States, in an opinion to the President, in which he declares that it does not prohibit an alien from acquiring a leasehold property in the District of Columbia or in the Territories for a reasonable term of years; the terms of the Act construed literally would have prevented any foreign legation from making leases from year to year in Washington City for the purposes of its residence. The Attorney-General also holds that it does not prevent the leasing of mines for a reasonable period of time.

This Act, of course, will have to be amended, and several bills are pending to secure this end, so as to except from its operation, mines, particularly those of precious metals, and in order to allow, in the District of Columbia, which contains the City of Washington, the seat of Government, foreign legations to acquire lands for purposes of their residence.

This legislation will probably be the subject of still further amendments, and must necessarily give rise to considerable litigation, for the purpose of determining whether it was intended to operate upon contracts existing at the time of its passage, whether aliens may sell lands acquired before the Act took effect to other aliens, and for the purpose of limiting its operation by judical construction to the mischief which was intended to be reached, of the acquisition of vast tracts of territory withheld from market by foreign corporations and alien owners.

Chapter 396 of the laws of the 49th Congress, passed March 3d, 1887, provides for the recoining of the trade dollar and the repurchase at par of a coin of the United States, which, notwithstanding the larger quantity of silver that it contains as compared with the legal tender silver dollar, was selling theretofore at a discount.

An important concession was made by the United States Government by Chapter 359 of the laws of the 49th Congress, passed March 3d, 1887, in which general jurisdiction to entertain actions in all cases, except pension cases, was given to the Court of Claims, founded upon the Constitution of the United States or upon any regulation of an Executive Department, or upon any contract, express or implied, with the Government of the United States, or for damages, liquidated or unliquidated, in cases not sounding in tort in respect of which the party would be entitled to redress against the United States, either in a court of law, equity, or admiralty, if the United States were suable. An exception is made of war claims and such as arise from department regulations and such claims as had theretofore been reported upon adversely or rejected by Congress. This Act enables claimants against the United States Government to have their demands adjudicated by a Court of Justice, in the same manner as though the Government of the United States were a natural person and not a sovereign. In the same year a new Act providing for removal of causes from the State to the United States Court was passed, the main amendment in which is to guard against the abuse of the removal of causes on the ground of local prejudice by giving the Courts power to inquire into the truth of the affidavit alleging the existence of such local prejudice.

Probably the most important of the recent Acts of legislation of the United States Government is the Interstate Commerce Law which was enacted by the 49th Congress, Chapter 104, and signed by the President February 4th, 1887. This was the culmination of a long and persistent effort on the part of the people of the United States to subject the great railway interests of the country to some general regulation and control. This law provides that all charges for the transportation of passengers or property between the several States or from the several States into a foreign country, shall be reasonable and just. Special rates, rebates, drawbacks, and unjust discriminations, undue or unreasonable preferences, etc., are prohibited. It is made unlawful for any common carrier to charge or receive more or greater compen-

sation for the transportation of passengers or property for a
shorter than for a longer distance. The Commission created by
the Act is, however, empowered to suspend, in their discretion,
the operation of this clause. The pooling of freights by different and competing railroads is forbidden. Carriers are required
to print and make public their tariffs, including their rates to
foreign countries. These rates are not allowed to be advanced
except after ten days' public notice, but they may be reduced at
any time without notice. Copies of these tariffs and of all contracts between companies, joint tariffs and the like, are required
to be filed with the Commission. Complaints may be made to
the Commission by any person or corporation aggrievèd against
any railway company subject to the provisions of the Act, and it
is made the duty of the Commission to investigate the complaint
without reference to their sufficiency or to their accuracy. An
Interstate Commerce Commission of five members is created, to
be appointed by the President, by and with the advice and consent
of the Senate. It is made their duty to inquire into the management of railways subject to the Act, to keep themselves informed
as to their methods of doing business, to hear and determine complaints against common carriers for violation of any provisions of
the Act, and they are given the right in specified cases to apply to
the Circuit Courts of the United States for assistance in enforcing their decrees. Should the common carrier refuse to obey the
decrees of the Commission, the Commission may proceed by injunction or by attachment through a Court of the United States.
The Commission sits as a Court, in the City of Washington, but
may hold sessions elsewhere when the exigencies of the public
business demand it. A very important provision of the Act enables the Commission to require annual reports from the railways setting forth in detail their financial condition, and these
reports the Commission may require to be uniform. The Commissioners are to report to the Secretary of the Interior in writing
upon the first day of December in each year, and transmit to
him, for publication, whatever information and data they may
have collected during the preceding year, which may appear to
them to be of general interest.

Perhaps the most important provision, in the practical operation of the Act, is the one which authorized the Commission thereunder appointed to suspend the operation of the long and short haul clause section, and which reconciled the conflicting interests which threatened either to make the Act inoperative in a large number of cases by the evasion of its provisions, or to make it operate so harshly as to create a prejudice against the law and thus probably secure its repeal. The author of this treatise claims some credit for having suggested this mode of dealing with the subject to the Senate Committee, known as the Cullom Committee, which had the subject under consideration before the bill was enacted, and for having incorporated it in a redraft of the bill, which subsequently became law.

The Committee found that it was necessary to provide penalties against charging more for the lesser than for the longer haul, and yet were impressed by the railways that in certain instances such a course of conduct was not only to the best interests of the carrier but also to the community wherever competition of carriers by water at the greater distance made the law practically inoperative for good, and that inasmuch as the carrier by water was not subject to its provisions, the bill would, in that event, compel the railway carrier to go out of the business. Among other special circumstances which it was claimed would make the operation of such a clause oppressive were such as arose from the great expense of local traffic in the territories traversed by the Pacific roads.

To meet this conflict of interests, the author of this treatise suggested that the Commission be empowered to suspend the operation of the clause in all cases appealing to the discretion of the Commissioners. This suggestion met with the acquiescence of the railway interest as well as of the legislative Committee having the bill under consideration, and within the year that the Act has been in operation this power of suspension has been attended with good results.

In the way of propositions to amend the Constitution of the United States, many have been discussed since the first publication of this essay; but the only one which had some degree of legislative approval is that which was formulated by Senator Hoar, of Massachusetts, and which passed the United States Senate by a two thirds vote on the 18th of June, 1886, substituting the 30th of April for the 4th of March for the opening of each new Congress, and the inauguration of a President, thus extending all sessions of Congress by a period of eight weeks, and avoiding the extremely short term of the second session of each Congress, which terminates necessarily at the hour of midnight on the 3d of March. This amendment has not been acted upon by the House, and is, therefore, not yet before the people. It is in every way a desirable, but not a very important, constitutional provision.

In fiscal matters the only legislation of prominence may be considered to be the authority to issue silver certificates representing the actual silver accumulated, under the Bland Bill, in the vaults of the United States Government. These silver certificates are based upon the deposit of silver coin, and represent the actual silver reserve. They have added a considerable volume to the circulating medium of the country, but have created no financial disturbance or dangerous inflation, inasmuch as, by the rapid growth of commercial intercourse in the United States, this addition to the currency has been readily absorbed, and the dangers which, at the time of the passage of the Bland Bill, were apprehended in the then immediate future, have been, to some considerable extent, avoided by this substituted issue. This large part of the silver reserve has also been added to the currency without thereby disturbing the relations of the two metals constituting the coin of the United States, notwithstanding the very great discrepancy in actual value existing between silver and gold as compared with their currency value.

Among the additional acts of legislation of the country, of a public nature, which the author deems it proper to refer to herein, are the organization of a Bureau of Navigation, by Chapter 221 of the laws of the 48th Congress, passed July 5th, 1884; and the organization of a Labor Bureau for the collection of labor statistics, and the study and elucidation of labor problems, under Chapter 127 of the laws of the 48th Congress, passed June 26th, 1884.

288 ADDENDA.

The development of the Constitutional history of the United States is to be found, as already explained, in the text of the Constitution itself; in the positive enactments of Congress thereunder, and in the judicial interpretation by the Supreme Court of the United States of the validity and bearing of the Federal legislation, and of such State legislation as trenches upon Federal questions.

The leading decisions of the Supreme Court since the publication of the first edition of this book, elucidating and interpreting Constitutional questions, are both interesting and important. The Supreme Court of the United States in the Civil Rights cases, decided October 3d, 1883 (109 U. S. 3), has declared that the legislation of Congress requiring the like treatment of blacks with whites at theatres, inns, and railways within the States, passed March 1st, 1875, was unauthorized under the XIIIth and XIVth Amendments, and is, therefore, unconstitutional and void: that Congress was empowered to pass only such legislation as will prevent slavery and all badges of slavery; and that the Amendments prohibited all the States from passing any laws discriminating on account of color or previous condition of servitude against any class; but that Congress itself was not thereby authorized to prevent such discrimination by law, nor to impose upon the States, indirectly, legislation having that end in view.

In the case of Poindexter vs. Greenhow, 114 U. S. 270, known as the Virginia Coupon Case, it was held by the Supreme Court of the United States that a contract which had been made by a State by which it agreed to accept its coupons in payment of debts due to the State could not be impaired by subsequent legislation, and that such subsequent legislation was inoperative and void. In a recent case, however, re Ayres, 123 U. S. 443, it was held by the Supreme Court that it was not competent for the courts of the United States to issue mandatory process to compel the acceptance of such coupons by the State authorities, inasmuch as the State, under these circumstances, would necessarily be a party to the suit, and, by the XIth Amendment to the United States Constitution, jurisdiction in such a case is denied to the Supreme Court.

In the case of the Gloucester Ferry Co. vs. Pennsylvania, 114

U. S. 196, it was held by the Court that it was not competent for a State to impose, under the guise of a tax on the business or dividends of a ferry company engaged in interstate commerce, a tax on such interstate traffic; and that the power to regulate commerce between the States gave exclusive jurisdiction to the United States Congress, even when not exercised, and was an inhibition upon the States from enacting any such legislation; and reasserted the principle which secures to the people an interstate traffic and interchange of commodities unimpeded by any State regulation.

The same doctrine was restated and redeclared in Pickard vs. Pullman Car Co., 117 U. S. 34, in which a statute of the State of Kentucky, which imposed a tax upon each sleeping car carried by a railway train running through the State, was held to be inoperative and void as contravening the provision of the Constitution of the United States which was intended to secure to commerce between the States freedom from control on the part of the State authorities. To a like effect was the decision of Fargo vs. Michigan, 121 U. S. 230, which holds that a State cannot levy a tax upon the gross receipts of railroads, which includes interstate traffic, as that would be a tax upon such traffic.

Prior to the passage of the Interstate Commerce Act, in 1887, the various State Legislatures had passed laws organizing and appointing railway commissions for the purpose of regulating the railways chartered by the State governments respectively ; and the commissions imposed at times heavy regulative restrictions upon the railways within their borders. The authority of the States to pass such enactments was challenged by the railway companies, and those acting in their interest, on the ground that it was an impairment of the obligations of a contract, and therefore was forbidden to the States by the Constitution of the United States. It was held, however, by the Supreme Court of the United States in the case of Stone vs. Farmers' Loan and Trust Company, 116 U. S. 307, that the railway commission laws of the various States were, under that clause of the Constitution, not prohibited, and that they were a proper exercise of State legislative power.

The question came up in a different form before the Supreme

290 ADDENDA.

Court of the United States, when it was claimed and shown that some of the regulations attempted by the State commissions affected interstate traffic. It was then held by the Supreme Court of the United States, in Wabash Railway Co. vs. Illinois, 118 U. S. 557, that in so far as such regulations operated upon interstate commerce, it was not an impairment of granted rights or contracts, but was in contravention of the jurisdiction of the United States Government giving to it the exclusive power to regulate commerce between the States ; and that such regulation by statutes of interstate commerce traffic, either under the guise of commission laws or otherwise, was inoperative, unconstitutional and void. To the same effect is Western Union Telegraph Co. vs. Pendleton, 122 U. S. 347, as to the attempt by a State to regulate the interstate traffic of telegraph messages.

As an indication of the jealous care with which the United States Court protects the enjoyment of the interstate traffic, free from all restrictions attempted to be imposed by the different States upon the general commerce of one State carried on in another State, it is instructive to examine the Commercial Traveller's cases ; Corson vs. Maryland, 120 U. S. 502, and Robbins vs. Shelby County Taxing District, 120 U. S. 489. Several of the States, for the purpose of securing the commerce of the State within their own borders to their jobbers and importers, imposed license fees, for the doing of business by sample, in those States by persons not inhabitants thereof, but citizens of other States.

In the Shelby County Taxing District case, the Act which was under examination was passed by the State of Indiana, and did not in terms make any discrimination between the citizens of Indiana and those of other States, but simply demanded a license fee from all who did business by sample. The court, however, looked behind the act to its purpose ; examined the surrounding circumstances and conditions of commerce, and held that inasmuch as the citizens of Indiana having their warehouses and stores and commodities therein exposed for sale within the limits of the State did not require to do business by sample, the Act was intended to operate against persons who resided in other States and concurrently doing business in the State of Indiana, and who necessarily were doing such business by sample. This was practically, therefore, a discrimination by law against citizens of other States, and denying that privilege in their State which is secured by the Constitution to each of the citizens of the States in the other States ; it was an attempt to regulate commerce between the several States by one of the States ; and although the law in terms was made generally applicable to its own citizens as well as to citizens of other States, it was nevertheless an attempt to regulate commerce between the States, and was therefore void. There was a dissent from this decision by three of the judges, including the Chief Justice.

But in the Maryland case, 120 U. S. 502, the Court was unanimous. There a tax was imposed by the State, calculated upon the amount of the stock in trade in the State in which the person selling by sample resides and has his principal place of business ; and the judges dissenting in the Shelby County Case acquiesced in this decision ; holding distinctly that such legislation was unconstitutional, on the ground that it laid a tax on interstate commerce, and that the charge for the privilege to the person subject to the license is measured by his capacity for doing business all over the United States, and without any reference to the amount done or to be done in Maryland.

In the case of Walling vs. Michigan, 116 U. S. 446, it was held that a tax imposed upon an occupation which necessarily discriminates against the sale or production of another State is repugnant to the Constitution of the United States. In this case a tax was imposed upon persons who were vending spirituous and malt liquors from other States, and although it was shown that by subsequent legislation a heavier tax was imposed upon the citizens of Michigan than upon non-residents doing a like business, it was notwithstanding held by the Supreme Court of the United States that the first enactment which imposed upon citizens of other States such a tax was inoperative and void.

In the case of Sprague vs. Thompson, 118 U. S. 90, it was decided that a pilotage law of Georgia which in effect required vessels from one State to pay a pilotage different, or imposes a duty differing, from that imposed upon vessels from another State, is in conflict with the Constitution of the United States, and inoperative and void, and is also in conflict with the United States laws and regulations as to pilotage.

Corporations stand upon a somewhat different footing as to their rights in different States. In the case of the Philadelphia Fire Association vs. New York, 119 U. S. 110, the question was whether a law of the State of New York was constitutional which imposed upon a Pennsylvania fire insurance company a tax based upon the amount that the State of Pennsylvania exacted from New York companies; although such tax differed from and was more oppressive than that which was imposed by New York upon corporations from other States, it was held by the Supreme Court of the United States that as a foreign corporation could be permitted to do business only upon such conditions as the State tolerating such corporation sees fit to impose, as a matter of comity between the States, legislation making wide discriminations is not beyond the State authority, and is, in so far as the Constitution of the United States is concerned, valid.

A different rule was suggested in the San Mateo cases upon argument, and distinctly decided in the case of Santa Clara County vs. Southern Pacific R. R. Co., 118 U. S. 394, in which it was held that a discrimination between corporations and natural persons who were all citizens of the same State, in the exercise of the taxing power, was repugnant to the Fourteenth Amendment of the Constitution of the United States requiring equal treatment before the law of all citizens of the State, and that a corporation was in that respect a citizen; but the distinction is clear, although not very logical, of the rule of conduct to be exercised by a State as to all its citizens, corporations, and natural persons, as contradistinguished from the recognition to be extended or treatment accorded to a corporation extra-territorially.

Among the recent decisions of the Supreme Court of the United States are, however, several which incidentally affect interstate commerce, holding that certain enactments of the States were within their legislative power as coming within the police power of the State. Such is the case of Morgan Steamship Co vs. Louisiana Board of Health, 118 U. S. 455, in which it was held that the States may pass quarantine laws under the police powers of the States, and charge vessels for services rendered to them and to the State without thereby infringing upon any provisions of the Constitution of the United States, although such vessels may carry interstate or foreign traffic.

In the case of Boyd vs. U. S., 116 U. S. 616, an important principle securing individual liberty was established by the Supreme Court of the United States.

Under the revenue laws which had for many years been upon the statute books, the United States District Attorney was authorized to compel a production of books, invoices and papers by a demand for them in a civil or criminal proceeding against an importer; and the refusal to obey such order or subpœna for their production was to be taken as a confession of the allegations of the complaint or indictment. It was held, that when by the exercise of such a power a verdict was secured against an importer, it was an unconstitutional and illegal conviction and in contravention of the IVth and Vth Amendments to the Constitution of the United States, protecting a citizen against unwarrantable search and seizure of papers, and that no person shall be compelled in any criminal case to be a witness against himself. The Court very wisely interpreted the power of coercion contained in the United States Revenue law as in effect a seizure and a search for books and papers, and a compulsion of their production under a threat of a most severe penalty, which, though not mechanically and physically a seizure and search, produced practically the same results, and was clearly within the spirit of the prohibition of the IVth and Vth Amendments to the Constitution.

Among the most interesting cases recently decided by the Supreme Court of the United States is the case of Yick Wo vs. Hopkins, Sheriff, 118 U. S. 356. Prejudice against the Chinamen in the city of San Francisco had led to the passage of a municipal ordinance which was intended to deprive many Chinamen of their means of subsistence and employment. San Francisco is largely composed of wooden structures, and Chinamen notoriously live almost exclusively in wooden houses. The municipal ordinance was adroitly worded and effected its object without seeming to discriminate against Chinamen. It provided that the business of washing and ironing in houses built other than of stone or brick could only be thus carried on upon the condition of obtaining a license therefor from the Board of Supervisors. This looked like a regulation for the safety of the city against fire. The Chinamen applied for licenses, and were denied. They then either offered to comply, or did comply, with all the requirements of the prior ordinances to guard against dangers of fire. They carried on the business without a license, and were arrested.

The question whether the ordinance was in violation of the XIVth Amendment to the Constitution of the United States was presented to the Supreme Court of the United States in that case, and it held the ordinance to be inoperative and void, inasmuch as it practically was a discrimination of an unequal and oppressive character against the Chinamen by reason of the arbitrary manner of its execution ; and the manner of its execution was, in the interpretation of the Supreme Court, a guide to the intent of the passage of the ordinance. The court says that if laws which are seemingly fair are applied with a mind so unequal and oppressive as to amount to a practical denial by the State of the equal protection of the laws, and practically to make an unjust and illegal discrimination, then such denial of equal justice is still within the prohibition of the Constitution, intended to secure equal rights, which prohibits States from doing any act which shall deny to any person within their jurisdiction the equal protection of the laws.

Just and humane as the decision is, it will doubtless return to the Supreme Court of the United States to plague it, inasmuch as the execution of the law is ordinarily regarded as a matter foreign to the purpose of its enactment. This ruling, however, opens very wide a door for a question of what is and what is not within the limits of securing the equal protection of the laws to the inhabitants of the State, and thus makes a boundless preliminary investigation necessary as to the manner of the execution as well as the terms of the enactment of a law to determine its constitutionality.

Of more interest than the constitutional history of the country, since the first publication of this volume, are the political history and the development of public opinion within the past five years.

The political contest of 1884 between the Democratic and Republican parties was one of extraordinary interest, and will for this generation mark the dividing line between the sentimental politics of the past few decades and the commencement of struggles for political power, dependent upon economic and social questions.

The Republican party invited the voters to give to it their electoral ballots in that year, with James G. Blaine as its standard-bearer, the Democratic party with Grover Cleveland as its chief. Mr. Blaine was the incarnation of all the good and all the evil of the Republican organization. He, as much as any surviving statesman of the period immediately succeeding the War of Secession, aided in framing the legislation which resulted in the perpetual extinguishment of slavery, and made its return in the crude form of human bondage thenceforth impossible. On the other hand, those organizations which were developed outside of governmental institutions, but which possessed vast influence and strength, such as the railway corporations and the large landed property organizations, the telegraph and other instrumentalities of commerce, more or less dependent upon congressional favor or congressional non-action, for their financial success, had in him a steadfast ally. His administration of the office of Secretary of State under President Garfield was also of a character to give conservative men considerable apprehension.

During the period from 1865 to 1884, the greatest extravagance with reference to gifts of land and concessions to corporate greed prevailed and was indulged in by the national legislature. It is true that in that period no well-formed public opinion antagonized this abuse of power, inasmuch as the danger resulting from these aggregations of capital and *quasi* public trusts in the hands of persons not responsible to the people was not at that time felt, or had, at all events, not so clearly manifested itself as during a later period.

Mr. Blaine was, during the whole of this period, an active legislator and political leader, and was, therefore, most vulnerable to criticism by a better-informed public opinion in consequence of his participation in this mischievous drift of public legislation.

Mr. Cleveland, on the other hand, had held no public office which required him to take any position upon any of these questions or concerns. He had been Governor of the State of New York just prior to his nomination for President, had proved an excellent official, and except the objection to his inexperience in federal affairs, no fact could be laid at his door which involved reproach.

Aside from the accidents incident to every political campaign, which sway a few hundred or a few thousand votes one way or the other, Mr. Cleveland represented more thoroughly than did his adversary the growing feeling of the community, of having done with the questions which arose from the war issues and war results, and to deal with political matters upon the basis of the interests of the whole community, instead of the interests of classes.

The result was the election of Mr. Cleveland by an electoral majority of 37 votes out of 401, and a plurality of 62,683 of the popular vote.

This installed the Democratic party in power in 1885, after an exclusion of twenty-four years. That this result could not have been achieved without the aid of many citizens who had theretofore been in accord with the Republican party, is a manifest and conceded fact. The dissatisfaction of these Republicans arose partly from their discontent with the methods of the administrations beginning with President Grant down to the close of Mr. Arthur's term of office, and partly from their distrust of the standard-bearer of their party.

Mr. Cleveland was but a short period in power before it became manifest that the principles of civil service reform would be more earnestly put in practice during his administration than they had been theretofore, and that this would be done under circumstances of greater difficulty ; that the dangers which were supposed to be incident to the installation of the Democratic party in power, from such concessions to the South as would practically reimburse it for losses incurred in the war, were wholly illusory, and that that portion of the American community which had been practically excluded from power during a generation, slavery being extinct, could bo as safely intrusted with the national administration as that party which had for a generation, beginning with 1861, controlled its destinies.

The attitude of criticism of the institutions of America which had been previously indulged in only by profound students of political economy, and from time to time timidly suggested from the rostrum of professors at colleges, and from the platforms of lecturers, became more widespread, and thenceforth a most distinctive awakening of public sentiment in relation to politics may be traced.

Colleges organized departments of political philosophy and constitutional history. Two publications, comparing favorably with corresponding European journals, the "Quarterly Journal of Economics" and the "Political Science Quarterly," respectively published by the faculties of Harvard University and Columbia College, have taken their places, it is to be hoped permanently, in the field of political journalism, philosophically to examine public affairs, and to give the results of such examination to the people; political economy societies have sprung into existence, and there is a general disposition to examine and to study political conditions independent of party, untrammelled by the old ties arising from acts anterior to the war and conditions of slavery, and to further such wholesome and useful innovations in the political structure of the country as will bring it in harmony with its most advanced thoughts, and have it no longer governed by the old fetish, that institutions, however wisely planned, are not properly subject to the changes and modifications required by the growing wants and necessities of an advancing and progressing society.

Professor Von Holst says that during the first half of the century the ultimate question in American politics was, What did the framers of the Constitution mean? That question answered was supposed to be the solution of every political problem that arose. Different parties meant simply a different interpretation of the purposes of the founders, and the thought never took hold

of the statesman of that period that constitutional changes were
necessary to keep the institutions of the country in harmony with
the growth of popular society.

Toward the close of the nineteenth century this disposition is
in so far modified that, with an intelligent reverence and a keen
appreciation of the great work accomplished by the framers of
the Constitution of 1789, it is now almost universally conceded
that the present is also a formative period which requires for its
proper guidance a light which owes not all of its effulgence to
the ideas engendered in the last quarter of the eighteenth century.

The hoard of silver dollars, laid up in the treasury, intrinsically
worth 30 per cent. less than their face value, threatened for a
time, under the operation of the Gresham law, to displace gold
as a basis of the national currency. And yet the development of
commercial intercourse between the States, together with the
general growth in population, as well as wealth, of the country,
has so thoroughly kept pace with the increasing volume of this
debased currency, that it has found a place practically as a sub-
sidiary coinage without driving gold to a premium.

It has been the discovery and claim of Protectionists that there
is a special political economy for the United States as against
that which is applicable to the other countries,—a theory laughed
at and ridiculed by all students of that science, and yet which,
judged by the light of experience since 1861, has an element
of truth. The rush of progress and the development of the
material resources in the United States is so great, the wine and
strength of youth is still so active in this country, that the departure from sound economic principles, either in taxation, in
currency emissions, or in the distribution of wealth, does not
bring with it the immediate punishment resulting therefrom in
other and older countries, the resources of which have been ex-
ploited almost to their fullest capacity. In that respect, the
United States resembles a vigorous young athlete, who laughs to
scorn the advice of physicians, and who may commit excesses

without any visible diminution of strength, indeed accompanied even with a growth of strength, and who is thereby led to believe that the laws of hygiene are not for him. That a subtle and secret undermining of the constitution of this athlete takes place through his non-observance of the laws of hygiene is doubtless true, but he is so little sensible of the fact, and it is so little apparent during his youth, that it seems as though he could safely scoff at the suggestions of wisdom and of prudence.

Shrewd political economists who believed in the universal application of the Gresham law of currency, saw in the refusal of Congress to suspend the coinage of depreciated silver dollars an inevitable suspension of the gold payments by the treasury. Nevertheless the coinage has been permitted to continue, and yet the evils anticipated by past experience in other countries have not taken place, and are not likely to take place in the near future if the development of the country keeps pace with the putting out of this debased currency. It must, however, always be borne in mind that the extraordinarily adroit administration of the Treasury Department, since the inauguration of President Cleveland, in minimizing as much as possible the effect of unwise fiscal legislation, had much to do to avoid many of its evil effects.

One of the questions which has agitated the public, and which sooner or later will find its way into legislation, is that of a limitation of the traffic in alcoholic liquors. Although the ultra-prohibition element, looking at the growth of the popular vote upon the subject, is relatively weakened, the temperance question has gathered force by a movement taken part in by a large number of people who have no sympathy with prohibition, but who favor high license, which in its practical effect restricts the temptations put in the way of the workingmen and laborers, lessening the number of saloons, and thereby also lessening the influence of the dramshops and of their proprietors in local politics.

The success which has attended the constitutional amendment in the State of New York, by which the veto power of the Governor of that State is extended to separate items in the Supply Bill instead of as theretofore being compelled to choose between letting them all pass or vetoing the necessary with the prodigal or corrupt supplies, has awakened an agitation in favor of giving to the President of the United States a like power in reference to the annual Appropriation and Supply Bills that are passed by Congress. The demand for this amendment is much encouraged by the abuses and scandals incident to the appropriations in what is known as the River and Harbor Bill, which contains a few useful and beneficial appropriations for the improvement of the rivers and harbors of the United States, coupled with a vast number of appropriations made solely with a view of creating a political fund for distribution in localities, under the guise of improvements of rivers and harbors, the improvement of which can never be made to pay any return to the people commensurate with the expenditure thus incurred.

Without entering into a discussion upon the expediency of this measure, it is proper to draw attention to the fact that there is a great difference between the Supply Bills of the State of New York and the Supply Bills of the Government of the United States, in the enormous volume of arbitrary expenditures involved in the latter as compared with the very limited amounts dealt in by the former. A President armed with the power to determine what elements of the Supply and Appropriation Bills shall or shall not pass finally into the statute book, giving him absolute control of the purse-strings of the United States, could so use this veto as to fasten upon the country a political organization by a new influence more potent than all the existing elements of patronage and political power combined, and an ambitious incumbent of the presidential chair could make through it his re-election almost a certainty, and opposition to him would disappear as chaff before the wind.

———

The contest for right and justice, and the enforcement of the principles of common honesty embodied in the claim for an International Copyright, is now prominently before the public. The educational influence exerted by the American and Publishers' Copyright Leagues and the consideration given to their bill in Congress give hope that ere long the demand for the protection of private property in foreign authorship will receive the sanction of law ; and that the people of the United States will no longer be permitted to appropriate without just compensation, the work of foreign brains, any more than they are now permitted without such compensation to possess themselves of the work of the hands of foreigners.

The woman suffrage question, though not as actively agitated as heretofore, is still sufficiently in the forefront of discussion to justify a passing notice.

In Wyoming the experiment has been tried to an extent both to disappoint the enemies and friends of the movement. The political millennium did not come to the Territory in consequence of allowing women to vote ; nor have any marked changes for the worse appeared. Inasmuch as women vote, on the whole, pretty much as the men do, who are the bread-winners of the household, it was found in practice to be a mere duplication of the vote of the community, with some incidental advantages and some incidental disadvantages. In any event, until a vote will have been discovered which is simply protective in character, and which has not the element of aggression upon the rights of others contained and involved in the present ballot, the exercise of the suffrage cannot be claimed as a right.

Indeed, in practice (without a property qualification) the introduction of the reform would, in the first instance, be a duplicating of the vote of the lower classes, intellectually considered, rather than of the better classes. The prejudice against the exercise of the suffrage by educated women—involving walking to the polls for the purpose of depositing their votes under the gaze and criticism of large numbers of men—is sufficient for many years to come to deter a majority of the more refined women from participating in the privileges of suffrage, should it be conferred on them; whereas, on the other hand, these deterring influences do not exercise so strong a sway upon the lower classes, and particularly not where to counteract this influence a candidate bids for the votes of the working classes by the promise of large expenditures of money by the municipal government. The wives, sisters, and remoter female relatives of men connected with the public departments, and of the laborers employed through the instrumentalities of the vast expenditures of the city government, would be active at the polls :—whereas the women of the households of the tax-paying element would be more or less indifferent, in contradistinction to the female surroundings of the tax-eating elements.

Another question which has been, by recent utterances, presented with much force to the community, is the improvement of our methods of election. It is proposed that the public shall pay for the printing of the ballots and their distribution, instead of leaving it, as heretofore, to private enterprise. The activity and influence of the " halls " (or in other words, the local organizations of politics), arise in large part from the fact that they perform this service for the candidates at some expense to the candidates, it is true : but nevertheless it is a machinery which arises from an absence of proper provisions therefor in the public law; it is a machinery organized for agitation and for the best and most effective distribution of ballots now at hand, and for bringing out the voters.

Candidates hire this machinery, or are hired by it ; in any event there is an action and reaction between the candidates and the machinery, made necessary by the neglect on the part of the State to provide that kind of organization for the public. That the managers and *entrepreneurs* of this private machinery charge a high price for its activity, insist upon a profit on the investment represented by this machinery (for which the public is eventually to pay), is not to be laid at the door of the machinery, because in that respect its managers are governed by ordinary human motives, but should induce the public to perform an obvious duty so as to eliminate the political manipulator.

What is known as the Australian system, or more properly speaking the English system, is recommended for adoption. Substitution of the public performance of a public duty is an unquestioned improvement over existing methods of election, which is the performance of a public duty by private interests.

Methods of legislation are still in a colonial and undeveloped condition in the United States. The fact is that both the National and State legislatures grind out laws without direct responsibility as to their substance or form on the part of any one, and without notice to any interests affected, however seriously detrimental to such interests any proposed legislation may become or threatens to become. The party having the majority of the legislative body has no leadership organized in the shape of a ministry, directly in contact with legislation, and therefore no one is responsible for public legislation. The proposition to give Cabinet officers seats in Congress, and to so organize the State executive departments as to have a like direct contact by responsible executive officials with the State legislatures, will, if carried out, have a tendency to create, what is now so wofully lacking, some degree of responsibility for lawmaking.

In regard to private and local legislation a radical change must, sooner or later, be made in our method of producing laws. No bill of' a local or private character should under ordinary circumstances be considered unless it has been filed a proper length of time before the meeting of the legislative body, the expenses of its consideration provided for by the parties in interest; assurance afforded that proper notice to every interest that may be affected thereby has been given, and a trial secured of the objections interposed to such proposed legislation. This reform should be inaugurated by the adoption of a system of procedure analogous to that established by the standing rules of Parliament, by which private and local legislation is subjected to scrutiny and trial through the instrumentality of a parliamentary bar instead of a lobby, the sinister elements of a bill are eliminated, and thus the public weal protected and a machinery organized for the ascertainment of the effect of bills upon other interests, both public and private before they become law, so as to bring them in harmony with existing legislation and limit their mischievous results. Governor Hill's recommendation in the State of New York in favor of a counsel to the legislature, is a wholly inadequate, but a tentative step in the right direction.

The vast prizes that can be obtained in connection with the use of the public streets of cities for railway, telegraph, telephone, heating, and other purposes, offer, by the passage of laws subversive of public interests and destructive to private property rights

a constant temptation which can be prevented only by an organization of the public opposition in as continuous and powerful a
shape as the schemes for plunder are organized. This can be
done only by the securing of adequate notice of intent to apply
for such laws and public trial of them after application is made.
The divorce of public from private legislation would both improve
and purify our system of law-making, and operate to give it
both harmony and character wholly impossible now in the scramble for privileges to be obtained by means of the law, and by the
subversion of private interests. This scramble almost always
brushes aside and puts to naught the efforts of those who seek to
elevate our public law by far-reaching beneficial methods of codi-
fication and elbows to the rear those who seek to secure legislative
attention for the introduction of remedial measures against public evils that have sprung up in the community, for dealing with
which the existing body of the law is inadequate.

Through the advocacy of a single man, equally powerful upon
the platform as with the pen,—Henry George,—a proposition
to use the instrumentalities of taxation for the purpose of confiscating private property in land, particularly in densely populated
centres, has found a large number of adherents, and has been
made sufficiently prominent in the discussions of public questions to require notice in this book.

This theory is attempted to be justified by the proposition that
land is limited in quantity, and therefore partakes of a monopolistic element; that its owners, by the growing density of population alone, and by no effort of their own, receive an annual increment of value, which is abstracted from the community, but which
is earned by the community by mere addition to population; that
this increment of value created by the whole should belong to the
whole, and should not be permitted to become private property;
that to do away with this so-called " unearned increment " there is
but one arm which can be used with effect, and that is taxation;
and that in taxing unimproved property to the full extent of its
market value, a practical confiscation takes place of that value for
the benefit of the State, and it thus becomes the property of the
people.

To enforce the soundness of this doctrine, illustrations are used showing the enormous growth of the values of some particularly choice residential or business quarters in the city of New York, which, more than any other city in the United States, has enjoyed an almost uniformly progressive increase of real estate values ; and it is supposed that the case is made out when this constantly progressive increase in value is shown. This programme of confiscating under guise of taxing the unimproved property is accompanied by a proposition that the improvements thereon in the way of houses shall not be taxed.

The proposition as to farm lands may be left to itself. The farmers of the Eastern States have, in consequence of the competition of the Western States, been almost as little prosperous as the farmers in England and Germany, in consequence of the competition they suffer under with the great productivity of the virgin soil and the low cost of land in the Trans-Mississippi States and Territories. Any suggestion to add, by the way of taxation, to their burdens will find so little response from the voters of the United States, the majority of whom are farmers, and allied to the farming interest, that it is scarcely worth while to discuss the theory, inasmuch as in its application to that class of property it is wholly chimerical and impossible by the bar of personal interest to the contrary. The first step towards achieving its success would have to be the disfranchising of the farmer, as he would never by his own vote surrender his ownership to the State ; more particularly as in nine cases out of ten he has but a mere equity therein, and he is obligated on his bond, accompanied by a mortgage for a very considerable proportion of the value of his farm, to some capitalist. The personal bond in the hands of the capitalist cannot be cancelled, although the collateral may be deprived of value.

The theory, however, has its dangers in municipalities, partly by the discontent which it engenders among half-educated workingmen, and in the fact that the lower class vote which outnumbers the property-holding class, may, if thoroughly imbued with this idea, make an effort sooner or later to put these theories into practice in urban districts. In the first place any effort of that kind could result in a tax levied for once and once only upon unimproved property, because if sufficiently radical, it would cause as a consequence of this practical confiscation a surrender to the city, and it would thereafter be city property, and not property of individuals, and thenceforth cease to be an element of taxation. How the city expenses are to be defrayed with such an element of taxation removed from bearing its proportion of charge, is difficult to determine, except that the city shall in turn derive a revenue from the land, equivalent or more than equivalent to its former power of taxation, by reletting it on building leases. The result in that case is therefore mere destruction of private wealth and the substitution of the city government as the holder of this wealth for the private individual.

The tendency of modern civilization has all been toward the development of private wealth as against the aggregated wealth of governments. The great outcry against the surplus of the United States, and the demonstrably demoralizing effects arising from such a surplus, would seem to be lesson enough to any theorist that a proposition which substitutes public accumulation for individual wealth is a move in the wrong direction.

It is impossible to conceive how Mr. George and his adherents propose to deal with the fact that almost all of this property, the subject matter of his confiscatory theories,—the unimproved lots of the city—are already mortgaged to a vast number of institutions, particularly life insurance companies, and form a great part of their aggregated wealth, upon the safety of which investment is dependent the provision for the numberless widows and orphans who are the final objects of the distribution of their assets. The confiscation would have to operate on the mortgage titles precisely as it would upon the mere equity left in the hands of the owners.

If the land is not wholly confiscated, then the additional value giving to it in consequence of the exemption of the building erected or to be erected, from all taxation, puts, substantially by reason of this perpetual exemption from taxation, such an enhanced value upon the privilege of putting a house upon a lot as to make the lot as valuable thereafter as the value of the lot was before the tax, and it would be coined into money by the owner precisely as the real estate speculator now coins advancing values into money.

This scheme would also impose upon the city treasury all the expenses which are now borne by the property owners themselves, such as the regulating and grading of streets, the sewering thereof, and their pavement. If the history of a city lot could be written, it would be manifest even to the most obtuse that the present owner of the property, who stands in the shoes of the successive owners for several centuries, excepting possibly only in a few of the most favored localities of the city, such as Wall Street, Fifth Avenue and Broadway, has paid in assessments and taxes for two centuries, with interest added thereto, more than the present value of the property.

A revolution in the right to property, confiscating private ownership and substituting the municipality as such owner, would, owing to the sinister influences of political parties, produce corrupting consequences many times worse than those incident to private ownership. The favoritism and correlative oppression that would attend such a condition of affairs would indeed be a serious step backward in civilization.

It is easy, of course, to criticise any of the existing institutions of society. There is scarcely a social organization which, if the eye is directed only to the evils incident thereto, is not equally open to the same kind of arraignment to which private ownership of land is made subject by this agitator. The man who looks at the divorce proceedings alone, without taking into account the vast number of happy homes, where the thought of separation would be pain, and its suggestion an affront, could condemn the marriage tie with equal success.

The institution of private property is not based upon principle, but is conventional. It is the best that society can do with its property. India, Morocco and Egypt are illustrations of the utter paralysis of all enterprise, arising from public ownership of land. The experiment has been tried in those countries upon a scale so large, and for so many years, that it is no longer experimental. The Mir ownership of Russia is a further illustration, if any more be needed.

No man who does not own the land is willing to make lasting or permanent improvements thereon. It is better by far, therefore, to accept the incidental discomforts which attend private ownership, and to suffer them whatever they be, rather than to return to conditions which are known to be the inevitable concomitants of public ownership. Indeed the whole drift for eight hundred years past has been toward securing private ownership; and human nature would have to be changed in all of the social elements which constitute it, a change not likely to take place for many hundreds of years to come, before the public can be trusted to administer landed property as fairly and with as much regard to principles of justice as it is now administered in private hands.

The extraordinary growth of values in the city of New York arose through the exceptional opportunities for capital and for employment in the city, and its great commerce. No injustice, in allowing the increment of values arising therefrom to remain private property, is thereby done, as in great part these owners and their predecessors have given the impulse to and directed the energies of this development. But even then ownership of unimproved property in that city is attended with so many demands of taxation, assessments, and so many incidental expenses, that as a whole the speculator in unimproved property in the city of New York is a loser rather than a gainer by his operations. In other cities the doubtful profitableness of land speculation is not only equally true, but more largely true than it is of such operations in the city of New York.

The organization of laborers and mechanics has been carried in the United States to such a point as to create a sharp antagonism between employers and employed ;—this more emphatically in large cities than in villages and agricultural communities.

The growth of capital, and its administration by corporations instead of private individuals, have more and more widened the gulf between employer and the employed. The acts of personal kindness arising from personal relations which formerly had place between large individual employers of labor and their employed, are not practicable when the employer is a great corporation.

The success which has attended the trades union and knights of labor movements in raising prices of labor in the past twenty years has become an encouragement to further efforts in that direction. Of course the laborer does not see that every rise in the price of labor has a tendency to raise the price of every commodity consumed by him, and whether he is better off than before is to be determined only by the purchasing power of the money that he earns. Yet from causes counteracting this law within the past fifteen years the price of commodities has been sinking, while labor has been the only commodity going up in price. There is, therefore, no basis for discontent on the part of the laboring people. On the contrary, as compared with the capitalist class, they are better off, as all the politico-economical tendencies of this generation have worked to the lowering of interest and but few to the lowering of wages. The laborer's income, notwithstanding the competition of machinery, has been steadily on the increase for more than a decade past, and, with the exception of meat and house-rent, every article he consumes is from thirty to fifty per cent. lower than it was a decade ago.

This simultaneous reduction in values of commodities arising from causes far beyond the ken of the average labor agitator, while he has succeeded in raising the price of labor, makes him believe that continued agitation in that direction will produce continued beneficial results. Already, however, a counter movement is taking place of a character which makes it very doubtful whether future movements to raise wages can be conducted with any such degree of success as has attended them heretofore.

The excessive production of commodities, which has reduced prices and has given adequate employment to labor, is being checked in one class after another of production and activity by the organization of "trusts" no longer limited to one State or country, but extending, as the copper trust does, over the whole surface of the globe, by which the prices of commodities are artificially raised, and the output limited. If this continues, laborers and mechanics will be largely the sufferers, and the prices of commodities will increase, while the demand for employment will be so far in excess of the demand for labor that the organizations which have hitherto held the labor element together will no longer be able to control it.

Against this organization of trusts there is but one possible efficient remedy,—to widen the field of activity of the law of competition by lowering the tariff. This lowering of the tariff adds to the difficulty of organizing such trusts an almost insurmountable obstacle of compelling the participants of the "trusts" to be held together in the whole civilized part of the globe.

Hence this new menace to the general interests of society, as involved in these trust organizations, can only be successfully met by a reduction of the tariff of all nations still maintaining a protective system. Few people, probably, know that there is a tariff of twenty and ten cents per bushel on cereals in the United States, and that the existence of that tariff made the wheat corner of 1887 possible. But for the fact that, under this protective tariff, wheat could not be imported, no effort would have been made to corner an article which on the mere difference of the cost of freight and a slight percentage of profit, moves freely from one part of the globe to the other.

To meet this new menace of trusts, it is necessary to have recourse once more to wise legislation, and not only to lower the tariff, but also to re-enact some of the laws which in the era of competition had fallen into discredit, against combinations to raise prices. Some of the old laws against forestalling must be enforced, and the common law must be brought to bear upon these new forms of engrossing.

The great municipal problem is still unsolved, and will probably remain so for a long period of time. Some good has been done by an awakening of public interest in municipal affairs, and there has been a very marked decrease in the malversations attending their administration. Of late years there has been a relative decrease in local indebtedness. This is somewhat due to the fact that there has been no general speculative period in the United States since 1881, with great enhancing of prices, and large accumulations of capital within short periods of time. When that period comes again, the attention of the public will be so diverted from public questions to private interests, that it will give full scope once more to political manipulators and rogues, and unless some marked legislative change in relation to municipal organizations is accomplished in the mean time, there is but little hope for improvement in the municipal governments of the United States for years to come.

There is little to be added by the author to the language of the text in this regard. Minority or totality representation has made but little or no progress since the writing of the text of this book in 1881. This greatest of all reforms in Democratic representative government is still awaiting public recognition of the manifold benefits which will ensue from its adoption.

The most extraordinary problem in the history of governmental public finance—indeed one of an unprecedented character —has been created by the annual accretion of an enormous surplus beyond the needs of the Federal Government, accumulating considerable currency and circulating medium in the hands of the Government of the United States, and thereby withdrawing it from circulation.

Taking into consideration that ten millions of dollars is about the margin dividing violent stringency from great ease in New York, the controlling money market of the United States, it can very readily be seen how the abstraction of from fifty millions to one hundred millions of dollars of circulating medium, which the Treasury of the United States accumulates, creates a dearth of money, and has a tendency to precipitate and bring about financial crises. It also makes the Treasurer, with a view of relieving this financial pressure, an adjunct of Wall Street, and gives to the Treasury Department of the United States a power over values which in unscrupulous hands would be sure to be abused, and in any event has a tendency toward corruption, and is therefore a constant menace to the welfare of the community.

These considerations are independent of all those which may be urged against the surplus on the ground of excessive taxation, and that the government has no right to and should not take from the community a larger sum of money than is necessary for its financial purposes.

The remarkable growth of all material interests in the United States has caused a yield of taxation beyond any estimate when

312 ADDENDA.

the tax was originally authorized, and has placed the United States in the anomalous and in some respects fortunate position of being probably the only government now existing which is embarrassed by a large excess instead of a deficit in its budget.

Many incidental evils, however, arise from this excess, inasmuch as Congress is beset by claims and schemes, to which it lends too willing an ear, to get rid of the surplus by improper appropriations.

The President of the United States has made the surplus the basis of a powerful appeal to the people of the United States to revise the tariff laws, and to prevent them from repealing the liquor and tobacco excise, which are ideal incidents of taxation.

A large addition to the free list of the raw materials of commerce, so as to enable the manufacturers of the United States to work on an equally advantageous footing with the manufacturers of other countries, and thereby increase our export commodities, was the main remedial suggestion to prevent the accumulation of the surplus, contained in the tariff message of the President.

It is also suggested to reduce the tariff on wool and other articles of necessity, so as to reduce the taxes on the poor man's clothing; and to make the tariff in many particulars far more just and equal in its operation.

Inasmuch as the Republican party has unequivocally proclaimed itself in favor of a protective tariff, and will resist every effort to reduce its schedule of rates, and as by this step of the President, as the representative Democrat, the Democratic party is pledged to a reformation of the tariff on a revenue basis, the political contests of the Union will, for the next decade, turn upon fiscal and economic questions arising from this sharp division of parties upon these lines.

APPENDIX.

ARTICLES OF CONFEDERATION AND PERPETUAL UNION BETWEEN THE STATES.

TO ALL TO WHOM THESE PRESENTS SHALL COME, WE THE UNDERSIGNED DELEGATES OF THE STATES AFFIXED TO OUR NAMES, SEND GREETING.—Whereas the Delegates of the United States of America in Congress assembled did on the 15th day of November in the Year of our Lord 1777, and in the Second Year of the Independence of America agree to certain articles of Confederation and perpetual Union between the States of New Hampshire, Massachusetts-bay, Rhode-island and Providence Plantations, Connecticut, New-York, New-Jersey, Pennsylvania, Delaware, Maryland, Virginia, North-Carolina, South-Carolina, and Georgia, in the words following, viz.

"ARTICLES OF CONFEDERATION AND PERPETUAL UNION BETWEEN THE STATES OF NEW-HAMP-SHIRE, MASSACHUSETTS-BAY, RHODE-ISLAND AND PROVIDENCE PLANTATIONS, CONNECTICUT, NEW-YORK, NEW-JERSEY, PENNSYLVANIA, DELAWARE, MARYLAND, VIRGINIA, NORTH-CAROLINA, SOUTH-CAROLINA, AND GEORGIA.

ARTICLE I. The Stile of this confederacy shall be "The United States of America."

313

ARTICLE II. Each state retains its sovereignty, freedom and independence, and every Power, Jurisdiction and right, which is not by this confederation expressly delegated to the united states, in congress assembled.

ARTICLE III. The said states hereby severally enter into a firm league of friendship with each other, for their common defence, the security of their Liberties, and their mutual and general welfare, binding themselves to assist each other, against all force offered to, or attacks made upon them, or any of them, on account of religion, sovereignty, trade, or any other pretence whatever.

ARTICLE IV. The better to secure and perpetuate mutual friendship and intercourse among the people of the different states in this union, the free inhabitants of each of these states, paupers, vagabonds, and fugitives from Justice excepted, shall be entitled to all privileges and immunities of free citizens in the several states; and the people of each state shall have free ingress and regress to and from any other state, and shall enjoy therein all the privileges of trade and commerce, subject to the same duties, impositions and restrictions as the inhabitants thereof respectively, provided that such restriction shall not extend so far as to prevent the removal of property imported into any state, to any other state of which the Owner is an inhabitant; provided also that no imposition, duties or restriction shall be laid by any state, on the property of the united states, or either of them.

If any person guilty of, or charged with treason, felony, or other high misdemeanor in any state, shall flee from Justice, and be found in any of the united states, he shall upon demand of the Governor or executive power, of the state from which he fled, be delivered up and removed to the state having jurisdiction of his offence.

Full faith and credit shall be given in each of these states to the records, acts and judicial proceedings of the courts and magistrates of every other state.

ARTICLE V. For the more convenient management of the general interest of the united states, delegates shall be annually appointed in such manner as the legislature of each state shall direct, to meet in congress on the first Monday in November, in every year, with a power reserved to each state, to recal its delegates, or any of them, at any time within the year, and to send others in their stead, for the remainder of the Year.

No state shall be represented in congress by less than two, nor by more than seven members; and no person shall be capable of being a delegate for more than three years in any term of six years; nor shall any person, being a delegate, be capable of holding any office under the united states, for which he or another for his benefit, receives any salary, fees or emolument of any kind.

Each state shall maintain its own delegates in any meeting of the states, and while they act as members of the committee of the states.

In determining questions in the united states, in congress assembled, each state shall have one vote.

Freedom of speech and debate in congress shall not be impeached or questioned in any Court, or place out of congress, and the members of congress shall be protected in their persons from arrests and imprisonments, during the time of their going to and from, and attendance on congress, except for treason, felony, or breach of the peace.

ARTICLE VI. No state without the Consent of the united states in congress assembled, shall send any embassy to, or receive any embassy from, or enter into any conference, agreement, alliance or treaty with any King prince or state; nor shall any person holding any office of profit or trust under the united states, or any of them, accept of any present, emolument, office or title of any kind whatever from any king, prince or foreign state ; nor shall the united states in congress assembled, or any of them, grant any title of nobility.

No two or more states shall enter into any treaty, confederation or alliance whatever between them, without the consent
of the united states in congress assembled, specifying accu-
rately the purposes for which the same is to be entered into,
and how long it shall continue.

No state shall lay any imposts or duties, which may interfere with any stipulations in treaties, entered into by the
united states in congress assembled, with any king, prince or
state, in pursuance of any treaties already proposed by congress, to the courts of France and Spain.

No vessels of war shall be kept up in time of peace by any
state, except such number only, as shall be deemed necessary
by the united states in congress assembled, for the defence of
such state, or its trade ; nor shall any body of forces be kept
up by any state, in time of peace, except such number only, as
in the judgment of the united states, in congress assembled,
shall be deemed requisite to garrison the forts necessary for
the defence of such state ; but every state shall always keep
up a well regulated and disciplined militia, sufficiently armed
and accoutred, and shall provide and have constantly ready for
use, in public stores, a due number of field pieces and tents,
and a proper quantity of arms, ammunition and camp equi-
page.

No state shall engage in any war without the consent of the
united states in congress assembled, unless such state be
actually invaded by enemies, or shall have received certain
advice of a resolution being formed by some nation of Indians
to invade such state, and the danger is so imminent as not to
admit of a delay, till the united states in congress assembled
can be consulted : nor shall any state grant commissions to any
ships or vessels of war, nor letters of marque or reprisal,
except it be after a declaration of war by the united states in
congress assembled, and then only against the kingdom or
state and the subjects thereof, against which war has been so
declared, and under such regulations as shall be established
by the united states in congress assembled, unless such state

be infested by pirates, in which case vessels of war may be fitted out for that occasion, and kept so long as the danger shall continue, or until the united states in congress assembled shall determine otherwise.

ARTICLE VII. When land-forces are raised by any state for the common defence, all officers of or under the rank of colonel, shall be appointed by the legislature of each state respectively by whom such forces shall be raised, or in such manner as such state shall direct, and all vacancies shall be filled up by the state which first made the appointment.

ARTICLE VIII. All charges of war, and all other expenses that shall be incurred for the common defence or general welfare, and allowed by the united states in congress assembled, shall be defrayed out of a common treasury, which shall be supplied by the several states, in proportion to the value of all land within each state, granted to or surveyed for any Person, as such land and the buildings and improvements thereon shall be estimated according to such mode as the united states in congress assembled, shall from time to time, direct and appoint. The taxes for paying that proportion shall be laid and levied by the authority and direction of the legislatures of the several states within the time agreed upon by the united states in congress assembled.

ARTICLE IX. The united states in congress assembled, shall have the sole and exclusive right and power of determining on peace and war, except in the cases mentioned in the 6th article—of sending and receiving ambassadors—entering into treaties and alliances, provided that no treaty of commerce shall be made whereby the legislative power of the respective states shall be restrained from imposing such imposts and duties on foreigners, as their own people are subjected to, or from prohibiting the exportation or importation of any species of goods or commodities whatsoever—of estab-

lishing rules for deciding in all cases, what captures on land
or water shall be legal, and in what manner prizes taken
by land or naval forces in the service of the united states
shall be divided or appropriated—of granting letters of marque
and reprisal in times of peace—appointing courts for the trial
of piracies and felonies committed on the high seas and establishing courts for receiving and determining finally appeals in
all cases of captures, provided that no member of congress
shall be appointed a judge of any of the said courts.

The united states in congress assembled shall also be the
last resort on appeal in all disputes and differences now sub-
sisting or that hereafter may arise between two or more states
concerning boundary, jurisdiction or any other cause whatever ; which authority shall always be exercised in the manner following. Whenever the legislative or executive
authority or lawful agent of any state in controversy with
another shall present a petition to congress, stating the matter in question and praying for a hearing, notice thereof shall
be given by order of congress to the legislative or executive
authority of the other state in controversy, and a day assigned
for the appearance of the parties by their lawful agents, who
shall then be directed to appoint by joint consent, commissioners or judges to constitute a court for hearing and determining the matter in question : but if they cannot agree,
congress shall name three persons out of each of the united
states, and from the list of such persons each party shall
alternately strike out one, the petitioners beginning, until the
number shall be reduced to thirteen ; and from that number
not less than seven, nor more than nine names as congress
shall direct, shall in the presence of congress be drawn out by
lot, and the persons whose names shall be so drawn or any
five of them, shall be commissioners or judges, to hear and
finally determine the controversy, so always as a major part of
the judges who shall hear the cause shall agree in the determination : and if either party shall neglect to attend at the day appointed, without showing reasons, which congress shall judge

sufficient, or being present shall refuse to strike, the congress shall proceed to nominate three persons out of each state, and the secretary of congress shall strike in behalf of such party absent or refusing ; and the judgment and sentence of the court to be appointed, in the manner before prescribed, shall be final and conclusive; and if any of the parties shall refuse to submit to the authority of such court, or to appear or defend their claim or cause, the court shall nevertheless proceed to pronounce sentence, or judgment, which shall in like manner be final and decisive, the judgment, or sentence and other proceedings being in either case transmitted to congress, and lodged among the acts of congress for the security of the parties concerned : provided that every commissioner, before he sits in judgment, shall take an oath to be administered by one of the judges of the supreme or superior court of the state, where the cause shall be tried, " well and truly to hear and determine the matter in question, according to the best of his judgment, without favour, affection or hope of reward : " provided also that no state shall be deprived of territory for the benefit of the united states.

All controversies concerning the private right of soil claimed under different grants of two or more states, whose jurisdictions as they may respect such lands, and the states which passed such grants are adjusted, the said grants or either of them being at the same time claimed to have originated antecedent to such settlement of jurisdiction, shall, on the petition of either party to the congress of the united states, be finally determined as near as may be in the same manner as is before prescribed for deciding disputes respecting territorial jurisdiction between different states.

The united states in congress assembled shall also have the sole and exclusive right and power of regulating the alloy and value of coin struck by their own authority, or by that of the respective states—fixing the standard of weights and measures throughout the United States—regulating the trade and managing all affairs with the Indians, not members of any of the states, provided that the legislative right of any state within its own limits be not infringed or violated—establishing or regulating post-offices from one state to another, throughout all the united states, and exacting such postage on the papers passing thro' the same as may be requisite to defray the expenses of the said office—appointing all officers of the land forces, in the service of the united states, excepting regimental officers—appointing all the officers of the naval forces, and commissioning all officers whatever in the service of the united states—making rules for the government and regulation of the said land and naval forces, and directing their operations.

The united states in congress assembled shall have authority to appoint a committee, to sit in the recess of congress, to be denominated "A Committee of the States," and to consist of one delegate from each state; and to appoint such other committees and civil officers as may be necessary for managing the general affairs of the united states under their direction—to appoint one of their number to preside, provided that no person be allowed to serve in the office of president more than one year in any term of three years; to ascertain the necessary sums of Money to be raised for the service of the united states, and to appropriate and apply the same for defraying the public expenses—to borrow money, or emit bills on the credit of the united states, transmitting every half year to the respective states an account of the sums of money so borrowed or emitted,—to build and equip a navy—to agree upon the number of land forces, and to make requisitions from each state for its quota, in proportion to the number of white inhabitants in such state; which requisition shall be binding, and thereupon the legislature of each state shall appoint the regimental officers, raise the men and cloath, arm and equip them in a soldier like manner, at the expense of the united states; and the officers and men so cloathed, armed and equipped shall march to the place appointed, and within the time agreed on by the united states in congress assembled: But if the united states in congress assembled shall, on consideration of circumstances judge proper that any state should not raise men, or should raise a smaller number than its quota, and that any other state should raise a greater number of men than the quota thereof, such extra number shall be raised, officered, cloathed, armed and equipped in the same manner as the quota of such state, unless the legislature of such state shall judge that such extra number cannot be safely spared out of the same, in which case they shall raise, officer, cloath, arm and equip as many of such extra number as they judge can be safely spared. And the officers and men so cloathed, armed and equipped, shall march to the place appointed, and within the time agreed on by the united states in congress assembled.

The united states in congress assembled shall never engage in a war, nor grant letters of marque and reprisal in time of peace, nor enter into any treaties or alliances, nor coin money, nor regulate the value thereof, nor ascertain the sums and expenses necessary for the defence and welfare of the united states, or any of them, nor emit bills, nor borrow money on the credit of the united states, nor appropriate money, nor agree upon the number of vessels of war, to be built or purchased, or the number of land or sea forces to be raised, nor appoint a commander in chief of the army or navy, unless nine states assent to the same: nor shall a question on any other point, except for adjourning from day to day, be determined, unless by the votes of a majority of the united states in congress assembled.

The Congress of the united states shall have power to adjourn to any time within the year, and to any place within the united states, so that no period of adjournment be for a longer duration than the space of six months, and shall publish the Journal of their proceedings monthly, except such parts thereof relating to treaties, alliances or military operations, as in their judgment require secrecy; and the yeas and nays of the delegates of each state on any question shall be entered on the Journal, when it is desired by any delegate; and the delegates of a state, or any of them, at his or their request shall be furnished with a transcript of the said Journal, except such parts as are above excepted, to lay before the legislatures of the several states.

ARTICLE X. The committee of the states, or any nine of them, shall be authorized to execute, in the recess of congress, such of the powers of congress as the united states in congress assembled, by the consent of nine states, shall from time to time think expedient to vest them with; provided that no power be delegated to the said committee, for the exercise of which, by the articles of confederation, the voice of nine states in the congress of the united states assembled is requisite.

ARTICLE XI. Canada acceding to this confederation, and joining in the measures of the united states, shall be admitted into, and entitled to all the advantages of this union: but no other colony shall be admitted into the same, unless such admission be agreed to by nine states.

ARTICLE XII. All bills of credit emitted, monies borrowed and debts contracted, by or under the authority of congress, before the assembling of the united states, in pursuance of the present confederation, shall be deemed and considered as a charge against the United States, for payment and satisfaction whereof the said united states, and the public faith are hereby solemnly pledged.

ARTICLE XIII. Every state shall abide by the determinations of the united states in congress assembled, on all questions which by this confederation is submitted to them. And the Articles of this confederation shall be inviolably observed by every state, and the union shall be perpetual; nor shall any alteration at any time hereafter be made in any of them; unless such alteration be agreed to in a congress of the united states, and be afterwards confirmed by the legislatures of every state.

And Whereas it hath pleased the Great Governor of the World to incline the hearts of the legislatures we respectively represent in congress, to approve of, and to authorize us to ratify the said articles of confederation and perpetual union. Know Ye, that we the undersigned delegates, by virtue of the power and authority to us gievn for that purpose, do by these presents, in the name and in behalf of our respective constituents, fully and entirely ratify and confirm each and every of the said articles of confederation and perpetual . union, and all and singular the matters and things therein contained: And we do further solemnly plight and engage the faith of our respective constituents, that they shall abide by the determinations of the united states in congress assembled, on all questions, which by the said confederation are submitted to them. And that the articles thereof shall be inviolably observed by the states we respectively represent, and that the union shall be perpetual. In witness whereof we have hereunto set our hands in Congress. Done at Philadelphia in the state of Pennsylvania the 9th Day of July in the Year of our Lord, 1778, and in the 3d year of the Independence of America.

On the part and behalf of the state of New Hampshire,
          Josiah Bartlett,
          John Wentworth, jun.,
                    August 8th, 1778.

On the part and behalf of the state of Massachusetts-Bay,
          John Hancock,
          Samuel Adams,
          Elbridge Gerry,
          Francis Dana,
          James Lovell,
          Samuel Holten.

On the part and behalf of the state of Rhode-Island and
Providence Plantations,

William Ellery,
Henry Marchant,
John Collins.

On the part and behalf of the state of Connecticut,

Roger Sherman,
Samuel Huntington,
Oliver Wolcott,
Titus Hosmer,
Andrew Adam.

On the part and behalf of the state of New York,

Jas Duane,
Fras Lewis,
William Duer,
Gouv^r Morris.

On the part and behalf of the state of New Jersey, November 26th, 1778,

Jn° Witherspoon,
Nathl Scudder.

On the part and behalf of the state of Pennsylvania,

Robt Morris,
Daniel Roberdeau,
Jon^a Bayard Smith,
William Clingan,
Joseph Reed,
22d July, 1778.

On the part and behalf of the state of Delaware,

Tho. M'Kean,
Feb. 12, 1779,
John Dickinson,
May 5, 1779,
Nicholas Van Dyke.

On the part and behalf of the state of Maryland,
        John Hanson,
                March 1st, 1781,
        Daniel Carroll,
                March 1st, 1781.

On the part and behalf of the state of Virginia,
        Richard Henry Lee,
        John Banister,
        Thomas Adams,
        Jn° Harvie,
        Francis Lightfoot Lee.

On the part and behalf of the state of North-Carolina,
        John Penn,
                July 21st, 1778.
        Corns Harnett,
        Jn° Williams.

On the part and behalf of the state of South-Carolina,
        Henry Laurens,
        William Henry Drayton,
        Jn° Matthews,
        Richd Hutson.
        Thos. Heyward, jun.

On the part and behalf of the state of Georgia,
        Jn° Walton,
                24th July, 1778,
        Edwd Telfair,
        Edwd Langworthy.

CONSTITUTION

OF THE

UNITED STATES OF AMERICA.

WE the People of the United States, in order to form a more perfect Union, establish Justice, insure domestic Tranquillity, provide for the common defence, promote the general Welfare, and secure the Blessings of Liberty to ourselves and our Posterity, do ordain and establish this CONSTITUTION for the United States of America.

ARTICLE I.

SECTION 1. All legislative Powers herein granted shall be vested in a Congress of the United States, which shall consist of a Senate and House of Representatives.

SECTION 2. The House of Representatives shall be composed of Members chosen every second Year by the People of the several States, and the Electors in each State shall have the Qualifications requisite for Electors of the most numerous Branch of the State Legislature.

No Person shall be a Representative who shall not have attained to the Age of twenty-five years, and been seven Years a Citizen of the United States, and who shall not, when elected, be an Inhabitant of that State in which he shall be chosen.

[Representatives and direct Taxes shall be apportioned among the several States which may be included within this Union, according to their respective Numbers, which shall

326

be determined by adding to the whole Number of free Persons, including those bound to Service for a Term of Years, and excluding Indians not taxed, three fifths of all other Persons.]* The actual Enumeration shall be made within three Years after the first Meeting of the Congress of the United States, and within every subsequent Term of ten Years, in such Manner as they shall by Law direct. The Number of Representatives shall not exceed one for every thirty Thousand, but each State shall have at Least one Representative; and until such enumeration shall be made, the State of New Hampshire shall be entitled to chuse three, Massachusetts eight, Rhode Island and Providence Plantations one, Connecticut five, New York six, New Jersey four, Pennsylvánia eight, Delaware one, Maryland six, Virginia ten, North Carolina five, South Carolina five, and Georgia three.

When vacancies happen in the Representation from any State, the Executive Authority thereof shall issue Writs of Election to fill such Vacancies.

The House of Representatives shall chuse their Speaker and other Officers; and shall have the sole Power of Impeachment.

SECTION 3. The Senate of the United States shall be composed of two Senators from each State, chosen by the Legislature thereof, for six Years; and each Senator shall have one Vote.

Immediately after they shall be assembled in Consequence of the first Election, they shall be divided as equally as may be into three Classes. The Seats of the Senators of the first Class shall be vacated at the Expiration of the second Year, of the second Class at the Expiration of the fourth Year, and of the third Class at the Expiration of the sixth Year, so that one-third may be chosen every second Year; and if Vacancies happen by Resignation, or otherwise, during the Recess of the Legislature of any State, the Executive thereof

---

* The clause included in brackets was superseded by the 14th amendment, 2nd section.

may make temporary Appointments until the next Meeting of the Legislature, which shall then fill such Vacancies.

No Person shall be a Senator who shall not have attained to the Age of thirty Years, and been nine Years a Citizen of the United States, and who shall not, when elected, be an Inhabitant of that State for which he shall be chosen.

The Vice-President of the United States shall be President of the Senate, but shall have no Vote, unless they be equally divided.

The Senate shall chuse their other Officers, and also a President pro tempore, in the Absence of the Vice-President, or when he shall exercise the Office of President of the United States.

The Senate shall have the sole Power to try all Impeachments. When sitting for that Purpose, they shall be on Oath or Affirmation. When the President of the United States is tried, the Chief Justice shall preside: And no Person shall be convicted without the Concurrence of two-thirds of the Members present.

Judgment in Cases of Impeachment shall not extend further than to removal from Office, and Disqualification to hold and enjoy any office of honour, Trust or Profit under the United States; but the Party convicted shall nevertheless be liable and subject to Indictment, Trial, Judgment and Punishment, according to Law.

SECTION 4. The Times, Places and Manner of holding Elections for Senators and Representatives, shall be prescribed in each State by the Legislature thereof; but the Congress may at any time by Law make or alter such Regulations, except as to the places of chusing Senators.

The Congress shall assemble at least once in every Year, and such meeting shall be on the first Monday in December, unless they shall by Law appoint a different Day.

SECTION 5. Each House shall be the Judge of the Elections, Returns and Qualifications of its own Members, and a Majority of each shall constitute a Quorum to do Business;

but a smaller Number may adjourn from day to day, and may be authorized to compel the Attendance of absent Members, in such Manner, and under such Penalties as each House may provide.

Each House may determine the Rules of its Proceedings, punish its Members for disorderly Behaviour, and, with the Concurrence of two-thirds, expel a Member.

Each House shall keep a Journal of its Proceedings, and from time to time publish the same, excepting such Parts as may in their Judgment require Secrecy, and the Yeas and Nays of the Members of either House on any question shall, at the desire of one-fifth of those Present, be entered on the Journal.

Neither House, during the session of Congress, shall, without the Consent of the other, adjourn for more than three days, nor to any other Place than that in which the two Houses shall be sitting.

Section 6. The Senators and Representatives shall receive a Compensation for their Services, to be ascertained by Law, and paid out of the Treasury of the United States. They shall in all Cases, except Treason, Felony and Breach of the Peace, be privileged from Arrest during their Attendance at the Session of their respective Houses, and in going to and returning from the same; and for any Speech or Debate in either House, they shall not be questioned in any other Place.

No Senator or Representative shall, during the Time for which he was elected, be appointed to any civil Office under the Authority of the United States, which shall have been created, or the Emoluments whereof shall have been encreased during such time; and no Person holding any Office under the United States shall be a Member of either House during his Continuance in Office.

Section 7. All Bills for raising Revenue shall originate in the House of Representatives; but the Senate may propose or concur with Amendments as on other Bills.

Every Bill which shall have passed the House of Representatives and the Senate, shall, before it become a Law, be presented to the President of the United States; If he approve he shall sign it, but if not he shall return it, with his Objections, to that House in which it shall have originated, who shall enter the Objections at large on their Journal, and proceed to reconsider it. If after such Reconsideration two-thirds of that House shall agree to pass the Bill, it shall be sent, together with the Objections, to the other House, by which it shall likewise be reconsidered, and if approved by two-thirds of that House, it shall become a Law. But in all such Cases the Votes of both Houses shall be determined by Yeas and Nays, and the Names of the Persons voting for and against the Bill shall be entered on the Journal of each House respectively. If any Bill shall not be returned by the President within ten Days (Sundays excepted) after it shall have been presented to him, the Same shall be a law, in like Manner as if he had signed it, unless the Congress by their Adjournment prevent its Return, in which Case it shall not be a Law.

Every Order, Resolution, or Vote to which the Concurrence of the Senate and House of Representatives may be necessary (except on a question of Adjournment) shall be presented to the President of the United States; and before the Same shall take Effect, shall be approved by him, or being disapproved by him, shall be repassed by two-thirds of the Senate and House of Representatives, according to the Rules and Limitations prescribed in the Case of a Bill.

SECTION 8. The Congress shall have Power

To lay and collect Taxes, Duties, Imposts and Excises, to pay the Debts and provide for the common Defence and general Welfare of the United States; but all Duties, Imposts and Excises shall be uniform throughout the United States;

To borrow Money on the credit of the United States;

To regulate Commerce with foreign Nations and among the several States, and with the Indian tribes;

To establish an uniform Rule of Naturalization, and uniform

Laws on the subject of Bankruptcies throughout the United States;

To coin Money, regulate the Value thereof, and of foreign Coin, and fix the Standard of Weights and Measures;

To provide for the Punishment of counterfeiting the Securities and current Coin of the United States;

To establish Post Offices and post Roads;

To promote the progress of Science and useful Arts, by securing for limited Times to Authors and Inventors the exclusive Right to their respective Writings and Discoveries;

To constitute Tribunals inferior to the supreme Court;

To define and punish Piracies and Felonies committed on the high Seas, and Offences against the Law of Nations;

To declare War, grant Letters of Marque and Reprisal, and make Rules concerning Captures on Land and Water;

To raise and support Armies, but no Appropriation of Money to that Use shall be for a longer Term than two Years;

To provide and maintain a Navy;

To make Rules for the Government and Regulation of the land and naval Forces;

To provide for calling forth the Militia to execute the Laws of the Union, suppress Insurrections and repel Invasions;

To provide for organizing, arming, and disciplining the Militia, and for governing such Part of them as may be employed in the Service of the United States, reserving to the States respectively, the Appointment of the Officers, and the Authority of training the Militia according to the Discipline prescribed by Congress;

To exercise exclusive Legislation in all Cases whatsoever, over such District (not exceeding ten Miles square) as may, by Cession of particular States, and the Acceptance of Congress, become the Seat of the Government of the United States, and to exercise like Authority over all Places purchased by the consent of the Legislature of the State in which the Same shall be, for the Erection of Forts, Magazines, Arsenals, Dock-Yards, and other needful Buildings;—And

To make all Laws which shall be necessary and proper for carrying into Execution the foregoing Powers, and all other Powers vested by this Constitution in the Government of the United States, or in any Department or Officer thereof.

SECTION 9. The Migration or Importation of such Persons as any of the States now existing shall think proper to admit, shall not be prohibited by the Congress prior to the Year one thousand eight hundred and eight, but a Tax or Duty may be imposed on such Importation, not exceeding ten dollars for each Person.

The Privilege of the Writ of Habeas Corpus shall not be suspended, unless when in cases of Rebellion or Invasion the public Safety may require it.

No bill of Attainder or ex post facto Law shall be passed.

No Capitation, or other direct, Tax shall be laid, unless in Proportion to the Census or Enumeration herein before directed to be taken.

No Tax or Duty shall be laid on Articles exported from any State.

No Preference shall be given by any Regulation of Commerce or Revenue to the Ports of one State over those of any another : nor shall Vessels bound to, or from, one State, be obliged to enter, clear, or pay Duties in another.

No Money shall be drawn from the Treasury, but in Consequence of Appropriations made by Law ; and a regular Statement and Account of the Receipts and Expenditures of all public Money shall be published from time to time.

No Title of Nobility shall be granted by the United States : And no Person holding any Office of Profit or Trust under them, shall, without the Consent of the Congress, accept of any present, Emolument, Office, or Title, of any kind whatever, from any King, Prince, or foreign State.

SECTION. 10. No State shall enter into any Treaty, Alliance, or Confederation ; grant Letters of Marque and Reprisal ; coin Money ; emit Bills of Credit; make any Thing but gold and silver Coin a Tender in Payment of Debts; pass any Bill

of Attainder, ex post facto Law, or Law impairing the Obligation of Contracts, or grant any Title of Nobility.

No State shall, without the consent of the Congress, lay any
Imposts or Duties on Imports or Exports, except what may be
absolutely necessary for executing it's inspection Laws : and
the net Produce of all Duties and Imposts, laid by any State
on Imports or Exports, shall be for the Use of the Treasury of
the United States ; and all such Laws shall be subject to the
Revision and Controul of the Congress.

No State shall, without the Consent of Congress, lay any
Duty of Tonnage, keep Troops, or Ships of War in time of
Peace, enter into any Agreement or Compact with another
State, or with a foreign Power, or engage in War, unless
actually invaded, or in such imminent Danger as will not
admit of Delay.

ARTICLE II.

SECTION 1. The executive Power shall be vested in a President of the United States of America. He shall hold his
office during the Term of four Years, and, together with the
Vice President, chosen for the same Term, be elected, as follows

Each State shall appoint, in such Manner as the Legislature
thereof may direct, a Number of Electors, equal to the whole
Number of Senators and Representatives to which the State
may be entitled in the Congress : but no Senator or Representative, or Person holding an Office of Trust or Profit under
the United States, shall be appointed an Elector.

[* The Electors shall meet in their respective States, and vote by Ballot for
two Persons, of whom one at least shall not be an Inhabitant of the same
State with themselves. And they shall make a List of all the Persons voted
for, and of the Number of Votes for each ; which list they shall sign and certify, and transmit sealed to the Seat of the Government of the United States,
directed to the President of the Senate. The President of the Senate shall, in
the Presence of the Senate and House of Representatives, open all the Certifi-

---

* This clause within brackets has been superseded and annulled by the 12th
amendment.

cates, and the Votes shall then be counted. The Person having the greatest number of Votes shall be the President, if such Number be a Majority of the whole Number of Electors appointed; and if there be more than one who have such Majority and have an equal Number of Votes, then the House of Representatives shall immediately chuse by Ballot one of them for President ; and if no Person have a Majority, then from the five highest on the List the said House shall in like manner chuse the President. But in chusing the President, the Votes shall be taken by States, the Representation from each State having one Vote ; A Quorum for this Purpose shall consist of a Member or Members from two-thirds of the States, and a Majority of all the States shall be necessary to a Choice. In every Case, after the Choice of the President, the Person having the greatest Number of Votes of the Electors shall be the Vice President. But if there should remain two or more who have equal Votes, the Senate shall chuse from them by Ballot the Vice President.]

The Congress may determine the Time of chusing the Electors, and the Day on which they shall give their Votes; which Day shall be the same throughout the United States.

No Person except a natural born Citizen, or a Citizen of the United States, at the time of the Adoption of this Constitution, shall be eligible to the Office of President; neither shall any Person be eligible to that Office who shall not have attained to the Age of thirty five Years, and been fourteen Years a Resident within the United States.

In Case of the Removal of the President from Office, or of his Death, Resignation, or Inability to discharge the Powers and Duties of the said Office, the same shall devolve on the Vice President, and the Congress may by Law provide for the Case of Removal, Death, Resignation, or Inability, both of the President and Vice President, declaring what Officer shall then act as President, and such Officer shall act accordingly, until the Disability be removed, or a President shall be elected.

The President shall, at stated Times, receive for his services, a Compensation, which shall neither be increased nor diminished during the Period for which he shall have been elected, and he shall not receive within that Period any other Emolument from the United States, or any of them.

Before he enter on the Execution of his Office, he shall take the following Oath or Affirmation:—

"I do solemnly swear (or affirm) that I will faithfully exe-
"cute the Office of President of the United States, and will
"to the best of my Ability, preserve, protect and defend the
"Constitution of the United States."

SECTION 2. The President shall be Commander in Chief
of the Army and Navy of the United States, and of the
Militia of the several States, when called into the actual Service of the United States; he may require the Opinion, in
writing, of the principal Officer in each of the executive Departments, upon any Subject relating to the Duties of their
respective Offices, and he shall have Power to grant Reprieves and Pardons for Offences against the United States,
except in Cases of Impeachment.

He shall have Power, by and with the Advice and Consent
of the Senate, to make Treaties, provided two thirds of the
Senators present concur; and he shall nominate, and by and
with the Advice and Consent of the Senate, shall appoint
Ambassadors, other public Ministers and Consuls, Judges of
the supreme Court, and all other Officers of the United
States, whose Appointments are not herein otherwise pro-
vided for, and which shall be established by Law: but the
Congress may by Law vest the Appointment of such inferior
Officers, as they think proper, in the President alone, in the
Courts of Law, or in the Heads of Departments.

The President shall have Power to fill up all Vacancies
that may happen during the Recess of the Senate, by granting Commissions which shall expire at the End of their next
Session.

SECTION 3. He shall from time to time give to the Congress Information of the State of the Union, and recommend
to their Consideration such Measures as he shall judge necessary and expedient; he may, on extraordinary Occasions,
convene both Houses, or either of them, and in Case of Disagreement between them, with respect to the Time of Adjournment, he may adjourn them to such Time as he shall
think proper; he shall receive Ambassadors and other public

13*

Ministers; he shall take Care that the Laws be faithfully executed, and shall Commission all the Officers of the United States.

SECTION 4. The President, Vice President and all civil Officers of the United States, shall be removed from Office on Impeachment for, and Conviction of, Treason, Bribery, or other high Crimes and Misdemeanors.

ARTICLE III.

SECTION 1. The judicial Power of the United States, shall be vested in one supreme Court, and in such inferior Courts as the Congress may from time to time ordain and establish. The Judges, both of the supreme and inferior Courts, shall hold their Offices during good Behavior, and shall, at stated Times, receive for their Services, a Compensation, which shall not be diminished during their Continuance in Office.

SECTION 2. The judicial Power shall extend to all Cases, in Law and Equity, arising under this Constitution, the Laws of the United States, and Treaties made, or which shall be made, under their Authority;—to all Cases affecting Ambassadors, other public Ministers, and Consuls;—to all Cases of admiralty and maritime Jurisdiction;—to Controversies to which the United States shall be a Party;—to Controversies between two or more States;—between a State and Citizens of another State;—between Citizens of different States;—between Citizens of the same State claiming Lands under Grants of different States, and between a State, or the Citizens thereof, and foreign States, Citizens or Subjects.

In all Cases affecting Ambassadors, other public Ministers and Consuls, and those in which a State shall be Party, the supreme Court shall have original Jurisdiction. In all the other Cases before mentioned, the supreme Court shall have appellate Jurisdiction, both as to Law and Fact, with such Exceptions, and under such Regulations as the Congress shall make.

The Trial of all Crimes, except in Cases of Impeachment, shall be by Jury, and such Trial shall be held in the State where the said Crimes shall have been committed; but when not committed within any State, the Trial shall be at such Place or Places as the Congress may by Law have directed.

SECTION 3. Treason against the United States shall consist only in levying War against them, or in adhering to their Enemies, giving them Aid and Comfort. No Person shall be convicted of Treason unless on the Testimony of two Witnesses to the same overt Act, or on Confession in open Court.

The Congress shall have Power to declare the Punishment of Treason, but no Attainder of Treason shall work Corruption of Blood, or Forfeiture except during the Life of the Person attainted.

ARTICLE IV.

SECTION 1. Full Faith and Credit shall be given in each State to the public Acts, Records, and judicial Proceedings of every other State. And the Congress may by general Laws prescribe the Manner in which such Acts, Records and Proceedings shall be proved, and the Effect thereof.

SECTION 2. The Citizens of each State shall be entitled to all Privileges and Immunities of Citizens in the several States.

A Person charged in any State with Treason, Felony, or other Crime, who shall flee from Justice, and be found in another State, shall on Demand of the executive Authority of the State from which he fled, be delivered up, to be removed to the State having Jurisdiction of the Crime.

No Person held to Service or Labour in one State, under the Laws thereof, escaping into another, shall, in Consequence of any Law or Regulation therein, be discharged from such Service or Labour, but shall be delivered up on Claim of the Party to whom such Service or Labour may be due.

SECTION 3. New States may be admitted by the Congress into this Union; but no new State shall be formed or erected within the Jurisdiction of any other State; nor any State be formed by the Junction of two or more States, or Parts of States, without the Consent of the Legislatures of the States concerned as well as of the Congress.

The Congress shall have Power to dispose of and make all needful Rules and Regulations respecting the Territory or other Property belonging to the United States; and nothing in this Constitution shall be so construed as to Prejudice any Claims of the United States, or of any particular State.

SECTION 4. The United States shall guarantee to every State in this Union a Republican Form of Government, and shall protect each of them against Invasion, and on Application of the Legislature, or of the Executive (when the Legislature cannot be convened) against domestic Violence.

ARTICLE V.

The Congress, whenever two thirds of both Houses shall deem it necessary, shall propose Amendments to this Constitution, or, on the Application of the Legislatures of two thirds of the several States, shall call a Convention for proposing Amendments, which, in either Case, shall be valid to all Intents and Purposes, as Part of this Constitution, when ratified by the Legislatures of three fourths of the several States, or by Conventions in three fourths thereof, as the one or the other Mode of Ratification may be proposed by the Congress; Provided that no Amendment which may be made prior to the Year one thousand eight hundred and eight shall in any Manner affect the first and fourth Clauses in the Ninth Section of the first Article, and that no State, without its Consent, shall be deprived of its equal Suffrage in the Senate.

ARTICLE VI.

All Debts contracted and Engagements entered into, before the Adoption of this Constitution, shall be as valid against the United States under this Constitution, as under the Confederation.

This Constitution, and the Laws of the United States which shall be made in Pursuance thereof; and all Treaties made, or which shall be made, under the authority of the United States, shall be the supreme Law of the Land; and the Judges in every State shall be bound thereby, any Thing in the Constitution or Laws of any State to the Contrary notwithstanding.

The Senators and Representatives before mentioned, and the Members of the several State Legislatures, and all executive and judicial Officers, both of the United States and of the several States, shall be bound by Oath or Affirmation, to support this Constitution; but no religious Test shall ever be required as a Qualification to any Office or public Trust under the United States.

ARTICLE VII.

The Ratification of the Conventions of nine States, shall be sufficient for the Establishment of this Constitution between the States so ratifying the Same.

DONE in Convention by the Unanimous Consent of the States present the Seventeenth Day of September in the Year of our Lord one thousand seven hundred and Eighty seven and of the Independence of the United States of America the Twelfth **In Witness** whereof We have hereunto subscribed our names,

GEO WASHINGTON—
Presidt and deputy from Virginia.

NEW HAMPSHIRE.
JOHN LANGDON,   NICHOLAS GILMAN.

MASSACHUSETTS.
NATHANIEL GORHAM,   RUFUS KING.

CONNECTICUT.
WM. SAML. JOHNSON,   ROGER SHERMAN.

NEW YORK.
ALEXANDER HAMILTON.

NEW JERSEY.
WIL: LIVINGSTON,   DAVID BREARLEY,
WM. PATERSON,   JONA. DAYTON.

PENNSYLVANIA.
B. FRANKLIN,   THOMAS MIFFLIN,
ROBT. MORRIS,   GEO: CLYMER,
THO: FITZSIMONS,   JARED INGERSOLL,
JAMES WILSON,   GOUV: MORRIS.

DELAWARE.
GEO: READ,   GUNNING BEDFORD, Jun'r,
JOHN DICKINSON,   RICHARD BASSETT,
JACO: BROOM.

MARYLAND.
JAMES M'HENRY,   DAN: OF ST. THOS. JENIFER,
DANL CARROLL.

VIRGINIA.
JOHN BLAIR,   JAMES MADISON, Jr.,

NORTH CAROLINA.
WM. BLOUNT,   RICH'D DOBBS SPAIGHT,
HU. WILLIAMSON.

SOUTH CAROLINA.
J. RUTLEDGE,   CHARLES COTESWORTH PINCKNEY
CHARLES PINCKNEY,   PIERCE BUTLER.

GEORGIA.
WILLIAM FEW,   ABR. BALDWIN.

Attest: WILLIAM JACKSON, *Secretary.*

ARTICLES

IN ADDITION TO AND AMENDMENT OF

THE CONSTITUTION

OF THE

UNITED STATES OF AMERICA.

Proposed by Congress, and ratified by the Legislatures of the several States, pursuant to the fifth article of the original Constitution.

(ARTICLE I.)

Congress shall make no law respecting an establishment of religion, or prohibiting the free exercise thereof; or abridging the freedom of speech, or of the press, or the right of the people peaceably to assemble, and to petition the Government for a redress of grievances.

(ARTICLE II.)

A well regulated Militia, being necessary to the seuritcy of a free State, the right of the people to keep and bear Arms, shall not be infringed.

(ARTICLE III.)

No Soldier shall, in time of peace be quartered in any house, without the consent of the Owner, nor in time of war, but in a manner to be prescribed by law.

(ARTICLE IV.)

The right of the people to be secure in their persons, houses, papers, and effects, against unreasonable searches and seizures, shall not be violated, and no Warrants shall issue, but upon probable cause, supported by Oath or affirmation, and particularly describing the place to be searched, and the persons or things to be seized.

(ARTICLE V.)

No person shall be held to answer for a capital, or otherwise infamous crime, unless on a presentment or indictment of a Grand Jury, except in cases arising in the land or naval forces, or in the Militia, when in actual service in time of War or public danger; nor shall any person be subject for the same offence to be twice put in jeopardy of life or limb; nor shall be compelled in any Criminal Case to be a witness against himself, nor be deprived of life, liberty, or property, without due process of law; nor shall private property be taken for public use, without just compensation.

(ARTICLE VI.)

In all criminal prosecutions, the accused shall enjoy the right to a speedy and public trial, by an impartial jury of the State and district wherein the crime shall have been committed, which district shall have been previously ascertained by law, and to be informed of the nature and cause of the accusation; to be confronted with the witnesses against him; to have Compulsory process for obtaining witnesses in his favour, and to have the Assistance of Counsel for his defence.

(ARTICLE VII.)

In Suits at common law, where the value in controversy shall exceed twenty dollars, the right of trial by jury shall be preserved, and no fact tried by a jury shall be otherwise re-examined in any Court of the United States, than according to the rules of the common law.

(ARTICLE VIII.)

Excessive bail shall not be required, nor excessive fines imposed, nor cruel and unusual punishments inflicted.

(ARTICLE IX.)

The enumeration in the Constitution, of certain rights, shall not be construed to deny or disparage others retained by the people.

(ARTICLE X.)

The powers not delegated to the United States by the Constitution, nor prohibited by it to the States, are reserved to the States respectively, or to the people.

ARTICLE XI.

The Judicial power of the United States shall not be construed to extend to any suit in law or equity, commenced or prosecuted against one of the United States by Citizens of another State, or by Citizens or Subjects of any Foreign State.

* ARTICLE XII.

The Electors shall meet in their respective states, and vote by ballot for President and Vice-President, one of whom, at least, shall not be an inhabitant of the same state with themselves; they shall name in their ballots the person voted for as President, and in distinct ballots the person voted for as Vice-President, and they shall make distinct lists of all persons voted for as President, and of all persons voted for as Vice-President, and of the number of votes for each, which lists they shall sign and certify, and transmit sealed to the seat of the government of the United States, directed to the President of the Senate;—The President of the Senate shall, in presence of the Senate and House of Representatives, open all the certificates and the votes shall then be counted;—The person having the greatest number of votes for President, shall be the President, if such number be a majority of the whole number of Electors appointed; and if no person have

* In substitution of part of § 1, Article 2, of Constitution, as originally adopted.

such majority, then from the persons having the highest
numbers not exceeding three on the list of those voted for as
President, the House of Representatives shall choose immediately, by ballot, the President. But in choosing the President, the votes shall be taken by states, the representation
from each state having one vote; a quorum for this purpose
shall consist of a member or members from two-thirds of the
states, and a majority of all the states shall be necessary to a
choice. And if the House of Representatives shall not
choose a President whenever the right of choice shall devolve upon them, before the fourth day of March next following, then the Vice-President shall act as President, as in the
case of the death or other constitutional disability of the
President. The person having the greatest number of votes
as Vice-President, shall be the Vice-President, if such number be a majority of the whole number of Electors appointed,
and if no person have a majority, then from the two highest
numbers on the list, the Senate shall choose the Vice-President; a quorum for the purpose shall consist of two-thirds of
the whole number of Senators, and a majority of the whole
number shall be necessary to a choice. But no person constitutionally ineligible to the office of President shall be
eligible to that of Vice-President of the United States.

ARTICLE XIII.

SECTION 1. Neither slavery nor involuntary servitude, except as a punishment for crime, whereof the party shall have
been duly convicted, shall exist within the United States, or
any place subject to their jurisdiction.

SECTION 2. Congress shall have power to enforce this article by appropriate legislation.

ARTICLE XIV.

SECTION 1. All persons born or naturalized in the United
States and subject to the jurisdiction thereof, are citizens of
the United States, and of the State wherein they reside. No

State shall make or enforce any law which shall abridge the
privileges or immunities of citizens of the United States; nor
shall any State deprive any person of life, liberty or property
without due process of law, nor deny to any person within its
jurisdiction the equal protection of the laws.

SECTION 2. Representatives shall be apportioned among the
several States according to their respective numbers, counting the whole number of persons in each State, excluding
Indians not taxed; but when the right to vote at any election
for the choice of electors for President and Vice-President of
the United States, Representatives in Congress, the executive
and judicial officers of a State or the members of the Legislature thereof, is denied to any of the male inhabitants of such
State, being twenty-one years of age and citizens of the
United States, or in any way abridged, except for participation in rebellion or other crimes, the basis of representation
therein shall be reduced in the proportion which the number
of such male citizens shall bear to the whole number of male
citizens twenty-one years of age in such State.

SECTION 3. No person shall be a Senator or Representative in Congress or elector of President and Vice-President,
or hold any office civil or military, under the United States
or under any State who, having previously taken an oath
as a Member of Congress, or as an officer of the United States,
or as a member of any State Legislature, or as an executive or
judicial officer of any State, to support the Constitution of
the United States, shall have engaged in insurrection or
rebellion against the same, or given aid or comfort to the
enemies thereof. But Congress may, by a vote of two-thirds
of each house, remove such disability.

SECTION 4. The validity of the public debt of the United
States authorized by law, including debts incurred for payment of pensions and bounties for services in suppressing insurrection or rebellion, shall not be questioned. But neither
the United States nor any State shall assume or pay any debt
or obligation incurred in the aid of insurrection or rebellion

against the United States, or any loss or emancipation of any slave, but such debts, obligations and claims shall be held illegal and void.

SECTION 5. The Congress shall have the power to enforce, by appropriate legislation, the provisions of this article.

ARTICLE XV.

SECTION 1. The right of citizens of the United States to vote, shall not be denied or abridged by the United States, or by any State, on account of race, color or previous condition of servitude.

SECTION 2. Congress shall have power to enforce this article by appropriate legislation.

INDEX.

COMPILED BY L. E. JONES.

354

Pacific coast and Chinese question, 239–241.
Pacific railways, only ones chartered by natl. govt., 225; grants of land to, 246.
Panama Congress proposed, 167.
Panic of 1837, 172, 176; of 1873, 210.
Paper money, amount and redemption of Continental, 154; its excessive issue causes panic of 1837, 175–176; attempt to increase amount of irredeemable, 209–210; causes fictitious prosperity, 236; uniform character and value under natl. banking system, 244–245; basis, 246. *See also* Currency; Greenback party; Legal tender.
Pardoning power of Prest., 73.
Parker, I., proposed duty on importation of slaves, 151.
Parliament, denial of its power over colonies, 5.
Parties, their lack of principle, viii; nominations for Prest. by, 69–70; their influence in interpreting Const., 145–146; need of, 156; become more clearly defined, 157–158; in Jackson's adm., 172; originated in construing Const., 173–175; division in 1860 on slavery question, 192; their present demoralization, 220–221; demoralized by spoils system, 231; how to improve them, 231–235; their responsibility in special legislation, 259. *See also* Abolitionist; Anti-Federalists; Anti-Masonic; Democratic; Democratie-Republican; Federalist; Free Soil; Greenback; Know-Nothings; Liberal Republican; National Democratic; National Republican; Republican; Whig.
Patent Office, 94.
Patents, power of Congress over, 43–44, for land grants, 115, 116.
Pauper element, its influence in cities, 271.
Paving streets, 269.
Peace Congress of 1861, 195.
Penal law, use of States for, 223.
Pendleton, G. H., his civil service reform bill, 230.
Pennsylvania, form of colonial govt., 3; special legislation limited in, 258; minority representation in, 262; municipal govt. in, 273.
Pension Office, 94.
People, their ability to remedy evils, viii; rights reserved to, 15, 135–144; rights secured by Const. amends., 19–21; rights protected more by States than by natl. govt., 250.
Personal liberty, right of colonists to, 3; secured by Const. amend., 20;

how protected, 119, 121; protected more by States than by natl. govt., 250.
Personal rights guarded by amendments, 117.
Petitioning, right of, 19, 140, 251.
Philadelphia as site of capital, 152, 155.
Pierce, F., adm. of, 186–190.
Piracy, trials for, under Arts. of Confed., 10.
Place of meeting of Congress, 32–33; of trial, 120, 132.
Platt, T. C., resignation of, 77.
Police powers of States cannot be contracted away, 55–56.
Political assessments, 78, 228, 230.
Political hist. of U. S., 145–221.
Political institutions of U. S., interest in, iv; strain upon, caused by Civil War, iv–vi; their influence upon its prosperity, vi–vii.
Politicians, character of, 232–233.
Polk, J. K., adm. of, 179–181.
Population of U. S., increase up to Monroe's adm., 163; size in 1848, 182; its increase in cities, 270.
Post-const. hist. of U. S., 145–221.
Post-Office Dept., 84, 92–93; refusal to carry immoral publications, 138–139.
Postal powers under Arts. of Confed., 11; of Congress, 43.
Postmaster-General, 84; his duties, 92–93.
Potomac, as a site for the capital, 152, 155.
Preamble to the Const., 135; text, 288.
Presents. *See* Gifts.
President of the Senate, 34; to open electoral certificates, 66, 213–214; as acting Prest., 79–80.
President of U. S., commander-in-chief of army and navy, 45–46; his mode of requisition for militia, 46; mode of election, 65–72; term, 65, 72–73, 78–79; duties, 73–78, 81, 83–84; reelection, 79; vacancy, etc., 79–81; not subject to judicial interference, 79; impeachment, 81–82; power of creating vacancies, 82; his implied powers, 83–84; power of appointment, 83, 89, 90, 92, 93, 94, 126, 151; can require opinion of Attorney-General, 90; his order not a process of law, 119; influence of Washington in limiting term, 147–148; reeligibility, 152; change in mode of election, 160, 167, 169–170; amnesty power taken from, 203; power over army curtailed, 203.
President's official household, 73.
Presidents: Washington, 147–157; Adams, 157–159; Jefferson, 159–161; Madison, 161–163; Monroe, 163–166;

posed peace, 199 ; reconstruction,
200–202, 205–207. *See also* Confede-
rate.
Sovereignty. *See* State.
Spain, purchase of land from, 115, 116.
Speaker of House of Representatives,
32 ; as acting Prest., 79.
Special legislation, 257–260, 264. *See
also* Local bills.
Specie payments, resumption of, v,
209–211, 217.
Speech. *See* Freedom.
Spirits, duty on, 150.
Spoils system, 76–78, 169, 227–228, 230–
231. *See also* Appointing ; Civil ser-
vice.
Squatter sovereignty, 182–183.
Stamp act, cause of Continental Con-
gress, 5.
Standard silver dollars, 242.
Standing army, how controlled by
Congress, 46 ; not required by U. S.,
222.
Stanton, E. H., attempt of Johnson to
remove, 204–205.
State banks, evils of system, 244.
State conventions for amend. consti-
tutions, 253.
State courts, cases of concurrent juris-
diction with U. S. courts, 109–110 ; in-
dictments in, 118 ; appeals to Sup.
Ct. from, 127–132 ; writs of injunction from U. S. courts to, 132.
State Dept., 80, 84–85.
State engineers, 253.
State executives, 252.
State judges, 252 ; bound by U. S.
laws, 61–62 ; their election, 254–256 ;
minority representation in their
election in Penna., 262.
State legislatures, 252 ; power of colonial, 3 5 ; oaths of members, 63–64 ;
minority representation in their election in Ill., 262 ; biennial sessions,
264–266.
State officers, power of States over
salaries, 55 ; subject to mandatory
proceedings of Sup. Ct., 110 ; provisions for appointment in State
consts., 251–252.
State prison inspectors, 253.
State rights doctrine, 158, 173–175,
215.
State senates, 252.
State sovereignty, 7, 15, 24–26.
State surveyors, 253.
States, powers of, under Arts. of Confed., 10 ; their reserved rights, 15, 21,
118–117, 143–144, 250; their inde-
structibility, 15–16; equal suffrage in
the Senate, 17–18, 24, 33; admission
of, 17, 19; to give credit to acts of
one another, 18, 57–59; cannot be
divided without their own consent,

19 ; suits against, by citizens, 21,
103, 110 ; apportionment of Congressmen, 31 ; cannot levy same taxes as
natl. govt., 39; cannot be taxed by
Congress, 39–40 ; power of Congress
to organize govts. after Civil War,
48; privileges prohibited, 52–57, 62–
63; their right of eminent domain,
55; cannot limit power of natl. govt.
over public lands, 60–61; their laws
subordinate to those of U. S., 61–63;
prevention of jealousy in choosing
Prest., 60; power of Prest. to recognize their govts., 83; parties to actions, 103, 105, 109, 126, 131–132; constitutionality of their actions judged
by Sup. Ct., 104–106; cannot modify
jurisdiction of U. S. courts, 108–109;
suffrage in, 113, 124; their control
over citizens, 114; lands given to,
for educ. purposes, 115; can pass
seizure laws, 118 ; cannot modify
power of natl. govt., 120; their penal
code cannot be modified by U. S.,
122: Sup. Ct. to determine constitutionality of their acts, 127–132; their
laws and procedure binding on U.
S. courts, 132; rights to militia,
140–141; their jealousy, 147; debts on
adoption of Const., 154; their assumption by natl. govt., 155; need of
a party to assert their rights, 156;
their increase in number, 163; weakening of their power, 223–225, 226.
See also Constitutions.
Statistics, Bureau of, 88.
Stephens, A. H., elected Vice-Prest.
of Confederate govt., 185.
Story, J., quoted, 12, 136, 137.
Streets, laying out and paving, 269.
Strict construction of Const., 174, 215–
216. *See also* Limited.
Suffrage, 124; right of States to limit,
113; its extension to freedmen, 200–
203, 205; secured by State consts.,
251; need for its limitation in cities,
270. *See also* Ballot.
Sumner, C., assault upon him by
Brooks, 189.
Sumter, Fort, surrender of, 196.
Supreme Court, 102–106: decisions, 16,
38, 39–40, 41–42, 43, 48, 50, 51, 52–55,
56–57, 60, 63, 109, 111–112, 140, 190,
196, 224; influence of parties on, 145
–146; interpreter of the Const., 26,
62; coerced by Congress, 35: judges
appointed by Prest., 74; no authority
over Prest., 81; how it has interpreted Const., 125; its jurisdiction,
125–133; in control of Southern
States, 192.
Surveyors. *See* State.
Susquehanna, as a site for the capital,
152.

www.ingramcontent.com/pod-product-compliance
Lightning Source LLC
Chambersburg PA
CBHW030903270326
41929CB00008B/550